How It Works®

Science and Technology

Third Edition

Marshall Cavendish
99 White Plains Road
Tarrytown, NY 10591

Website: www.marshallcavendish.com

Third edition updated by Brown Reference Group plc.

Library of Congress Cataloging-in-Publication Data
How it works: science and technology.—3rd ed.
p. cm.
Includes index.
ISBN 0-7614-7314-9 (set)   ISBN 0-7614-7324-6 (Vol. 10)
1. Technology—Encyclopedias. 2. Science—Encyclopedias.
[1. Technology—Encyclopedias. 2. Science—Encyclopedias.]
T9 .H738 2003
603—dc21   2001028771

Consultant: Donald R. Franceschetti, Ph.D., University of Memphis

Brown Reference Group
Editor: Wendy Horobin
Associate Editors: Paul Thompson, Martin Clowes, Lis Stedman
Managing Editor: Tim Cooke
Design: Alison Gardner
Picture Research: Becky Cox
Illustrations: Mark Walker, Darren Awuah

Marshall Cavendish
Project Editor: Peter Mavrikis
Production Manager: Alan Tsai
Editorial Director: Paul Bernabeo

Printed in Malaysia
Bound in the United States of America
08 07 06 05 04   6 5 4 3 2

Title picture: Computer-assisted mapmaking, see *Mapmaking Techniques*

How It Works®

Science and Technology

Volume 10

Luminescence

Microsurgery

Marshall Cavendish
New York • London • Toronto • Sydney

Contents

Volume 10

Luminescence

Light can be produced by two processes that are fundamentally very different. If light results from something becoming hot, such as an electric lamp filament or a gas mantle, the process is called incandescence, whereas the emission of light without this intense heat is known as luminescence.

The earliest known form of luminescence, the glow emitted by fireflies and glowworms to attract their mates, was recorded over 3,000 years ago. Such bioluminescence in these and other species has been the subject of frequent literary musing but, until recently, evoked little scientific study. Of far greater interest was the first, accidental, synthesis of a luminescent material in about 1603 by an Italian alchemist and cobbler named Vincenzo Cascariolo. In his search for gold, he heated some barium sulphate (in the form of barite, or heavy spar) with coal. On cooling, he had a porous cake that looked ordinary by day but was found to give out a deep-blue glow at night. It was absorbing sunlight and giving a luminescent emission that was too weak to be seen except in the dark.

Luminescent materials

As a material is heated, its atoms become agitated and collisions occur between them causing the energy that has been put into the material to be emitted. This energy is normally noticed as radiant heat, but as the temperature rises, a proportion of the energy is emitted as visible light; in other words, the material becomes incandescent. In luminescent materials, the atoms are excited by the energy input to an internally unstable condition. They have an electron out of place and in this way are storing the energy, which is then emitted as visible light when the atom returns to its original state.

There are two forms of luminescence—fluorescence and phosphorescence. A simple distinc-

▼ In this ctenophore, a marine organism, the luminescent cells are situated in the hair-like cilia.

tion between these is that fluorescence stops as soon as the cause of excitation of the atoms or molecules is removed, whereas phosphorescence continues after such removal. Phosphorescence continues from a millionth of a second to days, depending on the material.

There are also several categories of luminescence, but they merely refer to the various ways in which the energy is supplied to the luminescent material. Thus, in chemiluminescence, the energy comes from a chemical reaction; in bioluminescence, the energy comes from a biochemical reaction; in photoluminescence, the energy comes from absorbed light; in electroluminescence, the energy is released as electrons pulled from atoms by an electric field combine with the ions produced to form neutral atoms; and in radioluminescence, ionizing radiation causes certain materials to luminesce—in the case of röntgenoluminescence (named for the German physicist Wilhelm Konrad Röntgen who discovered X rays in 1895), the energy comes from X rays.

Uses of luminescence

The most obvious use of a process that produces light is to provide enough light to act as a means of illumination. Bombardment of gas molecules by electrons in an electric fluorescent tube (discharge tube) causes excitation of these molecules, which then emit light. This is an example of electroluminescence. The first public lighting installation using fluorescent tubes was in 1904 at Newark, New Jersey, and the tubes contained air at low pressure. Today, fluorescent tubes use gases such as neon (for advertising signs) and sodium or mercury (for street lighting).

The color of the light emitted by a fluorescent tube is characteristic of the single gas used, but the color can be modified in a number of ways. A low-pressure sodium vapor lamp gives a monochromatic yellow light, but as the pressure is increased, the light emitted becomes whiter. By adding various metals to a high-pressure mercury discharge, in the form of their halide salts, a wide range of colored or white light sources can be achieved. These are known as metal halide lamps. The color of high- and low-pressure mercury fluorescent tubes, which produce a high output of ultraviolet radiation, can be modified and made more efficient by coating the outer bulbs or tubes with fluorescent materials generally known as phosphors. The coating, excited by the invisible ultraviolet radiation, emits visible light. Particularly in low-pressure mercury fluorescent lamps, by using mixtures of phosphors, a range of whites from warm (pinkish) to cool (bluish) color appearance can be produced. They can enable colored objects and materials to be seen either with acceptable fidelity for general lighting purposes or for the highest quality demands of accurate color matching. These are the fluorescent tubes currently in widespread use.

Applications of luminescence other than for lighting are extremely varied; the most important is probably in the cathode-ray tube, which is the basis of radar and television. The source of the picture that we see is cathodoluminescence, caused by accelerated electrons striking a screen of luminescent material at the end of the tube.

One of the most common uses of luminescent materials is in optical brightening agents for fabrics. Most fibers in their undyed state are slightly yellow, and the old method of whitening them was to add a trace of blue dye to counteract the yellow tint. The modern way is to add a fluorescent compound that absorbs the ultraviolet component of daylight and emits blue light to counter the yellow tint.

One advantage of luminescent materials is that minute quantities are more easily seen than the same amount of a dye of the same color. The luminescent organic compound fluorescein, for example, can be detected at a concentration of as little as one part in 40 million. This finding had led to the use of such materials in medical diagnoses, air-sea rescue, leak detection, and even confirmation of the source of the Rhône River in Europe.

Because luminescent materials are easily noticeable to the eye, they are sometimes included in paint compositions. Whereas an ordinary paint has a dye that reflects one color and absorbs the others, a luminescent paint additionally contains a luminescent material that emits the same color as the dye reflects, making the resulting paint unusually bright. The luminescent material can either be fluorescent or phosphorescent depending on the intended use of the paint. Fluorescent paints, for example, are used on road signs, while phosphorescent paints are used on instrument panels and luminous watches.

▲ In the luminous cells of a glowworm, the chemical luciferin is oxidized in the presence of the enzyme luciferase, and light is emitted.

SEE ALSO: CATHODE-RAY TUBE • DISCHARGE TUBE • ROAD SYSTEMS AND TRAFFIC CONTROL • X-RAY IMAGING

Lung

The lungs are the most important part of the respiratory system. All higher animals need oxygen to enable them to live, and it is the role of the respiratory system to take in this oxygen and dispose of particular waste products. Even a brief interruption in the supply of oxygen to the body can cause damage, or even death.

Air passages

Air travels to the lungs through the other parts of the respiratory system. Air is normally inhaled through the nose, which has a filtering system incorporated in the nasal cavity. The next stage on the journey is the pharynx, or throat, and to stop food from entering the lungs or air from finding its way into the stomach, a small flap called the epiglottis effectively divides the respiratory and the alimentary (digestive) systems.

Following the epiglottis, there is the glottis—the opening from the pharynx into the trachea, or windpipe. The trachea is stiffened by rings of cartilage so that it does not close up under the partial vacuums created by the flow of air to and from the lungs. The larynx, or voice box, which contains the vocal cords, is found just beneath the glottis in the trachea.

Physical facts

The lungs consist of right and left halves. In humans, the right lung is normally slightly thicker and heavier than the left, although the intrusion of the liver into the lower thorax makes it about 1 in. (2.5 cm) shorter. In adult males, the lungs weigh about 21 oz. (645 g) and in females slightly less. Lungs normally account for about $\frac{1}{37}$ of total body weight in the male and about $\frac{1}{42}$ in the female. Lung tissue is light and porous, and the texture spongy. Healthy lung tissue is buoyant in water; its relative density is between 0.126 (when fully inflated) and 1.056 (when deprived of air).

Linking the trachea to the two halves of the lungs are the branched bronchi. At the trachea end, the bronchi have similar rings of cartilage to the trachea, but once inside the main body of the lungs, the large bronchi begin to branch, making many small bronchi that can be described by comparing the structure with the stems of a bunch of grapes.

The smallest branches of the bronchi are called bronchioles. Finally, the airways end in alveoli, which are tiny air sacs. To continue the analogy with a bunch of grapes, the alveoli are the grapes themselves, and the exchange of gases occurs through the skin of the grapes. Although

◄ This cyclist is being monitored to find out how much oxygen he consumes during exercise.

each alveolus is extremely tiny, their enormous number (more than 700,000,000) amounts to a surface area of some 970 sq. ft. (90 m²), which is roughly the size of half a tennis court.

The alveoli are surrounded by a network of very fine blood vessels called capillaries. The capillary and alveolus walls are very thin and are made from only two layers of cells. Thus, gases are able pass through the walls easily.

As blood is pumped through the capillaries, its hemoglobin takes up oxygen (it becomes saturated at around 97 percent) from the alveoli. At the same time, carbon dioxide from the bloodstream migrates into the air in the alveoli. The gas exchange process will not work if the air in the alveoli becomes exhausted of oxygen and saturated with carbon dioxide. For this reason, the breathing action has to change the air at regular intervals.

Breathing

Three sets of muscles are involved in breathing. They are the diaphragm (the thin sheet of muscle stretched across the bottom of the ribs), the intercostal muscles (the muscles stretched between the ribs), and the sternomastoid muscles (attached to the breastbone and the shoulder blades).

When air is breathed in (inspiration) the intercostal muscles contract, causing the ribs to hinge upward and outward, and the diaphragm contracts. The effect is for the capacity of the lungs to increase and for a partial vacuum to be created so air is drawn into the lungs. Breathing out (expiration) involves relaxation of the muscles and a decrease in lung capacity, which pushes the air out.

When a person is relaxed and at rest, he or she takes between 15 and 20 breaths per minute, but

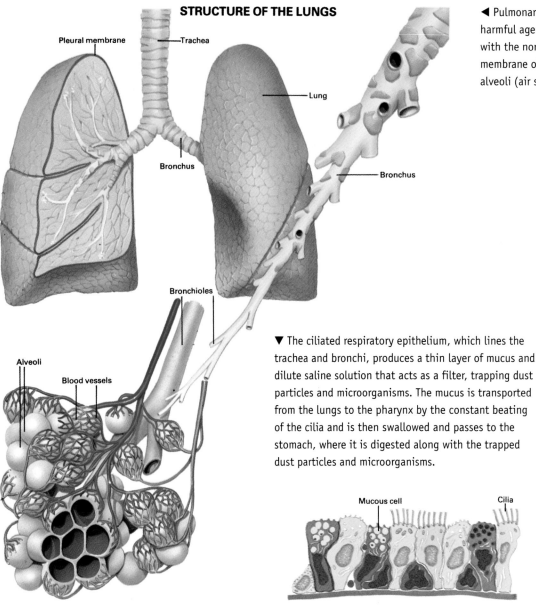

STRUCTURE OF THE LUNGS

Pleural membrane — Trachea

Lung

Bronchus

Bronchus

Bronchioles

Alveoli

Blood vessels

◄ Pulmonary disorders are caused by harmful agents in the air that interfere with the normal functioning of the mucous membrane of the bronchial tubes and the alveoli (air sacs) in the lungs.

▼ The ciliated respiratory epithelium, which lines the trachea and bronchi, produces a thin layer of mucus and dilute saline solution that acts as a filter, trapping dust particles and microorganisms. The mucus is transported from the lungs to the pharynx by the constant beating of the cilia and is then swallowed and passes to the stomach, where it is digested along with the trapped dust particles and microorganisms.

Mucous cell

Cilia

this number increases during exercise to increase the output of oxygen and the amount of waste carbon that is expelled. When a person is resting, tidal breathing moves about 1 pint (0.5 l) of air per breath. Deep breathing, however, moves about 1 to 1.3 gallons (3.5–5 l) of air, a characteristic called the vital capacity. The space left in the lungs after breathing out is called the residual volume.

When in the alveoli, the oxygen content of the air decreases from 20.9 percent of normal atmospheric air to 14 percent. Conversely, the carbon dioxide content increases from 0.03 to 5.5 percent. The expired air is also saturated with water vapor.

In every minute, about 0.5 pint (0.25 l) of oxygen is taken up by the bloodstream and exchanged for the same amount of carbon dioxide. The exact amount of gas exchanged depends on a number of factors, including metabolism, the acid-base (alkaline) balance in the blood, and the pattern of respiration.

Breathing control

Control of breathing is the responsibility of the respiratory center located in the medulla in the brain. Respiration has a basic rhythm, but different bodily demands impose the need for further modulation. The fine tuning of respiration comes from impulses in the vagus and glossopharyngeal nerves.

Nerves from the respiratory center pass through the spinal cord and are connected to the phrenic nerves in the diaphragm. The respiratory center nerves also connect to the anterior horn nerves, which control the intercostal and other muscles involved in respiration.

Further nervous control of respiration comes from nerve endings in the carotid and aortic bodies. These detect oxygen deficiency and send signals to the respiratory center. Receptors in the bronchioles are sensitive to lung distention during inspiration. When the degree of distention becomes too much, they too send signals to the respiratory center.

Respiration is not controlled by nervous mechanisms only; the carbon dioxide concentration in the blood also exerts control. Increases in the carbon dioxide concentration of blood passing through the medulla lead to an increase in the depth of respiration. If the carbon dioxide level drops, the depth of respiration is decreased.

Blood vessels

The capillaries around the lungs are branches of the pulmonary artery and narrow down from the large diameter of the main artery so that the capillaries around the alveoli are only 0.0084 mm in diameter. The capillaries are very closely spaced, with the spaces between them being even smaller than the diameter of the capillaries. The blood vessels fuse after leaving the alveoli and become larger, finally uniting in the pulmonary vein.

These pulmonary blood vessels differ from other blood vessels in the body because the roles of the arteries and the veins are reversed. The dark red deoxygenated blood is carried by the pulmonary artery, while the bright red oxygenated blood is carried by the pulmonary vein. The other major difference between the pulmonary veins and their counterparts elsewhere in the body is that they do not contain valves.

Altitude sickness

The demands placed on the lungs and the rest of the respiratory system are increased if the environment is changed, for example, if an athlete runs at a significant height above sea level where the air is rarefied. In extreme cases, humans experiencing depressurization in an aircraft flying above 16,000 ft. (5,000 m) without extra oxygen supplies will become unconscious, lose brain cells, and eventually die. In the case of mountain climbing, there is time for acclimatization, and the critical height is between 19,000 and 23,000 ft. (6,000 and 7,000 m).

Pollution

Since the industrial revolution, lungs have become exposed to air pollution, and although legislation has been passed in many industrialized countries to control air pollution, the air may still contain a mix of dangerous contaminants.

Fog can become contaminated with sulfur dioxide and dust. When it does, it becomes a serious danger to health by aggravating any existing lung disease. In cities such as Los Angeles, smog caused by a concentration of automobile exhaust gases is a danger to normal lung function. Cases of oxygen starvation, leading to brain damage in extreme cases, have been the result. In recent years, however, the introduction of cars that use

catalytic converters or that burn clean fuels, such as ethanol, has reduced this problem.

Cigarette smoke, inhaled both directly from smoking and indirectly from others smoking in the immediate environment, has been linked with chronic bronchitis and lung cancer. Cigarette by-products taken into the body through the lungs can lead to other serious effects, including coronary heart disease and heart attacks.

Although lung cancer is the biggest killer today among lung diseases, tuberculosis (TB) was the biggest killer until the 20th century. TB is caused by bacteria that destroy lung tissue. In industrial societies, improved hygiene and the development of effective drugs resulted in this disease becoming rare, until the 1980s, when incidence of the disease began to rise once more. This rise has been attributed to increased poverty, decaying health systems, and HIV, which increases vulnerability to TB. In many developing nations, TB remains a major cause of death.

In asthma, the muscles in the walls of the bronchioles contract in an allergic reaction. The narrowing of the bronchioles causes difficulty in breathing, resulting in wheezing. The condition can be alleviated with drugs, such as epinephrine, that relax the contracted muscles and allow normal breathing once more. Allergens responsible for causing asthma range widely from fungal spores and pollen to feathers and certain foods.

Those working in mining and related industries are susceptible to silicosis, a disease caused by inhaling fine particles of silica (silicon dioxide), released when many common rocks are cut. The effect of inhaling asbestos fibers has been well-documented, and chronic lung disease is one result, but 20 years after even a short exposure to asbestos people may develop mesothelioma in the pleura or peritoneum.

▼ The chest is a bony cage that contains the lungs, one of the most important organs in the body. The lungs are surrounded by a bell-shaped muscular bag that expands and contracts, sucking air into and expelling it out of the lungs. These X rays show how the chest expands when air is inhaled (below left), and contracts when air is exhaled (below right).

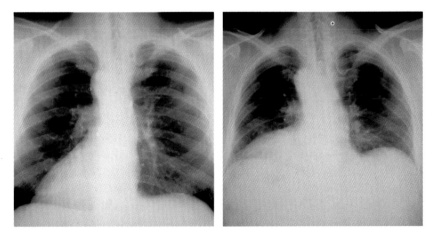

SEE ALSO: AIR • BRAIN • HEART SURGERY • MUSCLE • OXYGEN • POLLUTION MONITORING AND CONTROL

Machine Tool

A machine tool is a device used in workshops and factories to shape solid objects either by the systematic removal of material from a larger block—a process called machining—or by drawing or pressing a sheet of flexible material into shape in a machine press. Traditional machine tools use implements to remove material by mechanical means, while some modern machines use electrical discharges, electrochemistry, lasers, or ultrasound to remove material without direct mechanical contact with the workpiece.

Lathe development

A lathe is a machine tool that produces helical, or cylindrically symmetrical, pieces, such as bolts, drive shafts, locomotive wheels, and pulleys. A lathe spins workpieces between two rotating grips aligned on a common axis; its cutting tool tracks along the workpiece from end to end, altering its distance from the central axis according to the intended profile of the finished piece.

The lathe is the most widely used and the oldest of all machine tools—a lathe was depicted in an Egyptian tomb painting of around 300 B.C.E. Early lathes were used to produce wooden objects such as spindles and chair legs. One method of driving these early lathes was to wrap a cord around the workpiece and pull first on one end of the cord and then on the other, producing a back-and-forth turning motion. While one person operated the spindle in this way, another used hand tools to shape the workpiece. In the 15th century, treadle-operated lathes replaced cord driven machines. Using a principle similar to that of the spinning wheel, such machines turned the workpiece continuously in one direction.

By the 18th century, soft metals were being worked in the lathe using hand tools. Around 1770, a French engineer, Jacques de Vaucanson, designed an iron-framed lathe with adjustable head- and tailstocks to support workpieces of various sizes and a brass carriage that ran on iron guides to support the cutting tools.

By the end of the 18th century, the need for precision-manufactured components for steam engines and textile machinery was stimulating rapid advances in lathe designs. Important contributors to these advances were a British engineer, Henry Maudslay, and a U.S. inventor David Wilkinson, both of whom in 1797 designed power lathes whose cutting tools moved along the workpiece at a rate proportional to its turning speed. This feature made it possible to carve perfectly helical screw threads into shafts.

▲ A worker operates a metal-cutting lathe at the Electrosila works at Saint Petersburg, Russia. The rusty uncut surface of the massive steel workpiece is visible in the foreground at right, while the cut metal toward the rear of the scene has a bright-gray uncorroded surface.

In 1821, Thomas Blanchard, a U.S. engineer, invented a lathe whose cutting tool followed a template as it moved along the workpiece. This improvement enabled identical—and therefore interchangeable—components to be produced with relative ease. The ease of use of lathes increased further with the introduction of the turret lathe in the mid-19th century. Turret lathes have several cutting tools, each of a shape appropriate for a given cut. The tools are set around the edge of a circular mount and selected by rotating the tool mount to present the chosen tool to the workpiece. The mount is then locked in position.

With the development of the turret, the lathe had effectively arrived at its modern form. Subsequent developments increased the precision of cutting and the degree of automation.

Details of lathe design

The basis of a center lathe is a box-section metal bed that supports a pair of hardened and ground-guiding surfaces called slideways. Mounted at one end of the bed is the headstock—a casing that houses the spindle of the lathe and the transmission that delivers power from an electric motor to turn the spindle. A spindle can typically turn at between 30 and 2,000 rpm, according to the requirements of the job. The tip of the spindle is a 60-degree cone—the center—which fits into a

similar conical recess cut in the end of the stock, or uncut workpiece. The center ensures that the workpiece stays in position on the turning axis, while the stock is made to follow the spindle by attaching to it an L-shaped clamp—a lathe dog, catch, or dragger—that catches on a stud that protrudes from the side of the spindle.

Instead of centers, some spindles have notches or threads that allow for the attachment of various gripping devices to suit different types of stocks. A three-jawed chuck closes concentrically on round stock by the action of a single key, while each jaw of a four-jawed chuck operates by a separate key to secure irregular stock. Standard-size bar stock is secured by a collet, which is a split sleeve whose internal dimensions fit the stock perfectly when tightened in a chuck.

For short stock, a clamping headstock might provide adequate support for the workpiece during machining; for longer stock and other types of headstocks, the end of the workpiece far from the headstock must be supported by a tailstock. This device can be moved along the slideways and fixed in position to suit workpieces of various lengths. The end of the workpiece rests in a cylindrical sleeve, or quill, or on a conical center.

The height of the axis about which the workpiece rotates—the center height—is one of the basic specifications of a lathe and is around 6 to

▼ A typical workshop lathe has a three-jawed chuck headstock and a tailstock with center. Its operations include chamfering (1), which diminishes the diameter of the workpiece using a tool with a diagonal edge (2), and thread cutting (3). Facing off (4) and boring (5) operations are done with the tailstock removed. Deep cuts (6) are made at low turning speeds.

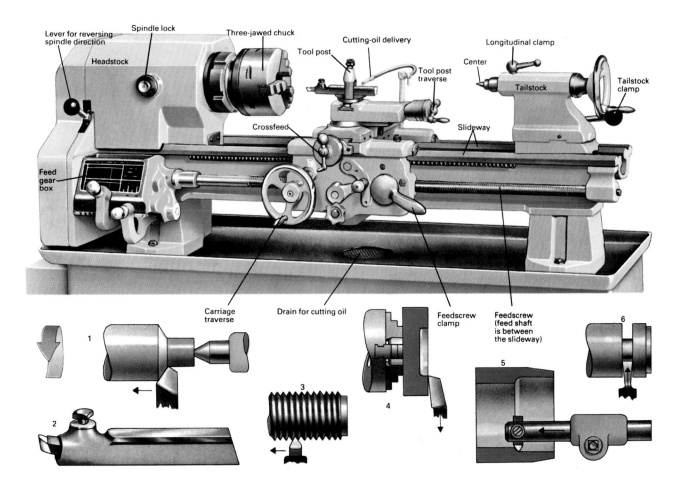

15 in. (15–38 cm) for a general-purpose device. However, it is more usual to specify the swing of a lathe—the maximum workpiece diameter that a lathe can accommodate with adequate clearance of the bed fittings. The swing is thus somewhat less than twice the center height.

The distance between the headstock and tailstock of a general-purpose lathe is typically around 40 to 60 in. (100–150 cm). Jewelers' lathes have much smaller dimensions and are usually small enough to fit on a desktop. Large lathes for heavy-duty engineering work can have swings of 10 ft. (3 m) or more and accommodate workpieces whose lengths can exceed 50 ft. (15 m).

The cutting operations of a lathe are performed by tools mounted on a carriage, called a saddle, that moves along the slideways in a motion called feed. The lower part of the saddle, called the apron, contains a cogged wheel that meshes with a rack in the lathe bed. Turning the cogged wheel causes the saddle to move along the slideway; the power for this motion can be supplied by a motor or by a hand-cranked wheel.

In the case of motor-driven feed, gears in the apron take power from one or other of two helical screws that project from the base of the headstock and pass through the apron. The screws are linked to the spindle drive by a feed transmission in the lower part of the headstock. One of them, the feed screw, is used for general feed purposes; the other, the leadscrew, is reserved for cutting threads in workpieces that have previously been cut to approximate size. This practice minimizes wear of the leadscrew, thereby maintaining its precision for thread cutting.

Depending on the type of lathe, the saddle may support a single tool holder into which tools of different materials and profiles can be clamped or a turret that holds several tools. The shape of tool for a given operation is determined by the shape of the required cut; the tool material can be a tough high-speed steel—a hard but brittle carbide of silicon or boron—or it may be tipped with a ceramic material or even diamond. In many cases, a stream of liquid coolant is directed at the cutting area to prevent its overheating.

The tool is pushed into the surface of the workpiece to perform the cut and progresses toward the turning axis as material is removed. Motion perpendicular to the turning axis is called crossfeed. In general, the workpiece is first cut to its approximate final shape using slow turning speeds and deep cuts. The precise dimensions are then achieved using high speeds and light cuts. Threads are cut by using a precise ratio of feed rate to turning speed and by using a tool whose profile matches the required thread.

A long piece of stock may flex when it comes in contact with the cutting tool; such distortion can be reduced by use of a support, called a steady, that holds the piece between three lubricated points. The three-point steady is mounted on the slideways, and its points are adjusted to the size of the piece. Two-point steady rests are sometimes used in thread cutting; the rest is fixed to the saddle and moves with the cutting tool.

Automatic lathes

The productivity and precision of lathes is greatly enhanced by integrating them with hydraulic and robotic systems that switch workpieces, tools, and spindle attachments under computer control. Similar controls set turning speeds and feed and crossfeed rates using information from position sensors to measure the progress of the cut. In computer-aided manufacture (CAM), all processes are controlled to achieve a specification produced by computer-aided design.

In older automated lathes, called tracer lathes, the profile of a workpiece reproduces that of a physical master, usually mounted in a copying machine behind the lathe from the operator's standpoint. A stylus traces the profile of the master as the carriage moves along the workpiece, and hydraulic or electric servomechanisms drive the cutting tool to match the original.

Surfacing tools

Shapers and planers are examples of surfacing tools. They are machine tools that carve flat surfaces in a reciprocating action that consists of a cutting stroke and a return stroke. Since the return stroke is nonproductive, the machine is designed to return rapidly. In a shaper, a moving tool cuts a stationary workpiece; in a planer, the the workpiece moves across a fixed tool.

▲ The abrasive wheel of a grinding machine forms a smooth surface on this metal workpiece. A stream of lubricant removes the debris from grinding and prevents overheating. The thread to the right of the wheel was cut into the shaft using a lathe.

The cutting tool of a shaper is mounted on the end of a ram, whose tip swivels to cater for various surfacing angles. The travel distance of the ram can be adjusted from zero to a maximum that depends on the size of the machine according to the intended dimensions of the cut surface. The workpiece is fixed by a vise to a table that can move in three dimensions. After each stroke of the cutting tool, the table moves so that the following stroke cuts a strip adjacent to the previous cut. The ram and table movements are driven by hydraulic or mechanical couplings that are designed to maximize the ratio of cutting time to tool-return and table-adjustment times in each stroke.

The planer performs a function similar to that of a shaper, but it is more suited to large pieces because of the simple back-and-forth motion of the table on which the workpiece is mounted. The cutting tool is repositioned between strokes so as to produce the required surface.

Milling machine

A milling machine differs from other types of machine tools in that it has multiple cutting surfaces in a rotating head rather than a single cutting point or surface. Milling machines are useful for machining noncylindrical components.

The two broad classes of milling machines are defined by the orientation of their rotational axes relative to the surface of contact with the workpiece: horizontal (parallel) or vertical (perpendicular). Horizontal types use cutting disks that have teeth or abrasive materials around their perimeters and resemble circular-saw blades; vertical types use an end mill, which resembles the bit of a household drill but has a flat tip and more teeth. Universal milling machines can be swiveled between horizontal and vertical orientations.

For some operations, the workpiece is clamped to a table whose traverse and crossfeed motions can be controlled manually or automatically; vertical milling heads can also feed up and down. For other operations, the workpiece is mounted in a chuck that rotates slowly as the milling operation proceeds. Cogs, spiral flutes, and elliptical surfaces are produced by synchronizing the chuck rotation with the orientation and movement of a horizontal milling head. The profile of the cut that results is determined by the edge profile of the cutting head.

Some vertical milling machines have an offset head feature, whereby the rotating spindle can move from its central position, allowing complex holes such as ellipses to be cut. Die sinking is an operation in which contoured surfaces can be machined using appropriately shaped cutters.

Grinding machine

A grinding machine is similar in construction to a horizontal-spindle milling machine, except that it has an abrasive wheel in place of the cutting disk of a milling machine. The abrasive wheel consists of an abrasive powder—usually corundum (aluminum oxide, Al_2O_3) or Carborundum (silicon carbide, SiC)—baked into a thermosetting resin, such as a phenol-methanal resin.

◀ The head of this cutting tool is equipped with a chip breaker so that the metal cuttings, or swarf, are ejected from the piece as fine particles rather than as slivers of metal.

The abrasive wheel is "dressed" (shaped) by trimming it with a diamond tool and must be redressed from time to time to restore its original edge profile. Straightforward grinding calls for flat-edged disks, but more complex edge profiles are available for grinding complex surfaces.

Grinding has several advantages over milling. It results in smoother surfaces, and soft materials such as plastics can be ground using light pressure, whereas a milling machine would tear such materials. The disadvantage of grinding is that the abrasive wheels must be stored under controlled conditions and need regular dressing.

Jig borer

Jig borers, mill borers, and boring mills are essentially large, high-precision, versatile milling machines. The spindle projects horizontally from a column that can be raised or lowered, and it can be advanced or withdrawn; there is also the usual traverse and crossfeed of the work table.

Some of these machines are as large as rooms. They use a variety of cutting tools with interchangeable collars, tapered sleeves, and so forth, to adapt the tools to the spindle. Large workpieces, such as machine-body castings, can be mounted on the table; holes, slots, and surface can then be machined to precise specifications.

Drill press

The simplest drill press, often found in a home workshop, is a clamp on a vertical column designed to hold an electric drill above a work table. The clamp travels up and down on a rack and gear that is operated manually; the drilling action occurs on the downward stroke.

Industrial drill presses have spindles powered by electric motors; drill bits of various sizes can be attached to the spindle, usually by means of tapered sleeves. For mass production, the table may have a fixture that allows for quick clamping and release of a specific type of component. The horizontal motions of the table and the drilling depth can be controlled by computer.

For precision drilling, a slightly undersized hole is drilled first and then brought to size using a reamer—a straight-fluted bit designed to remove only small amounts of metal. Drilling and reaming operations, especially at high speed, often require a stream of cutting fluid to carry away debris and the heat generated by friction.

Machine presses

Machine presses are used to form molded objects from sheets of flexible materials, principally metals and alloys. The tools of such machines are dies and punches. The external surface of the punch

◀ This vertical milling machine with end mill is being used to finish a machine body casting. By replacing the end mill with a drill bit, the same machine can be used as a drill press. The lever in the foreground is pulled to produce the downward stroke for drilling.

matches the internal surface of the die but is slightly smaller, and the sheet material is stretched over the punch during pressing. The power for the pressing operation is provided by a hydraulic ram or taken from a rotating flywheel by the action of a clutch mechanism.

Machine presses are used to form objects such as car door panels and some types of food cans in a single stroke. The lubricant, sheet material, pressing speed, and punch and die must be well matched to avoid tearing the sheet material.

Other machine tools

A variety of techniques exist for machining by using the localized application of heat to vaporize surface material in a controlled manner. The heat sources for such techniques include electrical discharges, electron beams, lasers, and plasma arcs.

In electrochemical machining (ECM), a metal workpiece is made the anode in an electrolytic cell with a shaped cathode and flowing electrolyte. The parts of the workpiece closer to the cathode lose metal at a faster rate, so the workpiece gradually assumes the form of the cathode.

In ultrasound machining (USM), a tool vibrates at ultrasonic frequencies near the surface of the workpiece. An abrasive powder suspended in liquid that flows between the tool and workpiece gradually erodes the workpiece.

 SEE ALSO: ABRASIVE • ELECTROLYSIS • KEY-CUTTING MACHINE • LUBRICATION • MASS PRODUCTION • METALWORKING

Magnetic Tape and Film

Methods of recording data magnetically began with a device invented by a Danish engineer, Valdemar Poulsen, in 1900. It consisted of a thin steel wire used to record sound magnetically. Engineers in the United States, United Kingdom, and Germany developed a variety of different methods for recording magnetically, but the magnetic tape was perfected by German engineers in the 1930s. This early design, called a magnetophone, was developed by British researchers in the 1940s to produce high-quality tape recording. The machines used large reels, and tape needed to be manually fed through the recorder and onto another reel. Used to record sound and computer data, these reel-to-reel machines have largely been superseded by audio cassette tape and, in the case of computers, with magnetic metal disks and optical media.

The use of magnetic tape for recording television programs was introduced in 1956 with the invention of the videotape recorder by Charles P. Ginsburg and Ray Dolby of the U.S. electronics company Ampex Corporation. This machine made possible the prerecording of television programs, which eventually replaced most live transmissions. The first video tape recorder for domestic use appeared in 1969.

Materials of magnetic tape

Magnetic recording tape consists of a layer of powdered magnetic material held together by a plastic binder, and coated onto a plastic base film, which provides support and mechanical strength.

The base film is usually made of a polyester material, the thicknesses used ranging from 0.002 in. (0.051 mm) in standard tapes to only 0.00033 in. (0.0084 mm) for the very thin tape used in C120 cassettes. The width varies from 0.15 in. (3.8 mm) for cassettes to 2 in. (51 mm) for professional studio and broadcasting tape used for sound and vision recording.

The magnetic coating is even thinner, between 0.000125 and 0.0005 in. (0.0032–0.0127 mm) thick, but every inch of the tape contains many millions of particles of the magnetic powder. These particles can be seen only with an electron microscope.

The magnetic material of most tapes is one of the oxides of iron, known as gamma, or ferric, oxide (Fe_2O_3), which gives the tape its characteristic brown color. Some tapes are black in color because finely divided carbon black has been added to conduct away any electrostatic charge that might accumulate on the tape as it moves

through the recording or playback equipment. New materials used to improve performance include cobalt iron oxides, chromium dioxide (CrO_2), and pure iron powders.

Recording

During recording, the input signals are amplified and fed to the recording head, essentially a coil of wire through which the signal current passes and which is wound round a core of magnetic material, creating an electromagnet. The core has a narrow gap cut into it at the point where the coated surface of the tape passes across it. As the incoming signal varies, so does the magnetization of the core, and a corresponding magnetic flux is created across and around the gap, setting up a similarly varying magnetic field in the coating of the tape adjacent to the gap.

The magnetic particles pass through the field at the gap as they are carried past it by the moving tape. The particles cannot physically move in the field, as they are fixed in the coating of the tape, but their magnetism is taken around a hysteresis loop and they leave the head having some remanent (remaining) magnetism, the strength of which depends on the strength of the field from the gap at the instant each piece of tape is in contact with it. The tape thus retains along its length a magnetic memory of the changes in the field, and therefore of the original signal.

▲ To enhance sound quality, professional recordings are made at a much faster speed than recordings made on an ordinary tape recorder at home. Because of this faster recording speed, the tape is stored not on spools but in a large container, which feeds the recorder more smoothly, minimizing fluctuations in the tension on the tape and further improving sound quality.

Playback

When the tape is played back by passing it across a replay head, similar to the recording head, the process is reversed. The varying magnetic fields on the surface of the tape head due to the remanent magnetism stored on the tape set up corresponding flux changes in the core and thus induce currents in the coils. These currents are amplified and will reproduce the original signals when played back through loudspeakers.

The magnetism in the tape remains unaffected by the replay process, and the signal can be replayed time and time again. The tape can be erased for reuse by passing it across an erase head, which has a larger gap than the recording or playback head and a high-frequency current flowing through the coils. As the particles move through the field from this head, their magnetism is taken round a series of hysteresis loops of progressively reducing size until no net magnetism remains.

Multitrack recording

By making the longest dimension of the head gaps much shorter than the tape width and including several gap, core, and coil assemblies magnetically screened from each other in one head unit, a number of tracks can be recorded on a single tape. This multitrack working can be used to increase the playing time of the tape by playing it through first on one track and then on another or to provide more than one signal at a time such as the two channels of a stereo recording or multiple instrument tracks in recording studios.

Uses of tape

One of the main uses of magnetic tape is for sound recording on open-reel tape or on cassettes or cartridges. Domestic video recorders use tape carried in cassettes. Computer backup data storage systems may use digital linear tape (DLT) to store the large amounts of data. A newer form of computer data storage technology, introduced in 1996, called advanced intelligent tape (AIT), is also available, with storage capacities of 15 to 50 GB.

By using a thinner polyester base, more tape can be wound onto a given size of reel. Standard play tapes are about 0.002 in. (0.051 mm) thick, and this tape is also used for professional sound recording. Long-play, video, and scientific information recording tapes are usually 0.0015 in. (0.04 mm) thick. Video tape is usually 0.5 in. (13 mm) wide. Double-play tape, used for home sound recording, is 0.001 in. (0.0254 mm) thick. For triple-play and C60 cassettes, 0.00075 in. (0.019 mm) thick tape is used, and the C90 and C120 cassettes use 0.0005 in. quadruple-play and 0.0033 in. quintuple-play tapes, respectively.

▶ Preparing leader tape, which is spliced to the ends of the magnetic tape. Open-reel tapes for sound recording usually have a red leader on one end and a green leader on the other.

▶ The tape is slit to the required width for use in cassettes.

▶ A bank of linked tape recorders, used to transfer an original sound track onto cassettes.

SEE ALSO:	Audio and video recording • Data storage • Magnetism • Plastics • Sound mixing • Video recorder

Magnetism

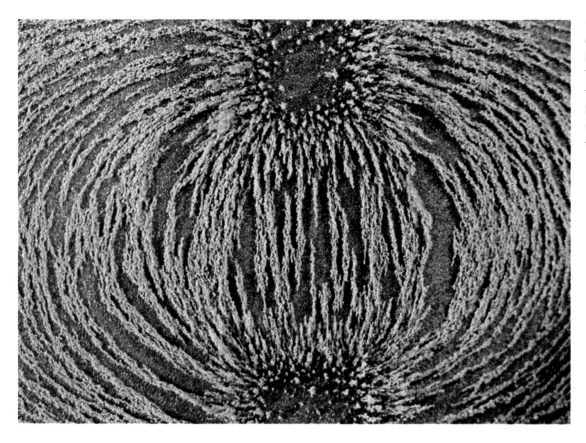

Magnetism is often thought of as a force in its own right, yet it is just one manifestation of the electromagnetic force. It is closely linked with electrostatic force: the difference is that while a stationary charged particle has just an electric field associated with it, a moving particle has a magnetic field as well. Yet it is possible to produce permanent magnets—indeed, these are the most familiar type—that have no apparent associated electric field.

In the 1830s, the British physicist Michael Faraday demonstrated clearly the relationship between electric charge and magnetism. When electric charge moves, it is said to constitute an electric current. When an electric current flows, it generates a magnetic field in the space around it just as if the current system had been replaced by a magnet system with a particular shape. It takes a force, analogous to the pressure needed to cause water to flow in a pipe, to make a charge move, that is, to produce an electric current. This force is known as an electromotive force (emf). Faraday showed that when an object capable of conducting electric current was moved through a magnetic field, an emf was set up in the conductor capable of producing electric current. He also demonstrated that a change in magnetic field produced an emf in a conducting object. So, electricity produces magnetism and magnetism produces electricity.

Magnetic circuits

The concept of magnetism existing only in closed loops is a useful one and was known to Faraday. It can be shown experimentally that the driving force in a magnetic circuit of an electromagnet (analogous to emf in an electric circuit) is proportional both to the number of turns that form the coil and the current in that coil. This phenomenon is called the magnetomotive force (mmf) and is measured in ampere turns. We then invent an imaginary substance that we consider to be the result of this mmf; we call it magnetic flux (or sometimes induction), which is measured in webers. Using these definitions we can write an equivalent of Ohm's law for a magnetic circuit and use it to calculate the mmf needed to set up a certain flux or the reverse. In electric circuits, emf equals current times resistance, and in magnetic circuits mmf equals flux times reluctance (the impediment to the flow of flux).

Permanent magnets

This tidy pattern of what is universally known as electromagnetism is, however, upset by an aspect of magnetism that has no precise counterpart in electricity. Some elements, having been placed in a magnetic field and then removed from it, adopt and retain an apparent internal source of mmf, and they continue to give a flux pattern in the

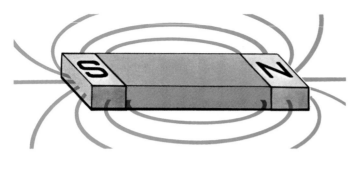

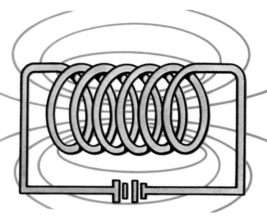

▶ A coil of wire (right) carrying an electric current sets up a magnetic field the same shape as that from a bar magnet (above).

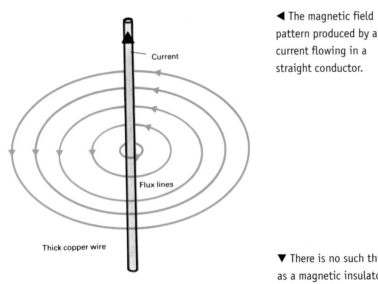

◀ The magnetic field pattern produced by a current flowing in a straight conductor.

space around them. They are called permanent magnets and the phenomenon, ferromagnetism, because the commonest element that displays ferromagnetism is iron (*ferrum* in Latin). The others are the less common metals cobalt and nickel and rarer elements such as gadolinium and dysprosium.

The fact that Earth itself is magnetized along an axis roughly corresponding to its axis of rotation was used by the ancient Chinese, who found that a freely suspended lodestone would always set itself in the same geographical direction. Simple rules were needed to deal with a simple action-at-distance experience, and soon the rule emerged that the lodestone has poles that point north and south, followed by the rule that like poles repel and unlike poles attract.

▼ There is no such thing as a magnetic insulator, and all materials conduct magnetic flux. Magnetic circuits are therefore like a conducting electric wire immersed in a salt bath: the current seems to have poles at X and Y.

The ready availability of permanent magnets focuses attention away from the closed-circuit nature of magnetism, a concept far more useful in engineering than is the pole concept. Arguments against the circuital concept are that, unlike electric circuits, magnetic circuits cannot be insulated because the corresponding magnetic conductivity of air or empty spaces is finite and only about a thousand times smaller than that of the best magnetically conducting steel. Faraday likened the design of magnetic circuits to the design of electric circuits, using bare copper wire in a bath of salt water (a good conductor of electricity). Although the electric circuits of most electrodynamic machines are complex and consist of coils with many turns of thin wire, their magnetic circuits are simple, short, fat and consist of a single turn.

The disadvantages of the pole concept are that it presupposes isolated poles in space, they have not been found despite searches (isolated electric charges, however, do exist), and troubles arise when trying to predict reactions between permanent magnets and other, initially unmagnetized, pieces of ferromagnetic material. For this purpose, the law of induced magnetism has been invented, implying that the proximity of a primary magnet pole to a piece of soft iron induces an opposite pole in the latter nearest to the magnet and a similar pole at the point most remote from the magnet. There are a number of experiments that are very hard to explain on the basis of poles alone, while the circuit concept sees no difficulty in such arrangements: the pieces will always take up a position of minimum reluctance (that is, minimum impediment to the flow of flux) within the prevailing mechanical constraints. The circuit theory sees a magnet's pole merely as a change in reluctance between different parts of a magnetic circuit.

The hysteresis loop

The difficulty with permanent magnets does not end here. The magnetic flux density B (the number of flux lines crossing unit area—measured as webers per square meter) that can be induced in a ferromagnetic material by imposing an mmf on it is not directly proportional to that mmf.

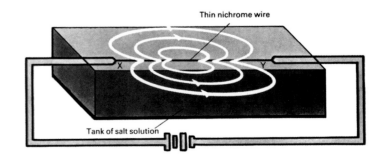

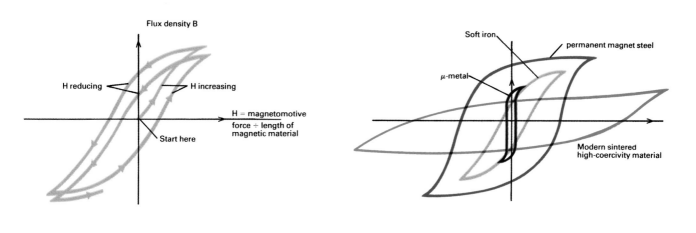

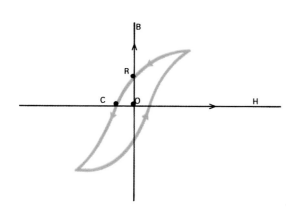

Furthermore, if flux density is plotted as a graph against magnetizing force *H* (a quantity obtained by dividing mmf by magnetic length and measured in ampere turns per meter), the state of magnetization of a piece of ferromagnetic material is seen to depend on its entire magnetic history. If such a material is taken through many magnetic cycles, the magnetization characteristic so obtained is called a hysteresis loop, whose area can be shown to be the work done in taking the magnetic material around one cycle and which appears as heat in the material itself.

The ratio *B/H* is given the name permeability (μ) but it is clear that μ is not constant as *B* varies. It is this aspect that becomes such an easy concept in magnetic circuits involving no ferromagnetic material, for μ is then constant and is the magnetic conductivity directly usable in the magnetic circuit version of Ohm's Law.

Theories of ferromagnetism

The behavior of ferromagnetics is one of the hardest phenomena to explain in terms of conventional physics. For several generations, the theory of the German physicist Wilhelm Weber that all ferromagnetic substances were effectively made of a mass of tiny particles, each of which was a permanent magnet, remained the only plausible model, but the concept had to be strained to

▲ Right: the shapes of hysteresis loops of various ferromagnetic materials useful in engineering. The total enclosed loop area for steels for permanent magnets should be as large as possible; for TV-tube electromagnets, the loop should be small. Top left: a typical magnetic journey as the result of an oscillating magnetomotive force in a ferromagnetic material. The ultimate steady cycle after millions of cycles is shown at bottom left. The point *R* is what remains of the flux density *B* after the magnetizing force *H* has been removed. The distance *OC* is called the coercivity, being the value of *H* required to demagnetize the magnetic specimen completely.

account for various degrees of difficulty being encountered in forcing the micromagnets to line up, as exhibited in the hysteresis effect.

The modern (domain) theory of ferromagnetism could be said to begin with the observation of the Barkhausen effect, whereby audible clicks were heard in a telephone receiver when connected to a coil of wire surrounding a ferromagnetic specimen that was being magnetized by a very gradually increasing mmf. Most of the pioneering work was done by a team of scientists at the Bell Telephone Laboratories in the United States. The technique that evolved, polishing the surface of a specimen and then etching it with acid, revealed patterns of walls, later to be called Bloch walls, dividing regions of different magnetic orientation. The theory of these domains was then built up to the following detailed picture.

Electron spin

A clue to the essential difference between a ferromagnetic element and a nonferromagnetic one is to be found in their atomic structures. The electrons orbiting the nucleus of an atom are arranged in shells, beginning with the simplest atoms filling the innermost shell, and shells of larger radius then being used for the electrons of elements higher in the periodic table, and therefore with more electrons. In order to balance the forces and energies within an atom, it is necessary to credit orbiting electrons with a spin (even though it is sometimes necessary to describe an electron as energy and therefore without shape).

One feature unique to ferromagnetic elements is that their atoms each have at least one electron with an uncompensated spin in one of the outer shells. Latching on to this phenomenon as the basis of the mechanism, scientists showed that atoms finding themselves in relative positions such that the axes of the uncompensated spins were parallel were likely to stay thus related and thereafter to regiment neighboring atoms in this direction. This build-up process is rapid and

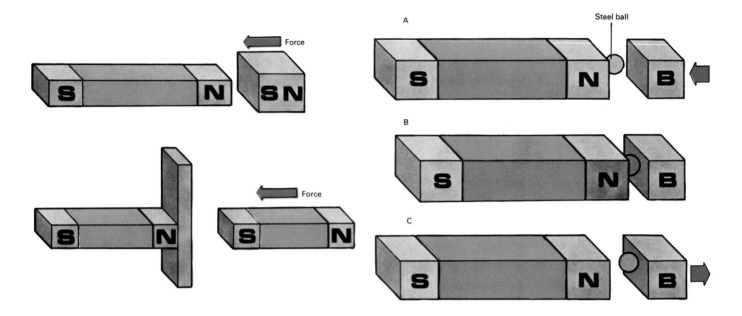

implies that every crystal of a ferromagnetic metal structure is self-magnetizing to saturation level.

In the case of each single crystal, however, what had hitherto been defined as the degree of magnetization was not due to each part of the crystal being magnetized to the same fraction of its saturation level. Rather, the crystal is divided into portions, or domains, each of which is selfsaturated, but not all the domains lie in the same magnetic direction. The rules for the domains can be investigated both experimentally, by the etching process, and theoretically, for the crystal as a whole tries to assume a pattern of minimum total energy.

The various forms of energy in a magnetic metal crystal may be classified as follows. First, there is magnetostatic energy, where the flux has to emerge from the crystal and pass through space. Second, there is magnetostriction energy due to the crystal increasing or decreasing in length because of magnetization, producing mechanical strain energy. Third, there is Bloch wall energy due to strain in the atomic lattice where, within a distance only a few atoms thick, the spin must reverse.

When a ferromagnetic metal is reduced to finer and finer particles, the minimum energy condition is reduced to magnetization in one direction only. This knowledge gave rise to a whole new magnet technology in which fine metallic powders were shaken so as to allow them to line up with each other (just as Weber's theory stated) and the whole then heated (sintered) to make a permanent magnet with a very large coercivity. (This is the magnetizing force required to pull the flux down to zero after its initial magnetization.) This technique can be extended to include substances other than pure metals, known as ferrites. These are ceramic materials consisting basically of iron oxide and small quantities of transition metal oxides, such as cobalt. It was found that, in the case of nonmetallic magnetic materials, not all the electron spins within a domain were aligned in the same direction. Instead, a portion of the atoms had their uncompensated spins aligned in one direction while the rest of the atoms had their spins aligned in the opposite direction. Externally, therefore, such materials cannot contain as high a flux level as can metallic substances. These ferrite substances are said to display ferrimagnetism. They are used in microwave apparatus, where it is essential that the substance is not capable of conducting electricity. The flux level can be controlled by mixing materials.

Recent developments have produced flexible and liquid magnetic materials by the powder metallurgy process, suspensions of barium ferrite and similar materials being held in a base of rubber, polyvinyl chloride, and other plastic materials.

Earth's magnetic field

Satellite MAGSAT was launched from Cape Canaveral in October 1979 and proved that Earth's magnetic field (the geomagnetic field) is decreasing in strength. If the field continues to decrease at its present rate, in a few thousand years, it will have disappeared altogether.

If Earth's field does decrease to zero, however, it is unlikely to stay there for long. According to archaeological evidence, it seems to have disappeared many hundreds of times in the past and always quickly returned. However, the new field has not always been in the same direction as the old. When the field returns, it could have the same direction as it had before it went away, but it is just as likely to have precisely the opposite direction. In other words, the geomagnetic field can, and does, reverse.

▲ Left: a permanent magnet induces poles in an unmagnetized piece of soft iron. The end nearest the north pole becomes a south pole, and the iron is attracted to the magnet. When a thin strip of steel is fixed to the north pole of the magnet, there is an attractive force on the north pole. Right: a steel ball, originally unmagnetized, can always be pulled off the primary magnet's pole by touching it with an unmagnetized piece of iron (B), that is then pulled away, as shown in the sequence (A) to (C).

When the magnetic field at Earth's surface is plotted on a world map, it looks highly complicated, although the complexity is largely an illusion created by a very small but highly irregular part of the field. About 5 percent of the field is nondipole, existing as local centers of varying strengths that grow and decay with time. Most of the geomagnetic field is that of a simple dipole, like the field produced by a bar magnet. The geomagnetic dipole lies through Earth's center and is currently inclined at 11 degrees to the rotational axis, but it oscillates very slowly and within strict limits so that it lies along the rotational axis when averaged out over time.

An axial dipole has two possible directions. At present, the south pole of Earth's dipole lies in the Northern Hemisphere. The north pole of a compass needle therefore points north, because only opposite poles attract. However, there is no obvious reason why the dipole should not point the other way, with its north pole lying in the Northern Hemisphere. In that case, of course, the north pole of a compass needle would point south. The field has been in its present direction for the past 700,000 years.

Geological evidence for field changes

Earth scientists have been able to discover that field changes have occurred because the ancient geomagnetic field is traceable in rocks. Many rocks contain small particles of magnetic material; these became magnetized in the direction of Earth's magnetic field at the time they were formed. Using sensitive magnetometers, scientists can now measure their fossil magnetism and hence determine what the direction and strength of the field were at various times in the past.

For example, at oceanic ridges—the vast mountain chains that rise from the floors of all the major oceans—hot, molten material from Earth's deep interior rises, cools, solidifies, and spreads away from the ridges on each side to form new oceanic crust. As it cools, it becomes magnetized in Earth's magnetic field, acting like giant tape recorders, creating a continuous record of any changes in field strength or direction. Huge strips of the crust parallel to the ridges become magnetized alternately in the normal and reversed direction. These strips then act as huge magnets themselves, giving rise at Earth's surface to a characteristic, striped magnetic field pattern that represents the way the geomagnetic field has frequently reversed.

By contrast, continental rocks (lava flows, for example) are produced at discrete times and thus only take snapshots of the field. Nevertheless, it is still possible to build up a good picture of the geomagnetic field reversal pattern. Indeed, continental rocks are essential most of the time, for they can be anything up to about 3 billion years old, whereas oceanic crust and sediments are all less than 200 million years old.

Putting together the information from all three types of rock, Earth scientists have been able to construct a polarity–time scale—a chart showing exactly when reversals took place.

▼ The axis of Earth's magnetic field is currently at an angle of 11 degrees to the axis of rotation. This angle gradually changes with time, and geological evidence shows that it may even completely reverse so that magnetic north becomes magnetic south, and vice versa.

FACT FILE

- *Ancient bricks have been found that give a record of Earth's magnetic field strength at the time they were made. The material became magnetized when the wet clay was thrown into the mold.*

- *Honeybee scouts indicate the direction of honey to other bees by performing a complicated dance that is governed by local geomagnetic fields. Magnetic variations as low as one-ten-thousandth of Earth's field can affect this dance.*

- *Dutch scientists have made monoatomic hydrogen by holding newly formed single atoms in a strong magnetic field at a supercold temperature to prevent them from combining into their natural H_2 form.*

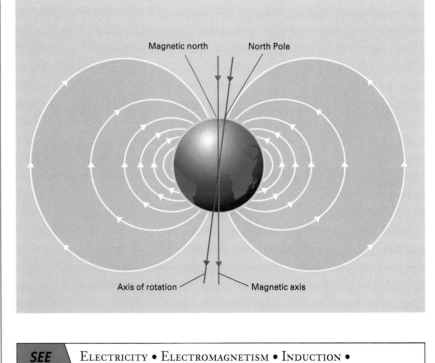

Magnetic north   North Pole

Axis of rotation   Magnetic axis

SEE ALSO: ELECTRICITY • ELECTROMAGNETISM • INDUCTION • MAGNETOHYDRODYNAMICS • MAGNETOMETER

Magnetohydrodynamics

Magnetohydrodynamics (MHD) is the study of how conductive fluids—gases and liquids—interact with magnetic fields when there is relative motion between the fluid and the field. Conductive liquids include metals—liquid mercury and molten sodium, for example—and ionic solutions, such as brine—sodium chloride (NaCl) solution—or seawater. Conductive gases are plasmas, substances in which neutral atoms or molecules have been caused to ionize by high temperatures or strong electrical fields.

Electromotive force

When a charged object moves through a magnetic field that acts at right angles to its direction of motion, that object experiences a force along a line that is at right angles to both the direction of its motion and the magnetic field. This force, called the electromotive force (emf), is the basis of how both motors and generators function. In a motor, moving electrons in current-carrying coils experience a force in a magnetic field that causes the coil to rotate. In a generator, the rotation of a conductive coil in a magnetic field causes the electrons in that coil to move in a current.

In the case of a conductive fluid, electrons and negative ions experience forces similar to those that act on electrons in the coils of motors and

generators. Positive ions, on the other hand, experience a force that acts in the opposite direction. As such, when a stream of charged particles moves forward through a vertical magnetic field whose north pole is uppermost, positively charged particles experience a force that drives them to the left, whereas negatively charged particles experience a force to the right.

MHD power generation

When a conductive fluid passes through a magnetic field, a voltage can be generated between a pair of electrodes so positioned as to discharge the charge carriers deflected by the magnetic field. In MHD power generation, the conductive fluid is a burning gaseous mixture of fuel oil, gas, or pulverized coal with air. At the combustion temperature—around 4500°F (2500°C)—a significant proportion of the gas is ionized. This proportion can be increased by seeding the fuel mixture with substances that ionize readily, although the recovery of such substances from the exhaust gases complicates and adds to the expense of the MHD generating process.

Once the combustion gases have passed through the MHD unit, water-filled heat exchangers extract energy from the hot gases to produce steam that is used to drive conventional

▼ In a combined-cycle MHD-thermal generating station, an MHD unit first extracts energy from the burning gases that pass through a magnetic field. The hot gases then give up some of their heat as they preheat air for the combustion process before providing heat to boil water for a conventional steam turbogenerator.

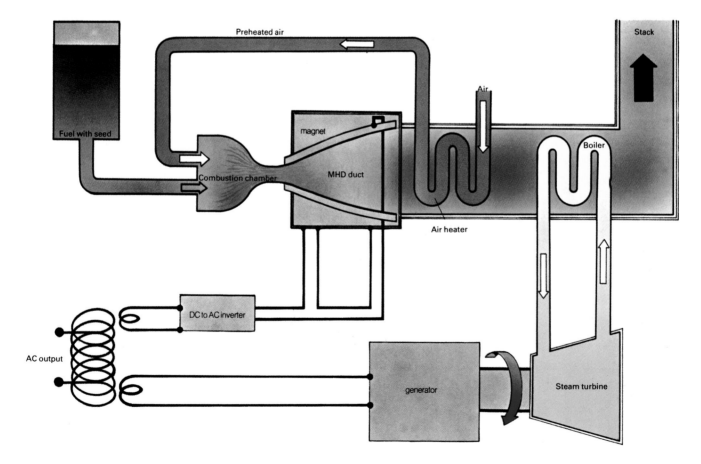

turbogenerator sets. At present, MHD technology is used to augment the power generated by turbines. A combined MHD and thermal generating unit converts around 50 percent of the energy content of fuel into electrical power, whereas a purely thermal unit converts just over 35 percent of the fuel's energy into electricity.

The power yield of an MHD unit could be increased by using higher combustion temperatures to achieve a greater degree of ionization. The higher temperatures could be achieved by burning fuel in preheated oxygen rather than air, for example. Powerful superconducting magnets could further increase the net power output by increasing the magnetic field strength and reducing the power used in energizing the electromagnets. Proportional heat and frictional losses could be reduced by increasing the scale of MHD units, thereby reducing the contact area with the electrodes and insulating walls in proportion to the volume of the combustion gases.

MHD generation could also be used to produce electricity from nuclear energy. In such a system, the heat released in a fission reactor can be used to vaporize sodium. Highly conductive sodium vapor would then generate a current as it passed through a magnetic field produced by the electromagnets of an MHD unit.

Electromagnetic propulsion

A conductive fluid can be made to flow by passing a current between electrodes at right angles to a magnetic field. In effect, this process is the reverse of what happens in an MHD generator. The phenomenon can be used to propel a craft by directing the fluid against the direction of travel.

The first ship to successfully use electromagnetic propulsion was the Japanese *Yamato-1*, an experimental vessel sponsored by the Nippon Foundation whose maiden voyage took place in 1992. The propulsion unit of the 204-ton (185 tonne) vessel consists of a cylindrical duct that runs from fore to aft below the waterline of the boat. Superconducting coils above and below the duct produce the magnetic field, and electrodes at the sides of the duct provide the current. The dissolved salts in seawater cause its conductivity.

Since an electromagnetic propulsion unit has no moving parts, it produces neither the noise nor the vibration associated with propeller action. The flow of water through the duct of an electromagnetic drive is streamlined. Consequently, it produces practically no wake and has none of the energy losses associated with the turbulent flow of water around a conventional ship's propeller. A further advantage is the ease of control and handling relative to propeller-driven craft.

▲ The *Yamato-1* is the first vessel to use magnetohydrodynamics as a means of propulsion. MHD ships have no propeller and so do not create any noise or vibration. The speed of the ship can be controlled simply by changing the strength of the electrical current. Another benefit of MHD ships is that there is less cavitation, so they can reach much higher speeds than conventional vessels.

Water treatment

Magnetohydrodynamics is used to reduce the concentrations of dissolved salts in water for industrial and residential hot-water systems. Electromagnetic coils placed at either side of a water pipe provide the magnetic field, and the circulation of water in the system provides the motion necessary for the MHD effect. As water flows through the field, the positive and negative ions of its dissolved salts are deflected to opposite walls of the pipe, where they are trapped.

The removal of dissolved salts inhibits corrosion and the formation of scale. This action is particularly important for boilers and industrial evaporators, where any dissolved salts become concentrated by the evaporation of water.

MHD in plasmas

An aspect of magnetohydrodynamics is the study of the motion of plasmas in magnetic fields. In the laboratory, MHD is used to confine the plasmas used in fusion experiments within toroidal (doughnut-shaped) circuits. The high temperatures of such plasmas would melt or vaporize conventional containers, thereby losing the heat necessary for fusion reactions to occur.

On a vastly greater scale, theoretical MHD helps astrophysicists understand the motion of radiation-ionized hydrogen plasma in interstellar space.

SEE ALSO: CONDUCTION, ELECTRICAL • ELECTROMAGNETISM • PLASMA PHYSICS • POWER PLANT

Magnetometer

The need to measure the strength of magnetic fields in science and industry has resulted in the production of magnetometers of many types. Early magnetometers consisted of spring-loaded magnets in which the field strength was measured by the extension of the spring. They were superseded by electronic systems, the most common being the proton, fluxgate, and Hall effect magnetometers.

Proton magnetometer

The proton magnetometer is probably the most accurate type of magnetometer available, and it relies for its operation on the alignment of protons—the positively charged particles in atoms—within a proton-rich source such as kerosene, which has a comparatively large number of hydrogen atoms. In one form of this instrument, suitable for measuring weak magnetic fields, the kerosene, which is contained within a bottle, is magnetized to a high level by means of surrounding coils. When it is fully magnetized, the protons are all aligned in the same direction. The moment the exciting field is removed, the protons begin to fall back to their original random orientation, and as they do so, they induce an alternating voltage in a sensing-coil system. The frequency of this voltage is a measurement of the surrounding magnetic field.

An alternative form suitable for use in strong fields employs a small sample of water or heavy water (D_2O). The sample is exposed to a radio frequency (RF) field (1 to 1,000 MHz). At one specific frequency, energy is absorbed from the radio frequency (RF) field. This frequency is again a measure of the field strength.

The main advantage of the proton magnetometer is that the frequency can be measured very accurately, and therefore a very precise field strength can be obtained. However, it cannot be used to measure a rapidly varying or alternating field, the field direction, or, because of the recycling time, the field at any instant in time.

Fluxgate magnetometer

The fluxgate magnetometer depends for its operation on the rapid alternating current (AC) magnetization of a pair of high permeability (easily magnetizable) cores. Each core has a primary and a secondary winding, one outside the other. An AC current applied to the primary magnetizes the core, which in turn induces a current in the secondary windings. If an external field is present, the core will be magnetized more, and by using two

cores arranged so that their outputs will reinforce each other, the signal is doubled for a given external field, showing up as an AC voltage of twice the original frequency.

Magnetometers based on this principle can measure fields over a small area, as small as 0.20 x 0.08 in. (5 x 2 mm), can detect rapidly varying fields, and can measure field direction as well. They are ideally suited to the detection of sunken objects such as ships, bombs, and mines. Their directional properties make them useful aboard aircraft as compasses, with one on each wingtip. Other uses include measuring magnetic fields in deep space and detecting weak magnetic fields in geological and archaeological specimens.

Hall effect

The principle of the Hall effect magnetometer was discovered in 1879, but it has only been applied quite recently with the introduction of semiconductor materials such as indium arsenide and indium antimonide. When a current is applied between two edges of a slice of the material, a voltage is induced across the other two edges by the movement of the electrons carrying the current through the magnetic field. This voltage can then be measured, and its magnitude is a measure of the magnetic field strength.

Such a device is particularly suitable for measuring strong magnetic fields and will work at frequencies up to one megahertz. Because the semiconductor material may be only 0.004 in. (0.1 mm) thick, it is ideally suited to measuring very strong fields in small spaces in machines such as electric motors.

▲ A diver uses a magnetometer in the Red Sea to look for the remains of sunken ships.

SEE ALSO: ARCHAEOLOGICAL TECHNOLOGIES • ELECTROMAGNETISM • INDUCTION • MAGNETISM • METAL DETECTOR

Mail-Sorting Machinery

◀ A mail segregator. Letters of the right size for automatic handling fall through the slots; the others have to be sorted by hand.

The aim of every mail service is to provide the most efficient delivery possible. Beginning in the middle of the 19th century, steps have been made toward the total mechanization of the postal system. Britain was the first country to frank (cancel) mail in 1844, with a rubber stamp showing the date and where the mail was posted. Initially, franking was done by hand, although a steam-powered machine was tried unsuccessfully in 1857.

The last few decades have seen the beginnings of radical changes in postal services worldwide, with business starting to adopt new technology in the shape of electronic mail (e-mail) as an alternative to conventional letters. For those without a computer, there are interesting hybrid systems that use electronics to send messages from place to place but can still physically deliver a letter to the recipient.

Automated canceling

The first franking and facing machines were introduced in the late 1940s and early 1950s. They used a light-dark scanning principle to detect a dark-colored stamp against the (usually) light-colored envelope. Unfortunately, these early scanners also reacted to labels and some writing.

Research turned to the stamps themselves. Graphite lines were printed on the backs of the stamps so that they could be detected as areas with higher electrical conductivity. However, this system was not totally successful. The lines were easily broken, causing loss of conductivity, and metal objects such as paper clips sent in the mail often fooled the machinery.

▶ Processing mail unsuitable for automatic readers. The machines can sort most typewritten mail; these operators read addresses that have been badly written by hand.

The system that finally brought success uses phosphorescent or fluorescent materials that become visible when bathed in ultraviolet light. Organic resins, or a mixture of zinc sulfide with a copper activator, rather than toxic phosphor itself, are incorporated in the stamp or printed on it.

Automatic sorting

Automation has advanced considerably in letter sorting, although the amount of automation still depends on the size of the sorting office and the volume of mail processed. In automated offices, the mail is first separated into letters that can be machined and those that cannot. In smaller offices, separation takes place at a table, where the letters are turned face-up by hand and then placed onto conveyor belts where the stamps are canceled. At the largest offices, mail goes through a segregator and then to automatic letter facing.

The key to all automated mail processing is the zip (zone improvement plan) code in the United States or the postal code in Europe. Similar systems are in use throughout the developed world. All the information needed for placing a letter in the right mailbag for the morning delivery is contained in the code. In the United States, the code is a five-digit number, and in Europe a five- to seven-character code is used.

In the U.S. zip code, the first three digits indicate where in the country the letter is destined to go—that is, they direct the letter to a section of a particular state—and the last two digits denote the specific city or town or post office if there is more than one in a city. To pinpoint a specific dwelling or company address, the house or build-

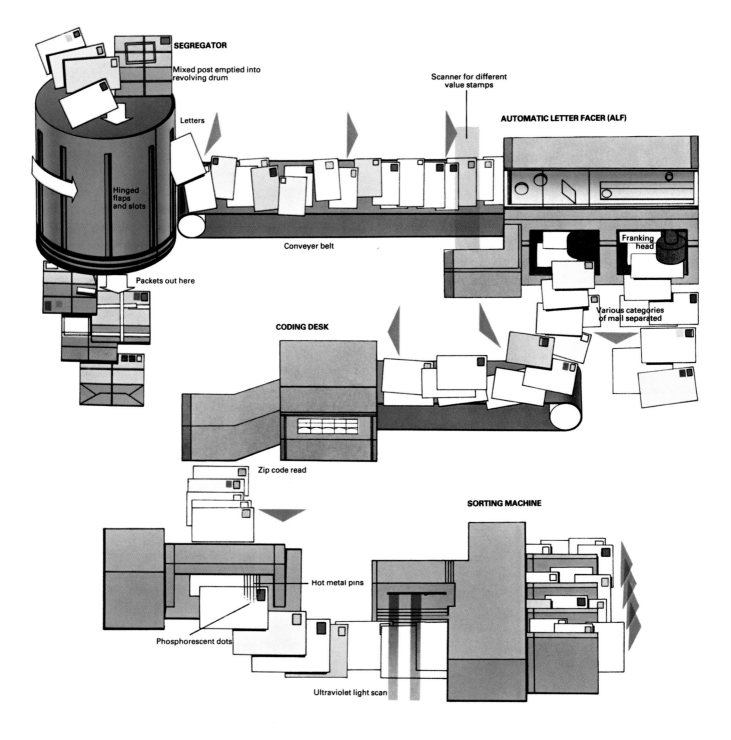

SEGREGATOR

Mixed post emptied into revolving drum

Letters

Hinged flaps and slots

Packets out here

Scanner for different value stamps

AUTOMATIC LETTER FACER (ALF)

Franking head

Various categories of mail separated

Conveyer belt

CODING DESK

Zip code read

SORTING MACHINE

Hot metal pins

Phosphorescent dots

Ultraviolet light scan

ing number included in the address normally has to be read, but this level of detail is not needed by the sorting system at the post office.

As well as zip codes, automation now means that in some countries, including the United States, automated post offices have bar code readers that can take address information from bar codes on envelopes. There are two elements to bar coding for letters in the United States—FIM (face identification marking) and POSTNET (postal numeric encoding technique). POST-NET was developed for use by the U.S. Postal Service to automate the sorting of mail. The code comprises two frame bars at the beginning and end, combinations of five long and short bars for

each of the zip code digits, and five more long and short bars for the check digit. Each digit from zero to nine is a unique pattern of long and short bars. The eleven-digit bar code is developed from the nine-digit zip code and the last two digits of the street address. POSTNET is a demanding system because the bar code has to be the correct size and in the correct place—it cannot be reduced or enlarged. Bar width, height, and spacing are all fixed.

FIM was developed as part of the POSTNET bar coding system. FIM is used by the canceling machines to sort mail according to whether or not it has bar codes and its postage requirements. There are three types of FIM, called FIM A,

▲ Mechanical handling of mail. After the letters have passed through the segregator, an automatic letter facer faces them and cancels the stamps. At the coding desk, the zip is typed in code in phosphorescent dots on each envelope so it can be read by the sorting machinery.

FIM C, and FIM D. FIM A means postage is required, but a POSTNET bar code is included. FIM C means postage is prepaid and a POSTNET bar code is included, and FIM D means postage required and a POSTNET bar code is not included.

Segregator

Mail collected from mailboxes is emptied into a hopper, from which it is carried by conveyor belt to the segregator—a slowly rotating inclined drum, some 4.5 ft. (1.5 m) in diameter and as long as a room. The aim of the segregator is to separate easily handled letters from less easily handled parcels and packets. The inside of the drum is fitted with hinged plates that form slots through which letters can slip onto vibrating rollers, which help to maintain a smooth flow of letters to the next stage.

Newspapers, small parcels, and letters thicker than 0.25 in. (6 mm) pass through the drum, ending up at another conveyor belt. About one-fifth of the mail separated in this way is nonmachinable and sorted by hand.

Automatic letter facing

The letters now pass to the automatic letter facer (ALF). First, the letters are aligned along their long edges, and then an optical scanner looks for phosphorescent lines printed on the stamp. If necessary, the letter is turned the right way up by the machine.

The next stage is for the machine to check whether a stamp is on the letter. A scanner in the ALF recognizes the afterglow excited by the ultraviolet light source and passes the letter to a franking head. If there is no stamp, the letter is rejected. In countries where a multitier postal system is operated, with first- and second-class mail at differing prices, this stage is more complex because letters have to be separated into differing priorities according to stamp value. This stage is also supplemented by bar code reading where it is available.

In Britain, first-class stamps are printed on phosphor-coated paper, while second-class stamps are on ordinary paper with one phosphor bar printed on them. If the scanner finds an afterglow, it switches off immediately. It opens again after 4.5 milliseconds, and if it still detects an afterglow, the letter is channeled to a franking device for first-class mail. If there is no further reaction, the letter goes to the second-class franking head. Each ALF is fitted with four franking heads and four boxes for receiving canceled mail; there is a fifth box for unrecognized letters, which must be dealt with manually.

Other kinds of scanners may be fitted to the ALF. For example, optical recognition devices may be fitted for detecting prepaid and official mail, which can have a number of dark printed bands to distinguish it from unstamped mail.

The coding desk

Ideally, post offices would like to have machines that can read all addresses on envelopes reliably, but the variety of typefaces and styles of handwriting mean that, despite advances in optical character recognition (OCR) technology, this is not always possible. However, OCR, also used in conjunction with computers to turn a written document into one that can be word processed, has advanced sufficiently to master most types of clear handwriting.

In a manual system, letters pass in front of the operator in a continuously moving stream at a rate regulated by typing speed. The operator reads the zip code and keys it into a computer with a large database containing all the zip codes that the system can handle.

The keyed code operates a translator (also called the electronic dictionary), which prints a phosphorescent code on the letter face by striking heated metal pins against a tape. The resulting pattern of dots is a binary representation of the zip code that can be read by machines. Two 14-bit patterns are used, each arranged as a start bit, a 12-bit code, and a parity bit, which can give more than 16 million possible combinations.

▼ The letter-coding machinery that prints the phosphorescent dots on the envelopes. The dots are printed in a computer code dictated by an electronic dictionary.

device in which the codes were represented by wires threaded through a magnetic core, but now the translator uses computer technology.

The incoming signal is compared with codes stored in a central computer. The computer is programmed to serve each sorting machine at regular intervals according to a time slot or timing pulse. During the time slot allotted to a particular machine, a question in the form of the binary address code (not to be confused with binary memory addresses in computer programming) is asked of the computer. The computer finds the code in its database, where it also finds routing instructions for that code. It sends back the routing instructions to the sorting machine, which operates mechanical devices in response.

Character recognition

Optical character recognition (OCR) systems can read typed or printed characters, dependent on the printing or typing quality. An OCR system can search in the body of the address or zip code to gather enough additional information to sort the letter accurately.

OCR equipment, operating at speeds of up to 30,000 items per hour, is being used in a number of locations in the United States, Japan, and several European countries. Typical OCR systems read the last three lines of the address and look for the zip code and the post town. The numbers in the zip code carrying the post town information are compared with the post town that the system has read. If they are the same, the phosphor code is printed on the letter ready for sorting. If the zip code is incorrect or missing, the

The phosphorescent materials used in stamps and those used in code printing are different, so the scanning head used to read the address code will not be confused by the phosphorescence from the stamp. In order to differentiate between the two codes, materials are used that phosphoresce in response to different wavelengths of ultraviolet radiation or different colors of visible light.

From the coding desks, the letters are fed into the presorter, which reads just the lower line of dots and can process letters at a rate of up to 30,000 per hour. From the lower line of dots, the machine can tell how far the letter has to travel and gives priority to those with the farthest distance by sorting the mail into a number of stacks.

▲ The control panel of an automatic address reader, which sorts and codes about 75 percent of the letters in this German sorting office.

▼ This letter-sorting system in Frankfurt, Germany, is integrated into an extensive tray conveyor system, so the transportation of the mail within the building is itself largely mechanized.

Letter-sorting machine

The stacks of letters are fed into automatic high-speed letter-sorting machines, which can process up to 16,000 letters per hour. The precise number of letters that can be sorted depends on the length of the envelopes being sorted. A space of about 2 in. (50 mm) is needed between each of the letters as they pass through the machine, and a machine processing mainly long business envelopes will therefore have a lower throughput than one processing mainly Christmas cards.

Each letter is passed under a code reader, where it is irradiated with ultraviolet light. A translator converts the code into a set of routing instructions, and the letters are sorted into a number—usually about 150—of sorting boxes.

Several machines used in parallel are needed to give all the possible code groupings. A single machine can be changed so that it can sort other codes by electronic switching within the translator. In the past, the translator was a threaded core

Chase Visa
P.O. Box 5111
New Hyde Park, New York 11042

FLUSHING
DROP SHIPMENT
AUTHORIZATION 15

ECB 1 REV. 3-80 PTG 11 85

FIRST CLASS

TONY WALTERS
158 BERRICK RD
FREEPORT NY 11520

◀ Automatic address readers can easily cope with a clearly typed address, as shown here. The zip code appears in the address and in coded form at the bottom of the envelope.

code of the post town only is printed. If the OCR fails to read the post town itself, the letter passes into the conventional sorting system.

Future developments

The long-term aim is to achieve completely automatic mail handling, so that a letter can be fed into the machinery and not handled until it gets to the mailbag. OCR technology has advanced considerably, but bar coding is seen as having the advantage of consistency and will probably prove more popular. In Russia, some steps have been taken to ensure conformity: the sender is required to print the postal code in standardized boxes on specially printed envelopes, so the address can be read easily by OCR technology.

Electronic mail

Mail has evolved fundamentally over the last few decades, thanks to investment in new technology. Predictions that letters themselves could disappear completely in favor of e-mails may not yet have come true, but the advent of e-mail has undoubtedly had a considerable effect on the amount of printed mail being sent, particularly between young people.

E-mail offers one real advantage over conventional mail: it is immediate. A message is typed into an e-mail program on a personal computer and then sent by a modem (standing for modulator-demodulator) link via the internet to a destination electronic mailbox—Internet service providers (ISPs) and company servers provide a central holding facility for subscribers or staff. When the recipient logs on to the system, the mail is waiting to be read. Instead of carrying tons of paper over many miles, the existing telephone system has become the medium over which many messages are sent. Another advantage is that

e-mailers can send attachments—either digitized photographs or other types of files, and computer programs, knowing that they will reach their destination quickly and conveniently.

Replacing the mailbox

Unlike conventional mail, there are many different programs for sending e-mail. Some are purely for e-mail, and others are part of the facilities of large database systems. Which is chosen depends on what other facilities are needed. Using electronic mail is not cheap, although the cost of personal computers, software, and modems has dropped considerably over the last few years. Flat-rate access charges or free local or cable calls also mean that running costs have reduced considerably. E-mail at best is almost instantaneous, and new high-speed lines are increasing the speed at which downloads and uploads can occur.

The middle course

For those who do not have access to computer technology, an alternative to electronic mail is still available. E-Com and Intelpost are a kind of hybrid of new technology and a traditional telegraph system. The system is spreading worldwide—most major European countries, as well as some countries in Africa and the Far East, are connected—and noncomputer owners can use it.

Other methods by which letters are now being sent include the fax—facsimile machine. Those with fax software on their computer can also send letters via the telephone system that can be accepted by a receiving fax machine in the same way as a normal sheet of paper.

SEE ALSO: Computer • Conveyor • Modem and isdn • Optical scanner • Telegraph

Manometer

A manometer is a device for measuring the pressure of a gas—essentially a pressure gauge. In its simplest form, it consists of a U-shaped glass tube filled with a liquid, such as mercury, water, or oil. A measurement of pressure is achieved by leaving one of the arms of the tube open to the atmosphere while the other is connected to the system to be measured. The pressure displaces the liquid in the tube, and the difference in the levels is a measure of the pressure relative to atmospheric pressure.

By connecting the arms of the manometer to two systems, it is possible to measure the differential pressure between the systems. Manometers can also be used for measuring vacuums.

Measurement can be simplified by making one of the arms of the manometer considerably wider than the other to give a well manometer. With this design, the fluid level in the large-diameter well does not change significantly when fluid is displaced up or down the narrow arm and so provides a more stable measurement indication. Increased measurement accuracy is given by the use of an inclined tube to provide an extended scale. In the piston manometer, or pressure balance, high pressures are measured by allowing them to act against a piston that is then balanced by the application of a force.

Uses

An example of a manometer is the Riva-Rocci sphygmomanometer, which is used by doctors to measure blood pressure in arteries. The manometer is connected by means of a flexible tube to an inflatable cuff positioned around the patient's upper arm. The cuff is inflated by means of a small hand pump until the pressure is just sufficient to stop pulsation in an artery in the forearm below the cuff. When this point is reached, the difference in mercury levels in the manometer is read off, and this gives the arterial blood pressure. A similar method is used to measure blood pressure in the veins, except that instead of a cuff, an inflatable rubber bag with a glass plate in its upper surface is used. The bag is positioned over a vein and inflated until the vein collapses, and the pressure is then read off.

In research and industry, processes are often carried out at low pressures, and a type of manometer called a McLeod gauge is sometimes used for measuring the pressure in such systems. McLeod gauges are commonly built to measure pressures of about 0.00005 in. (0.001 mm) of mercury. A McLeod gauge consists of a closed

A sphygmomanometer used to measure arterial blood pressure. The cuff is inflated around the upper arm and the pressure is then read off.

reservoir containing mercury that is connected by means of a tube first to a chamber of known volume having a closed glass capillary tube at its top end and, second, to the system whose pressure is to be measured. The tube to the system is provided with a capillary tube bypass, which runs parallel and close to the closed capillary tube; this measuring capillary is included to reduce measurement errors owing to capillary effects. Initially, the mercury level is below the junction of the measuring chamber and the system connecting tube so that the chamber is at the system pressure. Then the mercury level in the gauge is raised—either mechanically or by the application of pressure to the mercury reservoir—until the mercury level in the bypass capillary is level with the tip of the closed capillary. The volume of rarefied gas from the measuring chamber is thus compressed into the end of the closed capillary. The mercury level in the closed capillary gives a measure of the pressure in the capillary, and by Boyle's Law (pressure times volume is a constant), it is also a measure of the system pressure.

SEE ALSO: GAS LAWS • PRESSURE • PRESSURE GAUGE • SPHYGMOMANOMETER

Mapmaking Techniques

The task of the cartographer (mapmaker) is to represent the topographical (natural and artificial) features of Earth's surface at a greatly reduced scale in a convenient form, usually on flat sheets of paper. The first and fundamental difficulty arises from the curvature and irregularity of Earth's surface, and although the curvature can be ignored for maps of small areas, the surface irregularities—hills and valleys—make it necessary to show the ground features as plan projections on a plane (flat) surface. Therefore, unless the ground is level, the distances shown on the map do not agree exactly with those on the surface. With larger areas, such as the United States, the curvature has to be taken into account, and the plan projection is made on a curved surface conforming as nearly as possible to the shape of Earth; this surface is known as the spheroid of reference.

Projections

Maps on curved surfaces, however, are inconvenient objects to handle, and a transformation has to be made from the curved to a plane surface by means of a map projection. There are many different map projections, but they all result in distortion, in one way or another, of the pattern of features on the curved surface. This distortion is very obvious in atlas maps of the whole world (as on Mercator's or Mollweide's projections), but it is possible by using particular projections to retain some elements of correctness.

Orthomorphic projections are widely used for large-scale topographical maps. In an orthomorphic projection, the scale does not remain constant over the whole area, but at every point, the scale is the same in all directions for a short distance, thus preserving the correct shape in small areas. The orthomorphic transverse Mercator projection is used for the official maps of Britain, and in this comparatively small area, the scale variation caused by the projection does not exceed one part in 2,500, which is negligible for most mapping purposes.

The choice of the kind of projection chosen depends on the purpose of the map. The Mercator projection, devised by the Flemish cartographer Gerardus Mercator in 1569, is a kind of cylindrical projection that causes distortions at higher and lower latitudes. This projection has the advantage, however, of showing places of the same latitude positioned at the same height on the map. In the case of transverse Mercator projections, the cylinder is not tangential to the equator but runs along any other meridian, thus having

▲ A cartographer using a computer to create a digital map of Russia.

the effect of reducing distortion in the north–south direction around the chosen meridian.

Azimuthal projections produce circular maps that show Earth spreading out from one central point tangential to Earth. Maps of the Arctic and Antarctica are often depicted in this way. These maps become increasingly distorted toward the outer portion of the map.

Conic projections project an image of Earth onto a cone with its tip positioned above either the North or South Pole and with its sides tangential to Earth. These maps usually become increasingly distorted toward the bottom portion of the cone.

Primary mapping

A distinction must be made between the two classes of mapping. Primary mapping is produced directly from a topographical survey; derived map-

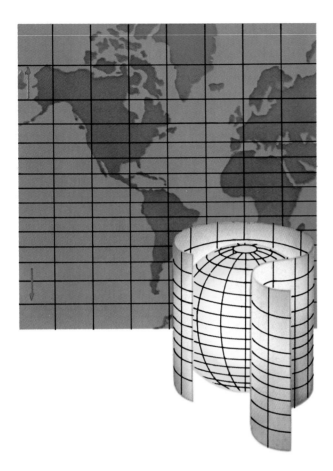

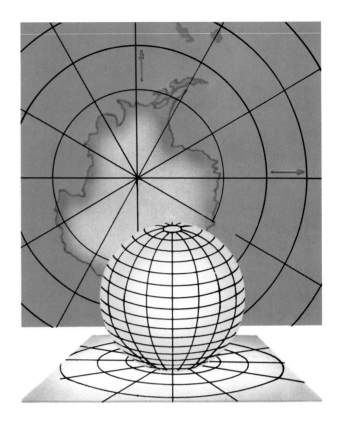

ping at smaller scale results from the reduction and generalizing of primary maps or from the compilation of material from either or both categories.

When undertaking primary mapping, it is not possible to fit together individual surveys of small areas in order to complete the survey of a large area. The errors in such independent local surveys would accumulate and produce discrepancies that would be unresolvable. A consistent framework has first to be constructed covering the entire area to be mapped. Constructing this framework, which must be located and oriented correctly on Earth's surface, is accomplished by astronomical observations at several points within it.

Since the middle of the 18th century, the classical control framework for mapping large areas has been produced by triangulation, in which the angles of a system of triangles are measured to a high degree of precision with a theodolite (an instrument consisting basically of a telescope moving around a circular scale graduated in degrees). The linear dimensions are determined by base measurement; that is, by measuring the lengths of several sides in different parts of the system, and thereafter by calculation. Accurate base measurement was first carried out in Britain with glass measuring rods on Hounslow Heath in 1784. At about the same time, great improvements were made in the design and manufacture of theodolites, particularly by the British designer

of precision mathematical instruments Jesse Ramsden, and the national triangulation of Britain was begun. The lengthy and laborious operation of base measurement with glass rods (1784), bimetallic bars (1826), and later, steel tapes suspended in catenary (the curve a string makes suspended between two supports) was gradually replaced from the 1950s onward by electromagnetic methods.

Instruments such as the tellurometer and geodimeter, which measure distance by recording the time taken for an electromagnetic wave to travel to and from a remote station, enable the whole operation to be completed in a few hours and make it possible to incorporate many more linear measurements into the triangulation framework. The subdivision of the main, or primary, triangles into secondary and tertiary triangles is continued until a density of fixed control points is obtained that meets the requirements of the topographical survey method chosen. A similar control network for heights above the sea level datum is obtained by a pattern of intersecting lines of spirit leveling.

Air surveys

The topographical survey can be undertaken on the ground or by means of aerial photographs. The ground surveys of the 18th and 19th centuries were carried out with compass, plane table (essentially a drawing board mounted on a tripod

▲ Left: cylindrical projection—still the most used mapmaking method. A light in the glass sphere casts the shadows of the parallels and meridians onto the surrounding paper. Right: If a sheet of paper were placed touching one of the poles, at a tangent to the sphere, the shadow would represent an azimuthal projection.

together with an alidade consisting of a rule with sights at both ends to give direction of survey points from the table), and chain; in the second half of the 20th century, new instruments that combined the theodolite with either an optical or an electromagnetic distance-measuring device came widely into use. The method most commonly practiced, however, in recent years for topographical mapping is air survey, because of its speed and economy.

Except when the ground is absolutely flat and when the photographic exposure is made with the camera pointing vertically downward, an air photograph cannot be used directly to make a map because of the scale variation caused by the ground relief and the tilt of the camera. To solve the problem, stereo plotting machines, such as the Wild photogrammetric instrument, are generally used. Pairs of overlapping air photographs are set up in the machine in accordance with the control data already obtained so that their positions and orientations in space at the two moments of exposure are recreated. It is then possible to create in the machine a three-dimensional model of the ground from which planimetric detail (distances and positions of features), contours, and spot heights can be derived. The model is formed by the intersection of the image of the two photographs.

In primary mapping, the task of the cartographer is to show all the information collected by the surveyor in the way that enables it to be most clearly and readily comprehended. With primary mapping at large scales (1:500 to 1:10,000), the preservation of positional accuracy is of first importance, and the cartographic process of generalization has little part to play.

Printing

One method commonly used in art studios for making a single-color primary map is to scribe the detail on plastic sheets. A clear plastic sheet is covered with a semi-opaque waxy coating on which the image of the surveyor's work is printed by a photographic process. The draftsperson cuts away the waxy coating along the lines of the surveyor's drawing, leaving very sharply defined lines of clear plastic. This operation produces a negative from which a positive on another sheet of film or plastic can be made by contact photography. Names and symbols are usually added at this stage; they are printed on strips of very thin film that are stuck to the film positive. A lithographic printing plate is made, for printing on a rotary offset litho machine.

The combination of scribing and photographic processes compares very favorably for speed and quite well for quality with the copperplate engraving used in the early 19th century for map reproduction. In this process, a hand-drawn tracing was made of the surveyor's drawing, and it was transferred to a copperplate that was coated with wax to take the transfer. The engraver then cut along the transferred lines into the

▼ Left: conic projection—the third main type of projection. Meridians project as straight lines and parallels as arcs on concentric circles. Right: since the middle of the 18th century, the classical control framework for mapping large areas has been produced by triangulation, by which an area is measured as a series of triangles, using a second set of triangles as a check.

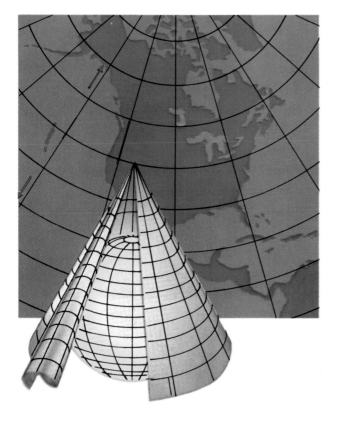

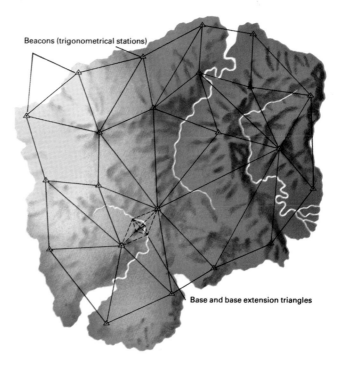

Beacons (trigonometrical stations)

Base and base extension triangles

copper; the outline, names, symbols, and ornamental drawing, including the hachures (lines used to shade a plan) representing the hills, were all engraved in this way. Ink was then rubbed into the engraved lines, and after the surface of the plate had been cleaned, impressions were taken on paper.

Derived mapping

Small-scale derived maps are made either directly from the primary mapping or from other derived maps. Here there is great scope for the cartographic designer, because it is generally necessary to make a selection of detail for showing at the smaller scale, to generalize the outline of some features, and to exaggerate the size of others so that they are given the prominence the designer requires. Because of the closeness of detail on small-scale maps, it is usual today to use colors to distinguish one type of feature from another, such as red for main roads, blue for water, and green for woods.

A typical procedure for making a smaller-scale derived map from primary mapping is as follows. From the primary mapping, reduced-scale film copies are made that are then built up into the new format. This compilation is then rephotographed into two scribecoats that allow the draftsperson to separate artificial and natural water detail. Contours are scribed separately later. Once the scribing is complete, these negatives are used to produce a series of masks. By removing the masking material where appropriate, color can be added to the detail, such as roads and water areas. From the negatives and masks, photo-

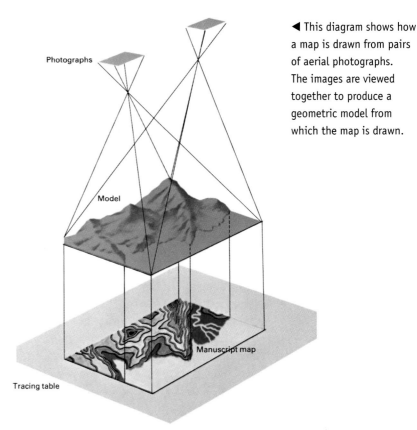

◄ This diagram shows how a map is drawn from pairs of aerial photographs. The images are viewed together to produce a geometric model from which the map is drawn.

Photographs

Model

Manuscript map

Tracing table

graphic positives are made onto which all the various symbols and names are applied. Although there can be many components, several will appear in the same color, so these are combined, resulting in a final set of negatives. Once cleaned of all marks, the printing plates are made, one for each color used.

Although each color is printed separately, it is possible to produce several shades of the same color by means of rulings or stipple. The relief of the ground, which in the 19th century was generally shown by hachures, is now normally depicted by contour lines, which may be enhanced by hill shading or by layer colors. In the latter method, the spaces between the contours are filled with a series of tints, often with green for the lowest level and deepening shades of brown for the higher levels.

Maps of sea areas, made for the guidance of mariners, are known as hydrographic charts. They show coastlines and coastal features, navigational lights and marks, and soundings and underwater contours. Because of the changing character of the seabed in coastal areas, up-to-date information is essential, and revisions must be distributed.

Digital mapping

Digital mapping is the application of computers and automatic drafting machines to mapping. It has been extensively studied since the late 1960s. Computer-based and topographical data

FACT FILE

■ Although Antarctica was officially discovered in 1818, maps from the early 16th century show detailed knowledge of the Antarctic coastline, though it has been obscured by ice since at least 4000 B.C.E. These maps may be based on far older charts from the famous library of Alexandria in Egypt, destroyed by fire in the seventh century C.E.

■ The last uncharted areas on Earth were mapped by the Landsat D satellite, which orbited the planet 14 times a day at an altitude of about 400 miles (640 km). Vast areas of Latin America, Africa, and Asia had not been mapped at scales larger than 1:1,000,000 prior to Landsat.

banks containing classified and coded information, any selection of which can be plotted at a wide range of scales, are of much use for the makers of atlas maps and for those responsible for topographical map series. The map detail is defined by recording strings of coordinates on magnetic tape. Once recorded, this information can be redrawn using an automatic plotter.

Digitizing tables are used to capture the map data and edit plots drawn for checking, and laserscan workstations are used for corrections and updating. Master plotters then produce the high-quality output directly onto photographic film for subsequent map production.

To capture data from a primary map, an enlarged negative is placed on a table and digitizing is carried out manually using a cursor. When the intersection of the crosshairs on the cursor is placed over a point of detail and a button pressed, then X, Y table coordinates of that point are recorded automatically on magnetic tape. A menu is used to code these coordinates so that different features, such as fences, houses, and road edges, can be recognized and extracted from the tape if required.

The computer processes the digitized map data to eliminate distortion from the source document, transforms all the table coordinates to national grid coordinates, links feature coordinates to feature codes, and gives each feature a serial number.

It is necessary to check the digitized data for correctness and completeness. This step is done after processing by producing a four-color ballpoint pen plot on paper using a plotter and comparing it, on a light table, with the source document. Editing, such as deletions, additions, changes of feature code, and moving of text, are carried out using interactive editing terminals.

Once accepted, the data representing the map are stored on tape in the databank. When a new edition of the map is to be published, the master plotter provides a positive of map detail, with a standard grid and names, direct from the digital data. Vegetation and other symbols are pasted onto the positive manually. A stipple mask is also prepared manually and is combined with the positive to produce the final negative used to make the printing plate.

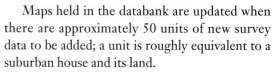

▲ Manual production of maps is a skilled technique requiring care and patience. Once the lines have been scribed onto the film, details can be added by pen. Maps can be prepared to a small scale for specialist use or to larger scales for general use.

▼ Names and symbols are applied to photographic positives once the main roads and water areas have been drawn.

Maps held in the databank are updated when there are approximately 50 units of new survey data to be added; a unit is roughly equivalent to a suburban house and its land.

Automation

Increasingly, the creation of maps using methods of automation are being developed to aid cartographers avoid much of the laborious and repetitive work necessary to produce new maps. These developments have been much aided by progress in the speed and power of computers over the last few decades. Automatic plotting of points and the use of devices that are able to scan stereo models and produce profiles of the contours reduce the work of the cartographers, leaving them to focus on areas that are not yet automated or where automation does not produce sufficient levels of accuracy, such as in the production of contours from automatically produced profiles. Using these techniques, it is possible for one cartographer to operate several map-producing machines.

Global positioning system

Highly accurate surveying can be achieved using the global positioning system (GPS). This system employs an array of 24 satellites owned and operated by the United States Defense Department. Coordinates are calculated using the difference between the time a radio signal is sent by one of the satellites and the time it arrives at a receiver on Earth. By using several satellites in the array, it is possible to accurately estimate the position of the receiver. Ordinarily, GPS gives an accuracy to either 330 ft. (100 m) or 66 ft. (20 m), depending on the service used. Map makers, however, require much greater accuracy than this and have devised a system that uses radio waves with modulated signals, called carrier frequency processing, which is capable of calculating coordinates to an accuracy of 0.4 in. (1 cm). The speed at which this data can be obtained has reduced the time taken for surveying and, therefore, the production of maps.

SEE ALSO: AERIAL PHOTOGRAPHY • ELECTROMAGNETISM • LATITUDE AND LONGITUDE • NAVIGATION • SURVEYING

Marine Biology

The sea covers over two-thirds of Earth's surface. In this vast range, there are more fundamentally different life forms than on land, including bacteria, plants, and animals, from tiny plankton to the largest animal in the world, the blue whale. Any aspect of a marine organism, from its biochemistry, physiology, behavior, and systematics to its ecology, may be investigated by marine biologists. In recent years, marine biologists have also begun to study the effects of pollution from sources such as oil tanker spills and the possible effects of global warming on marine environments, such as the death and decay of coral reefs.

The range of species

Compared with what is known about life on land, our understanding of marine life is much less complete because of the difficulties of working in the sea. Only about 10 percent of the sea has been sampled for living organisms.

The species studied by marine biologists fall into three broad categories: plankton, benthos, and nekton. Plankton are small to microscopic organisms that are carried by wind and ocean currents. These creatures live near the surface of water and are the most common organisms in the oceans, making up the diet of many other kinds of sea life, including the largest creatures on Earth, baleen whales (which include blue whales). Plankton live in abundance in the nutrient-rich waters of the Arctic and Antarctic Oceans, where currents caused by falling cold water and rising warm water bring nutrients to the surface. Plankton are eaten by larger creatures, which in turn provide food for fish and marine mammals. Thus, plankton are an extremely important element in the marine food chain. Plankton can be divided broadly into two types: those that are photosynthetic, known as phytoplankton, and those that are more animal-like, the zooplankton. In practice, plankton do not always fit neatly into either category and are often collectively known as protists.

Organisms that belong to the benthos (benthic species) are those that live on the ocean floor, This category includes, for example, starfish, sea cucumbers, seaweeds, and crustaceans. Benthic species that live on the surface of the ocean floor are known as epifauna, while those living under the surface in sediments are called infauna.

▼ Elephant seals sun themselves on Año Nuevo Reserve in California, while researchers attempt to attach time-depth indicators (TDI). Glued onto the backs of seals with a marine epoxy adhesive, the TDI will be removed in three months when the seals return to the nature reserve to molt. Devices such as these help marine biologists increase their understanding of marine life.

Nekton are those animals that are able to swim freely, independent of ocean currents. These include fish, whales, sharks, seals, squid, and turtles. Most nektonic species are either omnivorous or carnivorous, few are herbivorous.

Methods of exploration

The methods used by marine biologists to study the different forms of marine life often rely on deploying nets, dredges, and other devices from ships to retrieve samples. These samples may be studied on board ship or taken back to biological stations situated on the coast. Preserved specimens may be studied in museums. Since the second half of the 20th century, new techniques have enabled marine biologists to study species without removing them from their natural habitat, thus improving understanding of how species interact and how they form part of the food chain. The invention of the aqualung in 1943, by the French naval officer and ocean explorer Jacques Cousteau, enabled underwater environments to be studied in greater detail at depths down to 130 ft. (39 m). In addition, developments in piloted submersibles, such as submarines and bathyspheres, have allowed exploration of deep sea environments many thousands of feet below the surface, while unpiloted robot submersibles containing video cameras that relay information back to the surface may reach depths of 20,000 ft. (6,000 m). These techniques give marine biologists glimpses into some of the least explored environments on our planet. At depths such as

◀ The Galapagos vent was discovered in the late 1970s off Ecuador. Vent fields, or hydrothermal vents, such as this are places where hot or warm water wells up from the molten interior of Earth. The organisms that live around these vents, such as these tube worms, are able to live with very little light and withstand high temperatures and pressures.

these, where no sunlight can penetrate, sea creatures are often markedly different from those species that live closer to the surface, and some species, such as the deep sea angler fish, may even create their own light by using bioluminescence.

The use of piloted submersibles has led to the discovery of completely new animal communities around hot water vents in the ocean floor. The first hydrothermal vents were discovered in the late 1970s off Ecuador on the Galapagos Rift. Since then, expeditions have discovered life around vents in other areas of the Pacific and along the Mid-Atlantic Ridge. In the Marianas Trough, hairy snails and barnacles predominate; in the Mid-Atlantic Ridge, eyeless shrimp swarm over the vents; and in sites along the East Pacific Rise, there is a wide range of tube worms, clams, mussels, and white encrusting polychaete worms, plus thick mats of bacteria.

Instead of depending on plants to harness solar energy to convert carbon dioxide into organic material, vent communities depend on bacteria that live on the energy of hot water and the sulfur compounds it contains. Some animals around the vents feed directly on the bacteria. Others actually have bacteria living inside their tissues. The giant tube worms from the Galapagos vents rely entirely on these symbiotic bacteria. The mussel *Bathymodiolus* from the Galapagos has bacteria living inside its tissue but also filters food from the water.

FACT FILE

■ One technique borrowed from medical research, analytical flow cytometry, has been adapted for the rapid sorting and quantifying of planktonic protozoans. Protozoans in a seawater sample are passed through a laser beam, causing each protozoan to produce scattered or fluorescent light. Different protozoans produce different light signals that can be stored on a computer for laboratory analysis.

■ A further refinement is the use of fluorescently tagged nucleotide probes (based on short sequences of genes) that can target specific groups of microorganisms for identification. This technique allows population counts to be made every few hours or days, rather than every few weeks.

SEE ALSO: AQUALUNG • LUMINESCENCE • OCEANOGRAPHY • SUBMERSIBLE

Marine Propulsion

The power that propels a vessel through water can be obtained from three possible sources: from human power, from wind, or from fuel in an engine. When an engine provides the power, there are many different methods by which fuel energy can be converted into a driving force.

Paddles and oars

The earliest method for propelling a craft through water was by using paddles. A paddle has a blade at one end that is broad and flat or curved into a scoop; the other end is a rounded handle. The earliest paddles were wooden.

A paddler holds the handle in both hands and pulls the paddle back through the water with the hand closest to the blade. The other hand, which moves less, acts as the fulcrum of a lever that magnifies the motion of the pulling hand. The reaction against the paddle's backward force on the water is the force that drives the craft forward.

A development of the paddle was the oar, which has a longer handle and a longer, narrower blade than a paddle. Whereas a paddle moves freely, an oar rests in a notch or rowlock on the side of the boat, acting as a fixed fulcrum of a lever. Rowers face away from the direction of travel and pull the oar's handles toward themselves to push against the water. The narrow blade has to be raised only slightly to clear the surface of the water between power strokes.

In sporting boats, teams of up to eight rowers occupy seats that slide back and forth on runners. This mechanism enables rowers to increase the power of their strokes by pushing with their legs against stops fixed to the bottom of the boat.

Sails and airfoils

Sails are flexible sheets that catch wind to propel a vessel in a desired direction. A sail is held in place in the wind by a mast—a pole fixed securely through the deck and into hull of the boat. A sailboat may have one or more masts, and each mast may support several sails. The system of ropes or wires that raise sails into position against a mast and hold them there is called rigging.

Sails vary in shape, size, and material according to the vessel for which they are intended. Modern sails may be made of natural canvas or of a synthetic fabric, such as Dacron polyester. High-performance racing sails that are subjected

▲ A jet ski is powered by a propeller that forces water through a movable duct. The skier steers the craft by moving its handlebars, which control the direction of the water jet and, therefore, of thrust. The two-stroke engine that drives the propeller uses a mixture of gasoline and lubricating oil. Up to 30 percent of this fuel reaches the exhaust without burning and remains on the surface of the water. This pollution, together with the noise pollution caused by such engines and poor safety records, has led to calls for jet skis to be banned from lakes and coastal waters.

to extreme stress may consist of a Kevlar weave covered by a plastic skin. The Kevlar provides the strength, while the skin makes the sail airtight.

Sails are now mainly confined to sporting and leisure craft. Their use for cargo vessels started to subside with the introduction of steam and diesel power, which are immune to variations in wind strength and direction. However, some large cargo vessels now use rigid airfoils to supplement the thrust from other propulsion systems. Such airfoils have cross sections similar to those of aircraft wings but are mounted vertically to provide horizontal thrust rather than lift. Computer control ensures that the airfoils are faced in the best direction to extract thrust from a given wind condition, thereby maximizing fuel economy.

Steam power

As with land-based devices, the first engines made for marine propulsion used the expansion of steam in cylinder engines as their power source. At first, power from these engines was converted into thrust by paddle wheels, which have a series of blades mounted radially around their circumferences. The blades dip into the water one by one as the wheel rotates, thereby providing thrust. An example of a craft powered in this way was the *Charlotte Dundas*, a tug built in 1801 for use on the Forth and Clyde Canal, Scotland.

The first commercial inland paddle steamboat was the *Clermont*, designed by the U.S. engineer Robert Fulton and launched on the Hudson River, New York, in 1807. The *Clermont* was powered by an engine built by the British engineering company of Boulton and Watt. Its single 24 in. (61 cm) cylinder had a piston stroke of 8 ft. (2.4 m), and its power output of 19 horsepower (14 kW) drove two side-mounted paddles.

The type of screw propeller that now propels the vast majority of boats and ships was patented in 1836, first by the British engineer Francis Pettit Smith, then by the Swedish engineer John Ericsson. Smith used the design in the first successful screw-driven steamship, the *Archimedes*, which was launched in 1839. (A steamship is an oceangoing version of a steamboat—a vessel that plies inland waterways, such as rivers.) Appropriately, the ship was named in honor of the Greek inventor who in the third century B.C.E. demonstrated the ability of the helical blade to develop thrust in water. The engines of the *Archimedes* turned at 26 rpm, produced around 80 horsepower (60 kW), and were geared up to turn the screw propeller at around 140 rpm.

The engines of the first steamboats used steam generated by the heat from coal-fired furnaces—oil-burning furnaces were introduced in the 1890s and used a heavy fuel oil that became known as "bunker." In early engines, steam passed from a boiler to cylinders and was then released to the atmosphere. With the passage of time, boiler design improved such that higher steam pressures could develop. The exhaust steam from the initial cylinders could then be used to drive larger, lower-pressure cylinders so as to extract more energy from the steam. The first engines to use two stages of cylinders—double-expansion engines—were made in the 1850s. Triple-expansion engines followed in the 1870s. The improved fuel efficiencies of these designs significantly increased the ranges of steamships.

The first vessel to be powered by a steam turbine, rather than a reciprocating piston engine, was the *Turbinia*, launched in 1897. The engine of the *Turbinia* was designed by the British engineer

▼ Wind power is still a popular way to power boats, though continual improvements in boat design have done much to increase speeds by making it easier to handle sails and by streamlining the shape of hulls.

Charles Parsons. It had three separate turbines that used the steam in turn at successively lower pressures. Each turbine drove an associated propeller. The total output of more than 2,000 horsepower (1.5 MW) allowed the *Turbinia* to achieve a speed of 34.5 knots (40 mph, 64 km/h) at a royal naval review of 1897. This speed was significantly greater than that achieved by any other ship of the time and led to the rapid adoption of the steam turbine for marine use.

Internal combustion engines

Diesel engines were first used for marine propulsion in the early years of the 20th century, and their widespread adoption started in the 1920s. Diesel engines are ideal for marine use since they require little maintenance and function well under constant heavy loads. Diesel engines are also more efficient than steam engines; they produce power directly from burning fuel, rather than by using its heat to produce steam. This efficiency means that a diesel-powered vessel requires less fuel than a steamship for an equivalent voyage, leaving more room for money-earning cargo. Around 75 percent of heavy cargo vessels are now powered by diesel engines.

Modern marine diesel engines are either two-stroke or four-stroke engines, and they fall into two main types. Slow-running diesels drive the propeller shaft directly, while medium-speed engines drive propellers through reduction gears.

Slow-running engines turn at just over 100 rpm and normally use the two-stroke cycle with turbocharging to increase the power output. Typically, such engines have cylinder bores of 20 to 40 in. (51–102 cm) and strokes of 30 to 70 in. (76–178 cm). The power output of such a cylinder is 2,000 to 3,000 horsepower (1.5–2.2 MW), and a single engine may combine several such cylinders to drive a single shaft. Cylinders with even larger bores and strokes can be combined in a 12-cylinder arrangement that can have an output of 40,000 horsepower (30 MW) or more.

Medium-speed engines run at speeds of up to 1,000 rpm and commonly use four-stroke cycles. In general, such engines are used for

▼ A new era of water-speed-record breaking is dawning with boats such as the jet-propelled *Alton Towers*. The world's fastest boats are essentially hydroplanes; the *Alton Towers* skims along the water surface on three extremely small contact areas shaped like skis.

ships that have low-to-medium power requirements—around 10,000 horsepower (7.5 MW) is the upper limit for this type of diesel unit.

Other types of marine internal combustion engines include two-stroke and four-stroke gasoline engines and gas turbines. Gasoline engines are used for small craft such as motorboats; for larger craft, the superior fuel economy of diesel propulsion excludes the use of gasoline engines. Gas turbines that burn fuel oil are used where their ability to respond rapidly to high power demands is of benefit, such as for military craft.

Nuclear propulsion

Nuclear power has been used for marine propulsion since the late 1950s. In such systems, heat from fission reactors generates steam for turbines that are connected to the propellers through reduction gears. The water that produces this steam does not pass through the reactor core; rather, it acquires heat from reactor coolant in a heat exchanger.

The main advantage of nuclear propulsion is that it can generate great amounts of power from relatively little fuel and requires only infrequent refuelling. These characteristics have made it the system of choice for military vessels that could be isolated from friendly refuelling points for prolonged periods and for civilian icebreakers that require great power for long icebreaking missions in polar waters.

For submarines, nuclear propulsion has a second advantage: unlike combustion engines, a nuclear drive requires no air for the conversion of fuel, thus allowing nuclear-propelled submarines to remain submerged for longer periods than are possible with conventional submarines.

Electric motors

Although electric motors are perfectly capable of driving a vessel's propellers, their requirement for an onboard power source has limited their acceptance, because the power plant for generators can drive propellers directly or through gears, thus obviating the need to generate electricity for turning a motor.

An exception is the case of a conventional submarine, whose primary power source—diesel engines—cannot operate when submerged. Using

SMALL MOTORS

Small craft, such as motor launches, require suitably small motors for their propulsion. Some motors, such as that illustrated at right, are small four-stroke gasoline engines. Driven through gears, their propeller shafts pass through seals in the hulls of the vessels that they propel.

Other small craft use an outboard motor mounted on the stern. Power reaches the propeller through a vertical shaft outside the hull. This shaft is linked to the motor and propeller by bevel gears. The whole assembly of motor, drive shaft, and propeller can be dismounted for maintenance, storage, or replacement.

Until recently, outboard motors were almost exclusively two-stroke gasoline engines. Newer designs use more environmentally friendly four-stroke combustion cycles.

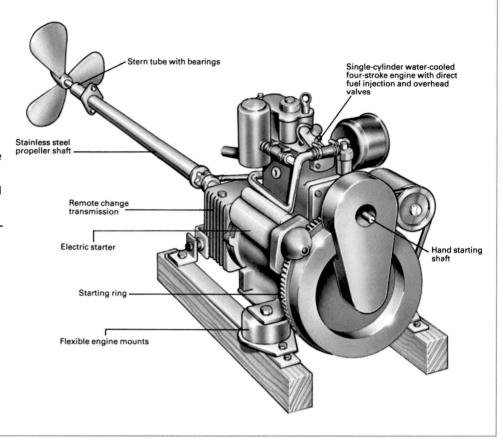

Stern tube with bearings

Single-cylinder water-cooled four-stroke engine with direct fuel injection and overhead valves

Stainless steel propeller shaft

Remote change transmission

Electric starter

Starting ring

Hand starting shaft

Flexible engine mounts

the engines underwater would quickly consume the breathable air in the vessel, and its exhaust gas bubbles would reveal the position of the craft—a strategic problem for naval craft. For these reasons, conventional submarines use their diesel motors when their proximity to the surface allows them to take in air for combustion and expel exhaust gases through snorkel tubes.

On the surface, a conventional submarine's diesel engines power a generator that provides power for general services, for its electric motors, and for charging its batteries. When submerged, the diesel engines are cut off and electrical energy stored in batteries drives the motors.

Prospective designs for future naval craft—surface and submarine—include electric motors for different reasons. The potential mechanical power sources for the generators associated with electric propulsion are many: they include economical diesel engines, steam turbines, fast-response gas turbines, and batteries and fuel cells.

The same basic motor can be built in several versions with different power outputs by using different numbers of stator-and-rotor modules. The modular composition makes such motors less vulnerable to battle damage, since any damaged modules can be removed or simply switched out of the control circuit. Also, the uniformity of controls means that a single personnel-training course would serve for a variety of craft.

Propellers and alternatives

A propeller is a collection of skewed teardrop-shaped blades mounted on a central shaft. When the shaft turns, these blades push water in a line parallel to the shaft, thereby converting torque into a thrust that acts on the water. By Newton's Third Law, this thrust is opposed by an equal force that acts on the shaft and thence on the hull.

Most propellers are mounted in the water outside the hull; the propelled water can be directed to some extent to aid steering by a rudder, a movable board behind the propeller or propellers. Some propellers are mounted in ducts that guide water through the hull of a vessel. The water can then be directed through a movable outlet nozzle, giving greater maneuverability than a rudder.

Hovercraft skim across the surface of water, so their propulsion comes from air propellers mounted atop the superstructure. The power plants of such craft are typically gas turbines.

Magnetohydrodynamic (MHD) propulsion dispenses with propellers altogether, using instead the electromagnetic properties of water to propel it between magnets and electrodes in a duct. Such systems create none of the vibration associated with propeller systems.

SEE ALSO: AIR-CUSHION VEHICLE • GAS TURBINE • INTERNAL COMBUSTION ENGINE • MAGNETOHYDRODYNAMICS • PROPELLER • SAILING

Mass Production

Although manufactured items of various types have been produced in large quantities almost since the start of organized production, this system was not mass production in the modern sense. The essential feature of modern mass production lies in the interchangeability of components, a system that allows any set of parts to be assembled together into the finished product.

This principle was first proposed by Eli Whitney, who started to apply the concept to the manufacture of flintlock muskets around 1800. For components to be interchangeable, they have to be produced to standard dimensions within allowed limits of tolerance, and Whitney used a system of gauges to ensure that components were manufactured to the correct size. At this stage, the gauges were comparative standards to check that all the components produced were the same, with the precise size being a secondary consideration, since standards were not generally available.

The ability to use unskilled labor was an important factor in the development of machine tools such as the milling machine and the turret lathe, which allowed parts to be machined to close tolerances. Previously, manufacturers such as Whitney had to rely on hand finishing by skilled craftsmen to obtain the tolerances needed for interchangeability. A further development was the introduction of machine tools, called "automats," that could carry out a series of operations on a part. One of the leaders here was Elisha Root, chief engineer of the Colt Armory, who around 1850 concentrated on using machine tools for mass production of the Colt revolver. Although much initial development of mass production systems was by the armaments industry, the techniques were quickly adopted by other industries, such as clock makers and sewing machine manufacturers. Mass production methods were fully established by the middle of the 19th century.

The final step in the development of modern mass production came with the introduction of the assembly line by Henry Ford. Here, the final stage of manufacture, the assembly of the product from interchangeable components, was split into a series of individual steps. The product (in this case, a car) was moved down the assembly by a conveyor system with a series of workers carrying out steps in sequence so that assembly was completed by the end of the line.

Standardization

Typically, parts can be produced with important dimensions to tolerances of ± 0.005 in. (0.1 μm) or so, while for critical components—such as automobile engine pistons—production tolerances of ± 0.0005 in. (0.01 μm) or less can be achieved.

Some components are common to a variety of products and so are in widespread use. The standardization of design and materials allows full interchangeability of such components within and between products and for specific applications. For example, size and thread characteristics for nuts and bolts are laid down in national and international standards, along with material specifications and finishes. The use of standard components and materials reduces costs and simplifies planning.

Planning

The development of a mass production system involves applying a range of different disciplines from the initial design of the product through to final distribution and marketing. In many cases, the process can involve adapting existing production arrangements, but the basic principles remain the same. Throughout the planning stage, considerable emphasis is placed on finding the most cost-effective ways of producing a part or carrying out an operation. When production quantities are measured in millions, even small savings of a fraction of a cent per item can add up to a substantial sum over a large quantity made.

An important part of the design stage lies in making sure the components are suitable for high-volume manufacture and assembly. For example, it may be necessary to modify the design of a part so that it can be readily clamped for machining or to provide alignment features for use in assembly. The planning for manufacture of an item is carried through into the production-engineering stage, which establishes the sequence of operations needed to manufacture the components and assemble them into the finished product. As a part of this process, tool engineering is applied to the design and production of the tools, assembly jigs, and other equipment needed to make the components. Often, special machines are used to carry out specific steps of the production process. For example, parts may be machined on transfer lines, where they are automatically transferred from one machining station to the next, emerging from the transfer line as a finished part. Quality-control systems with frequent inspections of parts and assemblies are planned into the process to ensure that the product meets the required standards throughout its production run.

At the same time, the production process is broken down into a series of small steps that can be carried out in a single machining or assembly stage. By reducing the process to small steps, the complexity of each step is considerably reduced so that an unskilled operator can be trained to do the work quickly and consistently.

In a major production facility, the complete process can be made up of an interlocked group of individual production sequences. For example, in an automobile factory, the main assembly production line will be fed by subsidiary lines producing major subassemblies, such as the body, engine, and transmission. In turn, these sublines are supplied with components and subassemblies themselves produced on other lines. Detailed planning and coordination of the production on all sublines is essential, since a problem in any single area can quickly bring the entire operation to a halt.

Production line

Early assembly lines, which provided the means to realize the full potential of the industrial revolution, were practically all run by manual labor. Most trivial tasks involved in the manufacture of even the most complicated objects were performed by hand. As each component was attached, the evolving assembly was passed on to the next stage of the line by hand, where it had a new part added before being passed on again.

The simplest improvement to the manual assembly line was the conveyor belt, which moves the components and the evolving product rapidly down the line. From one of these conveyors, a set of parts, possibly from a subassembly line, is picked up by the worker, plus maybe another

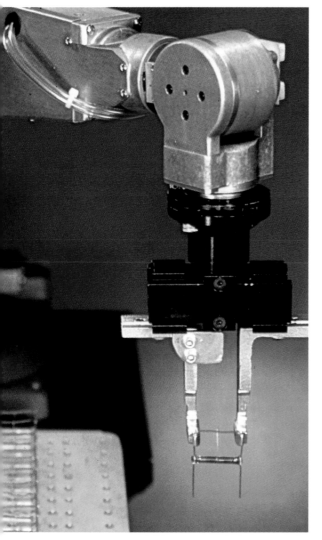

◄ Robots have made a huge impact on the production line because they can work in conditions that humans would find intolerable. They can also carry out delicate assembly work—this robot can handle fragile lightbulb filaments with ease.

◀ Research to improve methods of mass production is constantly undertaken, as in this ceramics factory where tableware is being made.

from an adjacent bin, and added to the main assembly. The semicompleted item is put on another conveyor and carried to the next stage of production.

In many ways the production line typifies the modern mass production process, with a steady stream of components and subassemblies being supplied to the line for assembly into the finished product. The assembly operations are carried out as the product is moved down the line on a conveyor system, with individual operations being planned using time and motion studies so that they fit in with the line speed. Owing to the interlinked nature of the operations, a production line has to be considered as a single unit, with the speed of the line establishing the output. By its nature the work involved on a production line is highly repetitive, leading to operator fatigue, loss of concentration, and possible disruption of the line operation. To minimize such problems robots are now in common use, for both repetitive operations and complex assemblies. In these operations, the robot manipulates a tool to perform a process on the part being manufactured. Applications include spot welding, continuous-arc welding, and spray painting.

Robots are also increasingly being used for inspection during factory operations. Typically, the robot positions a sensor close to a work part and uses the output from the sensor to determine whether the part meets the quality specifications for that particular element of the product.

Alternative approaches include the cell system. Here, product assembly is carried out by a team whose members share the work, each worker doing several jobs during the assembly.

However, although this approach enables high-quality products to be made, it is more expensive than the line system.

Batch production

Although many mass production processes are based on the production line, this is not the only technique used. Batch production methods are particularly suited to some products. As the name suggests, batch production involves the processing of a "batch" of products through the manufacturing process, all the items in a batch undergoing the same operation together.

Automation

While automatic machines have been an integral part of mass production systems from the beginning, a new element has been introduced by the use of "intelligent" systems such as numerically controlled machine tools and robots. Numerical control is a type of programmable automation in which machines are controlled by numbers and other symbols normally downloaded from a central computer via a SCADA (systems control and data acquisition) system, which sends and receives information through data lines not dissimilar to those used to connect computer peripherals. Numerical control was initially used in the machine tool industry to control the position of a cutting tool in relation to the part being machined. The coded numbers in the program provide coordinates in a Cartesian axis, which defines the positions of the cutting tool relative to the part. As the program is actuated by the central computer, it is called computer numerical control (CNC) or direct numerical control (DNC), if the commands are sent from one central computer to a number of individual machines. Electronic component assembly and drafting also use numerical control.

With CNC, it is much easier to introduce changes in a product, since the machines can be simply reprogrammed. By comparison, with a more traditional automated transfer line, such changes would involve complete retooling or the installation of a new line.

A flexible manufacturing system (FMS) enables several machine tools to be linked to a materials-handling system, with all elements controlled by a central computer. This system differs from an automated production line in its ability to process more than one product simultaneously. An FMS can also cope with different mixes of products and changes in schedule as demand patterns vary. New product styles can be introduced into production if they fall into the range that the system is designed to cope with. This kind of system is ideal where demand for the products is variable and "just in time" production is required to ensure efficient use of labor and materials. Stock updating can also now be tied into computerized systems, by use of bar codes and readers or other digital-input methods that can be interfaced with a computer system, thus enabling production of a product to be automatically triggered when particular stock levels are reached.

The high degree of automation and computer control that is now possible has given manufacturers the ability to produce a wide variety of options on a basic product. The most obvious example is in the automotive industry, where automobiles can be almost infinitely customized from one basic model, with optional extras being added as required and changes to paintwork programmed in to ensure an appealing variety of styles is available.

Robotics has also enabled manufacturers to ensure that their workers do not have to be exposed to dangerous working situations or hazardous substances during assembly. Such dangers in a mass production system can safely be consigned to robots. It is the ability to combine manual tasks with computer-controlled tasks and robotics that distinguishes the modern mass production process.

▶ Robots have had a considerable impact on mass production of goods. This seeing robot is inspecting tiny silicon chips for imperfections.

Mass customization

Customization may seem a contradictory concept in terms of mass production, but it is increasingly being adopted by companies keen to maintain a competitive edge over their rivals. Its main advantage is that the product is exactly what the customer wants rather than a "one size fits all" compromise. Behind this advance is the increasing flexibility that has been brought about by robotics and computerization of assembly lines. Use of bar code scanners means that manufacturers can monitor the use of every component in a factory, making stock control considerably easier and reducing the costs of warehousing large quantities of parts and finished products. The product too can be tracked from order to delivery, and an increasing number of orders are now being placed direct to the factory by customers using the Internet.

One of the early pioneers of the mass customization approach was Dell Computer, which saw its market share rise considerably through its ability to supply to the customer's exact specification. Dell builds its computers using modular parts but relies on sophisticated software systems to ensure that components are ordered and delivered to the right part of the production process only when needed. It is this information flow that has enabled the company to keep its inventory to a 6-day supply of parts, rather than the 31 of most other companies, and has allowed it to keep the cost of its product competitive.

Customization is not just restricted to the computer industry. Levi Strauss has introduced a custom jeans-manufacturing process, and Mattel has launched a customized Barbie doll offering 6,000 variations of hair, skin color, and clothing.

FACT FILE

- In 1808, Marc Isambard Brunel used mass production methods to make wooden pulley blocks for sailing ships. A number of specialized machines carved elm blocks and lignum vitae disks into shells and sheaves. The 43 machines produced 160,000 pulleys per year.

- The assembly line introduced by Henry Ford in 1913 was based on a combination of a railroad track manufacturing process and the overhead carcass trolleys of the Chicago meat factories. In 1912, Ford sold 82,000 Model Ts, but by 1919 monthly production was higher than this, culminating in a monthly record of 240,000 automobiles in November 1922.

- In 1951, Ford introduced 40 automatic machines to make engine blocks. The machines were capable of 500 distinct operations, from handling to machining, and converted a rough casting into a finished engine block.

SEE ALSO: COMPUTER • CONVEYOR • INTERNET • QUALITY MANAGEMENT • ROBOTICS • WAREHOUSING

Mass Spectrometry

A mass spectrometer is a device that separates mixtures of positively charged ions according to mass by first accelerating them through an electrical field and then deflecting them in a magnetic field. Mass spectrometry is the performance of such experiments and the interpretation of their results to gain such information as the formulas, structures, and isotopic compositions of compounds that yield ions in a mass spectrometer.

Principles

A mass spectrometer takes advantage of two basic electromagnetic forces: the force that a charged particle experiences in an electrical field and the force that a moving charged particle experiences in a magnetic field. When positive ions are introduced into the space between positive and negative electrodes, they experience a force that accelerates them toward the negatively charged electrode. If the negative electrode is annular (ring shaped), some ions are attracted to the center of the electrode and therefore simply pass through the hole in the ring.

The kinetic energy (K.E.) of a particle with charge q that has been accelerated by a voltage V is the product of charge and voltage: qV. Since the kinetic energy of a particle is related to its mass, m, and velocity, v, by the expression K.E. $= \frac{1}{2}mv^2$, charge, mass, velocity, and voltage are linked by the following expression:

$$(\text{K.E.} =)\ \tfrac{1}{2}mv^2 = qV$$

When the moving ion moves into a vertical magnetic field at right angles to its flight path, it starts to experience a sideways force, F, that is equal to the product of its charge, velocity, and the magnetic field strength (B): $F = qvB$. According to classical mechanics, the sideways force will make the particle move in a circular path whose radius, r, is related to the force, F, by the equation $F = mv^2/r$. Combining the two expressions for F,

$$(F =)\ mv^2/r = qvB$$
$$\text{so } v = qBr/m$$

Inserting this expression for v into the kinetic energy expression eventually gives a relationship between the fundamental properties of the ion—its charge and mass—and the conditions within a mass spectrometer—voltage, magnetic field, and the radius of curvature of an ion's path:

$$(\text{K.E.} =)\ \tfrac{1}{2}m(qBr/m)^2 = qV$$
$$\text{so } \tfrac{1}{2}qB^2r^2/m = V$$
$$\text{and } \tfrac{1}{2}B^2r^2/V = m/q$$

In a mass spectrometer, ions are detected only when the radius of curvature of their paths in the magnetic field deflects them by the appropriate amount to strike the detector. The value of r is therefore a constant for a given apparatus, and the charge–mass ratio, m/q, of a given ion is calculable from the strength of the electrical and magnetic fields at the time of its detection.

Practical details

The positive ions for a mass spectrometer are produced by vaporizing a sample and then ionized by bombardment with fast electrons or atoms or by a number of other techniques that result in vaporized molecules acquiring enough energy to lose one electron each to form positive ions.

In order for the ions to follow paths that are influenced by the electrical and magnetic fields alone, they must travel from the ionizer to the detector without colliding with other particles: a single collision would completely invalidate the charge–mass reading for an ion by knocking it off course. For this reason, the flight chamber of a mass spectrometer is evacuated to below 100 millionths of atmospheric pressure. At this pressure, the average distance of flight between collisions is around 16 ft. (5 m)—much greater than the distance between the ionizer and the detector, which is usually less than 20 in. (51 cm).

Many modern mass spectrometers use the magnetic field formed between powerful electromagnets to deflect beams of ions. The spectrum of charge–mass ratios is scanned by varying the intensity of the field so as to vary the extent of deflection. The precision of such instruments is largely determined by the uniformity of their magnetic field and how accurately the intensity of the magnetic field is measured.

In most instruments, ions are detected by an electron multiplier, which can amplify the electrical signal due to an arriving ion by as much as a million times. Electronic equipment displays the result of the analysis, and computers can be connected for automatic control and calibration of the data. Signal intensity is plotted against charge–mass ratio, producing a chart with numerous well-defined peaks. The height of each peak is proportional to the rate at which ions of that charge–mass ratio arrive at the detector.

Radio-frequency analyzers

An alternative to the magnetic analyzer already described uses a radio frequency signal to separate ions by charge–mass ratio. At any given frequency, only those ions with a specific mass pass through to the detector by oscillating at the same frequency as the applied signal; other ions collide with the walls and are absorbed. The particular mass that the analyzer allows to pass is inversely proportional to the frequency.

GAS CHROMATOGRAPHY-MASS SPECTROMETRY (GC-MS)

In industry and in research, it is desirable and often necessary to perform rapid and reliable analyses of mixtures. A routine method for performing such analyses is actually a hybrid of two analytical techniques: gas chromatography and mass spectrometry. This hybrid is conveniently referred to using the abbreviation *GC-MS*.

Gas chromatography (GC) is a highly effective means of separating mixtures of compounds. A sample is first injected into a stream of inert gas that carries it into a chromatography column. The column is maintained at high temperature in a precisely controlled oven. The components of the mixture repeatedly adsorb onto the internal surface of the column and then desorb. Those components of the mixture that have least affinity for the column material pass through the chromatography column in the least time, while other compounds take longer to emerge.

The relative retention time—the time spent in the column relative to a known standard material—is often sufficient to identify a material with reasonable certainty by comparing it with experimentally determined relative retention times. When more concrete identification of

compounds is necessary, it may be achieved by connecting the outlet of the gas-chromatography apparatus to the inlet of a mass spectrometer. Then, as each component of a mixture emerges from the GC column, it is immediately subjected to a mass-spectrometry analysis.

The molecular-ion peak of each compound identifies its molecular mass and probable formula. The fragmentation pattern then helps identify the structure.

One typical application of GC-MS would be to identify the product blend of a pilot-scale refinery process. Another use would be to identify potentially harmful impurities in pharmaceutical manufacture.

▼ A diagram of a GC-MS system. Such a system first separates a mixture by gas chromatography (top left), then identifies each component by mass spectrometry.

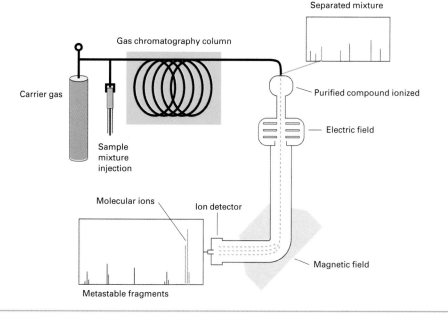

Separated mixture

Gas chromatography column

Purified compound ionized

Carrier gas

Electric field

Sample mixture injection

Molecular ions

Ion detector

Metastable fragments

Magnetic field

Molecular ions

A molecular ion is the first species produced when a molecule loses an electron in an ionizer. All the nuclei of the original molecule are present in the molecular ion, and its mass differs from the molecular mass only by the mass of one electron—a negligible amount in comparison with the total mass of a typical molecule.

In some cases, results from a high-precision mass spectrometer can identify the exact formula of a molecule, since only one combination of atoms corresponds to the exact molecular weight. Where ambiguity exists, the true formula can usually be deduced by examining the details of the mass spectrometer trace.

Fragmentation

A molecular ion tends to be an unstable species, since it has lost one of the electrons that participates in its bonding system. For this reason, many molecular ions break up into smaller fragments before they reach the analyzer.

The favorable pathways by which fragmentations occur are well documented, and they help a mass spectrometrist to deduce the structures of complex molecules. Branched hydrocarbons tend to fragment at their branching points, so one such fragmentation of 2-methylhexane—structural formula $(CH_3)_2CHC_4H_{10}$—will produce a mixture of CH_3^+ cations and $C_6H_{13}^+$ cations, depending on where the positive charge ends up. The detection of these two fragments in a mass spectrometer trace indicates a methyl branch.

Particularly stable fragments have the positive charge spread over a number of alternating double and single bonds or on the carbon atom of a carbonyl group. In these cases, the stability of the fragment is such that it may produce a stronger signal than the molecular ion itself.

Isotopes

One of the first uses of mass spectrometry was in the study of the isotopes of the elements. A compound such as chloromethane (CH_3Cl), for example, shows two distinct molecular-ion peaks: one at a charge–mass ratio of 50, the other at 52. These peaks correspond to molecules that contain chlorine-35 and chlorine-37, respectively. The height ratio for the two peaks is 24.6:75.4, which matches the relative abundances of the two chlorine isotopes in nature.

The multiple peaks for compounds that contain multiple-isotope elements reveal the abundances of isotopes in great clarity, whereas chemical analysis merely reveals a weighted average relative atomic mass—approximately 35.5 in the case of chlorine. Adapted mass spectrometers

◀ The ionizer filament of a mass spectrometer. The sample material can be seen on the middle of the filament.

can also be used to collect samples of isotopically pure materials. This technique is useful in the study of short-lived isotopes of artificial elements produced in nuclear reactions, for example.

The presence of multiple-isotope elements is also useful in the analysis of fragmentation patterns, because those fragments that contain one or more atoms of multiple-isotope elements exhibit multiple peaks in accordance with the relative abundances of the isotopes, whereas those fragments that contain only single-isotope elements show single peaks.

Applications

One of the great advantages of mass spectrometry as an analytical technique is that it is capable of producing highly informative results from minute samples. Flavor and perfume chemists can detect and identify active compounds in extremely small quantities using mass spectrometry, and research chemists can identify the components of the product mixtures from small-scale syntheses.

Portable and compact mass spectrometers are used routinely in a variety of applications, often by "tuning" the device to the charge–mass ratio of a key compound. Such devices can "sniff" key components of gasoline at the site of a suspected arson and monitor the atmosphere within occupied space vehicles. Pressure vessels can be checked for leaks by evacuating the vessel and attaching it to a mass spectrometer tuned to helium. A fine jet of helium is then played over the outer surface of the vessel, and the mass spectrometer triggers an alarm if the jet crosses a leak.

SEE ALSO: ATOMIC STRUCTURE • CHEMISTRY, ANALYTICAL • ELEMENT, CHEMICAL • ION AND IONIZATION • SPECTROSCOPY

Mass Transit and Subway

◄ Many European cities are adopting modern trams (streetcars) as a means of transporting large numbers of people. This system in Croydon, south London, made use of an old railroad to connect the town with nearby Wimbledon and added extra tracks to extend its run out to the east of the town. The tram route connects with a number of railroad stations that carry passengers into the center of London.

The first underground railways were those used in mines, with small trucks pushed by hand or, later, drawn by ponies, running first on wooden, then iron, and finally steel rails. Once the steam railway arrived, however, thoughts soon turned to building underground passenger railways, or subways, to avoid the traffic congestion that was occurring in city centers even in the middle of the 19th century. From such humble beginnings, the modern integrated mass transit systems of today have been developed.

There is no recognized definition of a rapid transit system, but it is generally accepted that it is an urban railway serving a city and perhaps its immediate suburbs and has relatively closely spaced stations to enable passengers to visit the city's focal points. This usually means there are stations to serve the main business district, shopping streets, and entertainment areas. If the city is large, there may be several stations in the center, and there will usually be others serving mainline railroad stations, major bus terminals, and also nearby airports.

There has been a marked expansion in such systems over the last couple of decades, generally in response to city center congestion, which is said to cost the United States $100 billion a year in lost productivity. An important feature of such systems is the provision of park-and-ride facilities—large car parks sited near the peripheral stations. Such facilities are sometimes teamed with disincentives

to driving into the city center, particularly in Europe where integrated public transport/mass transit/private transport systems have been put in place in a number of cities.

Many rapid transit railways have begun life as short underground or overhead lines serving the city center and have then expanded to connect surrounding suburbs. At one time, rapid transit railways were almost synonymous with underground railways, but today some rapid transit lines are not underground at all or are below ground only for short distances in the city center. Others are on overhead structures. Some combine all three structures to get the best possible route.

Although the term *rapid transit* normally refers to a railway, it is also accepted as applying to the type of service rather than the means of providing it. Thus, a rapid transit service may be provided by streetcars, either as single vehicles or coupled into trains, giving a service capacity about half that of railway rapid transit. Certain types of elevated rail systems or monorails, if they have sufficient capacity, could also give a rapid transit service, as could buses running on reserved tracks—roads reserved solely for their use.

Rapid transit, however, has always been taken to also mean "mass transit," that is, a system capable of carrying large numbers of people and moving them about a city quickly and efficiently. Such movements are often on a very large scale; for example the New York City Transit Authority was

◀ In densely populated cities such as Tokyo, subways can provide the fastest form of transport, despite speeds as low as 20 mph (32 km/h).

carrying over 900 million passengers a year in the early 1980s, while some stations on the Hong Kong system are designed for peak loads of over 800 passengers per minute.

Trains

Railway rapid transit systems often use trains with rapid acceleration and braking, and in these trains, electric traction is universal. Rubber-tired rolling stock is used in some systems, with the extra adhesion obtained giving higher acceleration rates (as well as increased passenger comfort). To save wear and tear on the brake blocks, the trains are provided with rheostatic or regenerative braking to take them down to low speeds, after which mechanical braking is used.

Rheostatic braking means the motors are used as generators, driven by the train wheels, to absorb the energy of the train's movement. The electric power generated in the process is dissipated as heat through resistances. Regenerative braking is similar, except that the power produced is fed back into the system to help to run other trains. Technical difficulties have made regenerative braking less attractive in practice than it sounds in theory.

Although the trains gain speed quickly and brake rapidly, the passengers must not be subjected to strains that would cause them to be flung about. As the distance between stations is short, very high speeds cannot be reached, and the most important factor affecting overall speed becomes the rate at which passengers can enter and leave the trains, because it dictates the length

of station stops. The overall speed on most rapid transit lines is not much more than 20 mph (32 km/h) unless the stations are an exceptional distance apart. If they are very close to each other, the speed can be much lower.

In congested city streets, however, the general speed of road traffic is very low, even for private cars or taxicabs. It was street congestion that caused the London Metropolitan Railway, the first underground urban passenger-carrying railway in the world and the forerunner of all rapid transit systems, to be built and opened as long ago as 1863. It was 3.75 miles (6 km) long, and ran from the main line railway terminal at Paddington to Farringdon Street in the business area of the City of London. Steam locomotives were used, and the track was built to the broad 7 ft. (2.13 m) gauge of the Great Western Railway, which supplied the rolling stock—

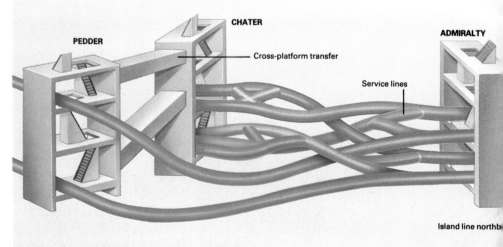

PEDDER
CHATER
ADMIRALTY
Cross-platform transfer
Service lines
Island line northb

TSUEN WAN/ISLAND LINE INTERCHANGE

though subsequently the standard gauge was adopted. Some of the trains ran from suburban stations on the Paddington main lines, but there was also a purely local service. The line was soon carrying over 27,000 passengers a day, and further underground lines soon followed in London.

Other European cities such as Budapest, Hungary; Berlin, Germany; Glasgow, Scotland; and Paris, France, also developed subway systems, followed later by cities in the rest of Europe, North and South America, Russia, and Japan. Subway lines continued to be built throughout the 20th century, both as extensions to existing networks and as complete new systems for city center transportation.

The trains themselves are generally of lightweight construction to permit rapid acceleration and save power, but they must still be strong enough to withstand possible collision—though rapid transit railways are probably the safest in the world. Seats are provided for a number of passengers, but during peak hours, there may be twice as many, or possibly even more, passengers standing as there are sitting down, within safety limits.

HONG KONG MASS-TRANSIT RAILWAY

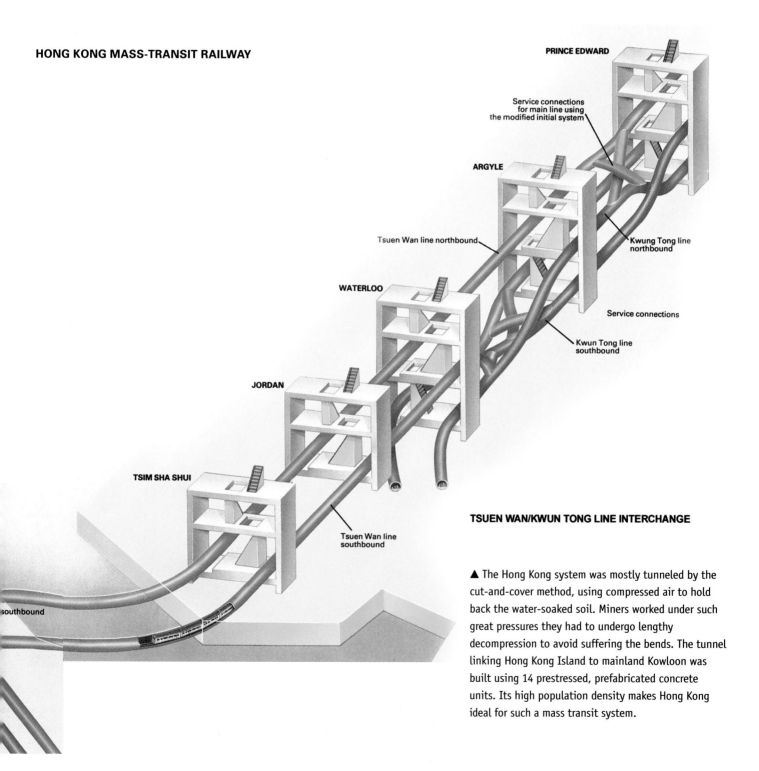

TSUEN WAN/KWUN TONG LINE INTERCHANGE

▲ The Hong Kong system was mostly tunneled by the cut-and-cover method, using compressed air to hold back the water-soaked soil. Miners worked under such great pressures they had to undergo lengthy decompression to avoid suffering the bends. The tunnel linking Hong Kong Island to mainland Kowloon was built using 14 prestressed, prefabricated concrete units. Its high population density makes Hong Kong ideal for such a mass transit system.

Automation

Speed of travel also means that passengers must not have to wait too long between trains, but to run a service frequent enough to carry all a city's peak-hour passengers means that coordination of train movements must be of the highest order, and signals must be obeyed promptly—with safety devices to bring the trains to a halt if they are not.

In traditional systems, signaling is done using colored lights with either two or three aspects, green and red or green, yellow, and red, and is automatically triggered by the trains themselves through track circuits provided by a low-voltage current passing through a section of running rail. This current is interrupted when a train is on the section in question, and through a system of electrical relays, this interruption sets the signals to danger behind the train and clears them again when the train has moved far enough forward.

On modern rapid transit railways, the visible signals are replaced by coded impulses—also controlled by track circuits—passing through the rails. They can be picked up by the following train or, more usually, a central computer-operated system control and data acquisition (SCADA) unit, which controls the signals to ensure that a train remains a safe distance from the one ahead. Other codes fed into the rails, either from fixed sources or by the computerized operation system, can be used to drive the train, as in the fully automated Docklands Light Railway in London and the Paris Meteor line, which opened in 1998. Only one person is then needed on the train to monitor the equipment, check passengers, and take control in an emergency.

The name Meteor comes from the line's direction, east to west (est-ouest), and is derived from the project's full name, Metro Est-Ouest Rapide. Meteor's operations are overseen by a state-of-the-art electronic control center at Denfert-Rochereau. It is fully automatic, but has

◄ The control center of the Washington Metropolitan Area Transit Authority, the linked subway and bus service system established in 1966 in Maryland, Virginia, and Washington, D.C.

▼ The heart of the Washington system is the Metro Center in downtown Washington, where all lines intersect. From there to Shady Grove, the farthest station 18 miles (29 km) away, takes only 35 minutes.

also been equipped with an incident management system to allow a control staff to intervene when necessary. The center has both audio and video links with all station platforms, as well as inside all of the trains, whether moving or stationary. Operations are overseen by a system known as SACEM, which has a high degree of automation, but is still compatible with the traditional signaling system used on other Metro lines.

The trains move under an advanced "moving-block" system. In this system, each train has a designated "safe space" around it, and only when this space is exceeded can another train move in behind it. It is more efficient than the older "static-block" system, which allocates one train per block of track and ensures no other train can enter that block before the train ahead of it has departed. This system creates larger gaps between trains than the moving-block system—with one train at the extreme end of a static block, the next train will be at least half a block farther behind than it would be in a moving-block system, creating unnecessary backlogs of traffic on the line. Similar systems are in use in Lille, France, Chicago in the United States, and Taipei in China.

Some entire transit systems are designed for remote operation under computer control. To ensure passenger safety at stations, the platforms are enclosed with doors that align with those of the trains and are only opened when a train is actually stopped at the platform.

Automatic systems are also used for fare collection, with some modern systems allowing the use of multijourney tickets. These tickets have a prepaid value, and the cost of each trip is deducted from the stored total when the ticket is used to operate the access gate.

Tracks

Streetcars used for rapid transit systems normally have their own specially designated tracks, even if these are in the center of wide highways. These tracks sometimes dive below ground in city centers. Such tracks and tunnels have been built for streetcars in a number of European cities, but allowance is being made for future expansion, and tunnels in particular are being built to full rapid transit railway standards so that, when the time comes, the changeover will be easy. These are often called pre-Metro systems and are seen as an intermediate stage, but other cities have decided to make the pre-Metro system the ultimate version of their transit network.

The integration of a rapid transit system into a city center is often difficult because of established structures. One solution is to take over existing, but underused, mainline railway tracks.

Maglev trains

Various alternative systems have been proposed to replace conventional wheel and track systems, with one of the most promising, but as yet underutilized approaches, involving magnetic levitation (usually known as maglev).

Leading the technology race is Germany with a design called the Transrapid. Transrapid technology uses conventional electromagnets and forces of attraction to levitate the train. Close behind Germany is Japan, which is working on an entirely different design involving superconducting mag-

nets to generate huge repulsive forces that levitate the train. Germany's technology is ready for commercial production, while Japan's technology is still in the experimental stages.

The Japanese system is being developed by the Railway Technical Research Institute at the Yamanashi Maglev Test facility. In April 1999, a five-car train achieved a new world speed record of 314 mph (552 km/h).

Because the operation of the vehicle takes place without any physical contact with the rail, high speeds are an inherent characteristic of maglev trains. Speeds up to 300 mph (480 km/h) are possible compared with commercial rail, which usually reaches 100 mph (160 km/h).

Independent experts have examined the safety of the maglev system and have found that it is currently the world's safest available means of transport. The Transrapid is 20 times safer than the airplane, 250 times safer than conventional railways, and 700 times safer than traveling by road. Despite the high speeds, passengers on board maglev trains do not need to wear seat belts and can move freely inside the vehicle. Derailments are impossible because the maglev vehicle surrounds its guideway, which is normally elevated and separate from other traffic, so collisions with other vehicles are impossible.

The intense magnetic fields required for magnetic levitation are confined to a very small region within the train around the rails. Outside the train and in the passenger compartment the effects are comparable with Earth's magnetic field and well below those of everyday household devices. Outside the vehicle, along the route, the magnetic fields are considerably lower. Therefore possible problems with the magnetic field affecting the operation of cardiac pacemakers or wiping credit cards can be ruled out.

Trams

A number of recent mass transit systems have taken a modern approach to an early-20th-century transport system—the tram. Original trams are still in use in a few European towns and cities, including Blackpool in the UK, but they are rapidly being augmented by modern systems, such as the new Tramlink in south London. Trams, like trains, have solid metal wheels that run on tracks or rails inset in the roadway. Like many trains, they derive their power from overhead electric catenary. Unlike trains, much of the track can be integrated into existing road systems or run parallel with it.

FACT FILE

- *Vancouver's Advanced Light Rapid Transit (ALRT) is an entirely automatic magnetic levitation (maglev) system serving 10,000 passengers an hour on a 13-mile (21 km) corridor. There are no drivers, and speed, direction, and location are constantly monitored via the induction loop, a cable laid between the tracks.*

- *Amsterdam is built on such waterlogged ground that when its metro system was built, large sections of tunnel had to be manufactured above ground from precast segments and then sunk to their final position—15 ft. (4.5 m) below ground level.*

- *In the early 1960s, there were cases of Allied Forces personnel being arrested in East Berlin after falling asleep on the subway in West Berlin and alighting at East Berlin stations. The two halves of the city shared a common system at that time.*

- *The first "tube," the City and South London Railway, which used electric locomotives of 150 horsepower to run under the River Thames, was opened in 1890. The Glasgow subway, which opened shortly afterward, was powered by a cable traction system.*

 SEE ALSO: Bus • Electric motor • Linear motor • Monorail system • Railroad system • Streetcar

Materials Science

Materials science spans a period of time from the Stone Age, when people learned to fire clay to make a durable material for containers, to the present Space Age. It has evolved to cover a wide variety of materials. In today's world, the traditionally separate subjects of metallurgy, ceramics, plastics, and glass technology combine to form the subject of materials science.

Materials scientists need a wide background, including physics, chemistry, and engineering, since materials are used for structural, electrical, optical, and medical applications. They have to understand the microstructure and properties of materials in order to face the challenges of developing new materials and processes and of improving existing materials.

New materials lie at the heart of many modern advances, including the demand for lighter weight transportation to increase fuel efficiency and reduce exhaust emissions, the need for materials capable of withstanding the hostile environ-

ment of space, and the requirement for computers and communication systems that operate faster. Recent years have seen the introduction of totally new materials with unusual structures and properties. They can even be custom-designed to fit a specific need. Beginning in the late 1980s, this approach was extended one step further, with materials that can even respond to their environment. These are known as smart materials.

Smart materials

What makes a material "smart" is its ability to react to changing conditions. This new class of materials arose from research begun by the Pentagon to make aircraft and submarines vanish from enemy radar and sonar detectors. Smart materials display a range of abilities. At its most basic, the material simply responds to variations in its external environment, such as the photochromic lenses in eyeglasses. At its most sophisticated, the materials form part of a complex feedback loop in

▲ The Lockheed F-117 Stealth Fighter. The use of radar-absorbent materials (RAM) combined with a surface profile free of right angles, which are strong reflectors of radar signals, results in this aircraft having the same radar visibility as a seagull.

which the material senses changes in the environment and triggers a response. Developing, improving, and finding new applications for smart metals, ceramics, and polymers constitute some of the challenges facing materials scientists.

Shape-memory alloys

A class of metallic alloys, known as shape-memory alloys, comprise one of the largest and most widely used smart actuator materials. When these alloys undergo plastic deformation, such as bending, at one temperature, they completely recover their original shape in a reversible transformation when raised to a higher temperature. If they are somehow restrained while recovering their shape, these alloys can also exert a force that varies with the temperature. These two characteristics enable shape-memory alloys to be used in a variety of applications.

The shape memory effect arises from a change in crystal structure with temperature. For this effect to occur, the alloy must possess a crystal structure that can shift into a configuration known as martensite. The transformation occurs upon rapidly cooling the alloy to a critical temperature. When this temperature is reached, the parent crystal structure spontaneously transforms to martensite by a coordinated movement of large blocks of atoms. The temperature at which a deformed alloy recovers its memory relates directly to the temperature at which martensite

formation begins or to the higher temperature at which the alloy reverts back to the parent crystal structure. The martensite transformation temperature depends on the composition of the alloy and can be shifted by an applied stress. The materials scientist designs shape-memory alloys with characteristics to fit specific needs, such as transformation temperatures ranging from 77°F (25°C) for switches for automatic greenhouse ventilation systems, to 250°F (120°C) for satellite couplings.

The shape-memory alloys available fall into two categories, ferrous (based on iron), and nonferrous. Ferrous shape-memory alloys include iron–platinum, iron–nickel–carbon, and iron–nickel–cobalt–titanium. Nonferrous shape-memory alloys such as nickel–titanium, copper–zinc–aluminum, and copper–nickel–aluminum are used commercially. The nickel–titanium system, known as Nitinol, has a transformation temperature range between –460 and 212°F (–273 and 100°C), produced by altering the nickel–titanium ratio or by incorporating small additions of other elements.

Scientists at Goodyear Aerospace Corporation developed a Nitinol antenna for small spacecraft. The antenna begins as a ball with a diameter of 2 in. (5 cm), crushed into shape at room temperature. As the temperature increases, the ball slowly unfolds, and when the temperature reaches 171°F (77°C), the antenna resumes its original unfolded shape with a diameter of 10 in. (25 cm).

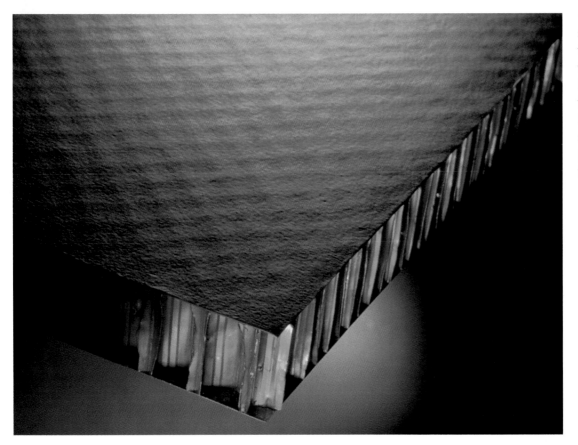

◀ A honeycomb sandwich structure made from titanium aluminide, an intermetal. Metallic bonding holds the atoms together in a crystal-like lattice. This panel has the strength of a solid metal panel but at a fraction of its weight.

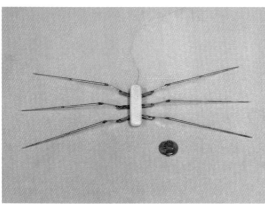

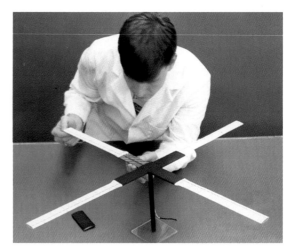

◀ A series of experimental devices made at the University of Kansas to show the potential of a ceramic material that flexes when current is applied to it. Top left: a solid-state aquatic vehicle that swims like a fish at up to 0.6 knots (1.1 km/h). Right: a smart rotor system for helicopters. When in production, rotors capable of tilting up to 9 degrees will give a smoother, more efficient ride. Bottom left: a walker, compared in size with a quarter, capable of moving spiderlike at 10 ft. per minute (0.22 km/h).

The versatile characteristics of shape-memory alloys such as Nitinol can also be exploited for medical applications. At present, cement forms the joint between artificial hip joints and bone. However, it causes problems of misalignment and loosening. By covering part of the prosthetic hip's surface with a shape-memory alloy with a transition temperature below body temperature, the alloy could be made to grasp the surrounding bone more firmly.

Liquid crystals

Metallic alloys and ceramics are generally composed of microscopic small crystals or "grains" within which the atoms are arranged in a three-dimensional periodic pattern repeated over long distances with a high degree of order. Liquids normally have at most short range order—the atoms or molecules may have a typical spatial relationship to their nearest neighbors but are uncorrelated over long distances. In a liquid crystal material, however, the shape of the molecules (rodlike or flat plates) imposes a partial long-range order, in that the molecules will in some phases have their axes aligned even though they do not sit at a particular position. They are thus said to exhibit orientational, but not positional, order. The alignment of the molecules can often be changed by imposing an electric field

around them, changing their reflectivity. Liquid crystals are widely used to display information using this effect in calculators and digital watches.

Smart polymers

Smart polymers are very large molecules that can change their internal arrangement of atoms in response to environmental conditions. Smart polymers developed by scientists at Pennsylvania State University have also found applications as coating materials that serve to make aircraft and submarines invisible to an enemy. These "active acoustic coatings" make submarines invisible by generating signals that act to neutralize reflections from sonar detectors.

Shape-memory polymers have also been developed that, like shape-memory alloys, are able to modify shape and stiffness in response to temperature changes. One example of this is a material produced by Mitsubishi called Diaplex that is produced as a textile capable of changing its breathability and water permeability.

Smart ceramics

Smart ceramics are mainly used in sensing and actuating systems. Some ceramics, such as zinc oxide, lose most of their electrical resistance when struck by lightning, and as a result, the current is grounded. This resistance change can be reversed so that it acts as a protection against current surges.

Lead zirconate titanate (PZT) is a piezoelectric material that has found a number of uses as a smart ceramic. Piezoelectric crystals are not in themselves a new development—they are found, for example, in mechanical gas lighters, in which pressure on a crystal makes it produce electric current. The explanation for this behavior is that a piezoelectric crystal has an asymmetrical distribution of positive and negative charges; that is, the centers of positive and negative charges do not coincide. In such a crystal, a mechanical stress alters the polarization of the crystal in the same way as an electric field would. Conversely, an electric field mechanically distorts the crystal.

One of the major implications of this behavior for smart ceramics involves the response of the material to an external electric field. Depending upon the direction of the field, the material either expands or contracts. The other important feature is the voltage change of the material in response to mechanical compression. These ceramics form major parts of sensing and actuating systems, such as rain sensors for automobile windshield wipers that detect the amount of rain falling and adjust the wipers to the optimum speed for the conditions.

Piezoelectric ceramics can also be used to control materials. Car shock-absorber systems that improve the handling of the automobile and at the same time increase passenger comfort utilize smart ceramics. In a system designed by Toyota, the road sensor consists of a five-layer piezoelectric ceramic mounted on the end of the shock absorber piston rod. When the car travels on a rough road, the sensor is mechanically compressed and the applied stress on the sensor creates a voltage. This voltage is then fed into a control unit, which amplifies it and feeds it into another piezoelectric ceramic that serves as an actuator. This voltage causes the actuator to change shape and therefore to exert a force on the hydraulic oil in the shock absorber, altering the ride from firm to soft. The process also considers the vehicle speed and, in total, requires 20 milliseconds to make the whole adjustment.

▶ A missile fin that warps to guide the missile as shown in the diagram, below. It has no mechanical linkages, yet will remain at full deflection in an airstream with a current consumption of a fraction of a watt.

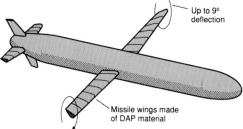

Up to 9° deflection

Missile wings made of DAP material

FACT FILE

■ *Composites are fiber-reinforced materials that ideally rival metals in their mechanical properties but are often limited by their failure under certain conditions. By embedding stress and temperature sensors into the composite material during its manufacture, subsequent stages in the processing of the composite, such as machining, assembly, and installation, can be monitored, and the production control data obtained can be used to optimize the composite.*

■ *One possible use for smart composite materials is in the construction of "smart structures" such as buildings, bridges, and aircraft that respond to their environment and warn of possible failure.*

Smart fluids and gels

Electrorheological and magnetorheological fluids are capable of becoming solid under certain conditions. In the case of electrorheological fluids, solidification occurs with the application of an electric field, and with magnetorheological fluids, it occurs with the application of a magnetic field. Both return to their fluid state when the field is removed. This technology has applications in vibration dampening and shock absorbers.

Polyelectrolyte gels are ionizable polymers that are capable of changing their shape and expanding their volume by up to 50 percent in response to temperature or pH change. Common forms of these gels are polyacrilonitrile-based gels. These smart polymers are being used to make musclelike materials that are up to 10 times stronger than human muscles, as well as grasping devices and controlled drug-release systems.

 SEE ALSO: ALLOY • CARBON FIBER • CERAMICS • MATTER, PROPERTIES OF • POLYMER AND POLYMERIZATION • SUPERCONDUCTIVITY

Mathematics

Mathematics is a language developed to aid precise and logical thinking about the relationships between physical and abstract objects. Many scientific disciplines rely heavily on mathematics although it is not necessarily these applications that motivate the mathematician. Computers now play a special part in mathematics. They can perform long and complex calculations very quickly, leaving the mathematician free to develop new theoretical ideas.

Mathematics has many branches, which are used according to the problem to be solved and the practical application of the results. Arithmetic is the most basic form of mathematics, dealing with whole numbers, fractions, and decimals and their manipulation through the processes of addition, subtraction, multiplication, and division. Algebra is used to solve problems with unknown quantities by using letters as substitutes for numbers. Geometry relates shapes and their positions in space, whether in two or three dimensions. Even the likelihood of an uncertain event happening can be calculated using probability and its related discipline, statistics.

Numbers

Arithmetic began with the natural numbers, 1, 2, 3, and so on, and the operations of addition and multiplication. The natural numbers are inconvenient because subtraction is not always possible: we can take 3 from 5 but not 5 from 3. Accordingly, the integers, or whole numbers (positive and negative), are defined to always allow subtraction, by the rule that since 3 from 5 is 2, 5 from 3 is to be written -2. This principle can be shown as:

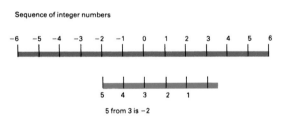

Sequence of integer numbers

5 from 3 is -2

The same problem arises with division and is again answered by inventing new numbers. Twenty-four divided by 4 gives 6 but divided by 5 does not give a natural number. The fractions, or rational numbers, were invented with the result that dividing 24 by 5 is written 24/5. The rational numbers are dense in the sense that between any two, there lies another (their average, for example); thus there is no "next" number.

The early Greek geometers thought that the rationals were all the numbers there were and set up their theory of similar figures on that basis. The idea was to represent numbers by suitable shapes; thus, we talk today of a number multiplied by itself as being its square, while a number multiplied by itself twice is the cube of the original number:

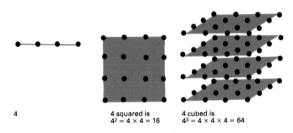

4

| 4 squared is | 4 cubed is |
| $4^2 = 4 \times 4 = 16$ | $4^3 = 4 \times 4 \times 4 = 64$ |

By this means, Pythagoras, or maybe his collaborators, were able around 500 B.C.E. to prove the theorem that the square of the longest side (opposite the right angle), the hypotenuse, in a right-angled triangle, is the sum of the squares on the other two sides. (A theorem is any proposition that is not obvious, but which can nevertheless be proved.)

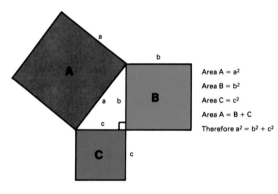

Area A = a^2

Area B = b^2

Area C = c^2

Area A = B + C

Therefore $a^2 = b^2 + c^2$

Pythagoras's theorem gives a good insight into the way mathematics relates to the physical world: the relationship $a^2 = b^2 + c^2$, which holds true for any right-angled triangle ever drawn, shows how to turn shapes into mathematics. It can be used to find unknown quantities—given any two sides, the third can be calculated—and so has immediate practical uses.

Applied to a square that has sides one unit long, the theorem says that the square of the diagonal must be 2 units; but no rational number can be squared to give the answer 2.

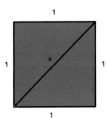

From Pythagoras' theorem
$x^2 = 1^2 + 1^2 = 2$
and so x is the square root of 2
$x = \sqrt{2}$

The proof that the square root of 2 (written $\sqrt{2}$) cannot be represented by a rational number was discovered by Pythagoras. A rational number is a number that can be represented as a fraction—that is, one integer (whole number) divided by another. In this way, the rational number 6.2 can be presented as $^{31}/_5$.

To prove the irrationality of $\sqrt{2}$, take two integers m and n such that m/n cannot be reduced to a fraction containing smaller integers—unlike, for example, $^{6}/_{10}$, which can be reduced to $^{3}/_5$, leaving its value unchanged, by dividing the top and bottom by 2. Therefore, m and n cannot both be even numbers or they would both be divisible by 2.

Now if $m/n = \sqrt{2}$, then $m^2/n^2 = 2$ and $m^2 = 2n^2$. But twice any integer is an even number, therefore m^2 is even, and thus m is also even (an even number multiplied by an even number gives another even number).

Thus, there must be another integer that is half of m. Call it p, and $m = 2p$, so $m^2 = 4p^2$. Substituting $4p^2$ for m^2 in the original statement $m^2/n^2 = 2$ gives $4p^2/n^2 = 2$. It therefore follows that $n = 2p^2$.

By the same argument, however, n^2 must therefore be even, and so must n; m has already been shown to be even. But m and n cannot both be even (see above), so there can be no rational number of the form m/n such that $m/n = \sqrt{2}$. Therefore $\sqrt{2}$ is irrational.

This result gave rise to the first of the great crises in the foundations of mathematics, which was solved by inventing yet more numbers—the irrationals. These and the rationals together form the real numbers—all numbers expressed by (finite and infinite) decimals. The number whose square is 2 (the square root of 2) is now 1.41421...

The square of 1.41421 differs from 2 by 0.0000100759; no matter how many more figures are taken, the square cannot quite be 2, but it can approach 2 as nearly as desired. The real numbers are the final step in constructing bigger number systems, so long as we restrict attention to numbers that are in some order (so that for any unequal pair, we can determine which is the greater). However, it became necessary from the 16th century onward to extend the number system one stage further, by giving up the requirement of ordering.

This need arose in the solution of equations and because of the double negative situation. In mathematics, as in any language, two negatives multiplied together produce a positive. If we ask what numbers when squared give the answer 1, the answer is twofold: 1 and –1. If we ask what numbers when squared give zero, there is but one, zero. But if we ask what numbers when squared

give –1, there are no such real numbers. It was possible to invent complex numbers, defined in terms of reals and one other unit, called i, with the property that i squared is equal to –1.

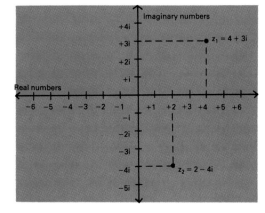

Argand diagram showing the complex numbers z_1 and z_2

Functions

A function is a rule that assigns to every element in a certain set, say X (called the domain of the function), one element in another set Y. Often the sets X and Y are sets of real numbers. For example, if X is the set of all real numbers, then f might take an element x of X and compute $2x^2$ (that is 2 times x times x), and we write $f(x) = 2x^2$.

Not all elements of Y need arise from an element of X, but those that do constitute the range of f. Well-known functions include the trigonometric functions, the study of trigonometry having been invented by Hipparchus (about 125 B.C.E.) and Ptolemy (about 150 C.E.). If two triangles have the same angles, but different sizes, their corresponding sides are proportional. Hipparchus realized that a table could be made relating the ratio of the sides to the angles in degrees. It proved sufficient to do this for right-angled triangles: the ratio of the side opposite one of the smaller angles (θ, say) to the hypotenuse is called the sine (abbreviated to sin) of the angle.

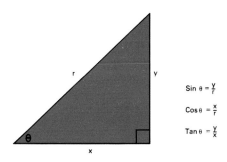

Since any triangle can be divided into two right-angled ones by forming a perpendicular from one corner to the opposite side, tables of sines of angles expressed in degrees suffice to calculate the ratios of sides for all triangles.

The Greeks were originally interested in trigonometry for astronomy: it was only much later that it was used for surveying Earth, as in the triangulation method used in mapmaking.

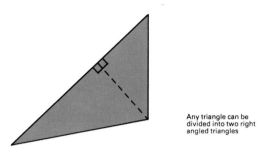

Any triangle can be divided into two right angled triangles

Often θ is expressed in radians. One radian is the angle subtended at the center of a circle by an arc whose length is the same as the radius of the circle. It is possible to extend the definition of sin, cosine (cos), and tangent (tan) outside the interval 0 degrees to 90 degrees (that is 0 to $\pi/2$ radians).

Functions can be demonstrated graphically. For any value of x, we plot the point $(x, f(x))$ on a graph. For example, if $f(x) = 2x^2$, we get a parabolic curve.

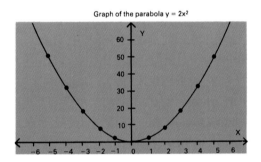

Graph of the parabola $y = 2x^2$

If the function $f(x) = \sin x$ is plotted against x, we get a sine curve, which periodically repeats itself at intervals of 2π radians. It was realized in the 18th century that almost anything that repeats itself periodically can be reproduced by adding together a sufficient number of sines and cosines of different sizes, this process being called Fourier analysis.

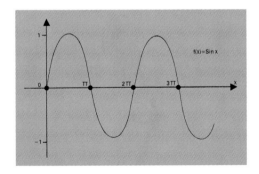

Calculus

Literally meaning "small stone," calculus was developed by Newton and Leibniz in the 17th century and is the study of infinitesimal changes in mathematical quantities. The key notion is that of the derivative of a function. If we plot a sufficiently smooth function $f(x)$ against x, we can draw a tangent to the curve at any point, say P, where $x = a$. A tangent is a line touching a curve.

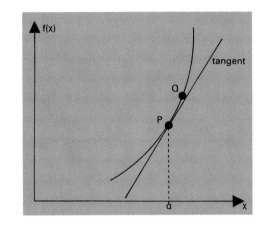

The slope, or gradient, of this tangent can be found by considering a chord PQ, where Q is the point on the curve for which $x = a + \delta$ where δ is very small. The slope of the chord is

$$\{f(a + \delta) - f(a)\}/\delta$$

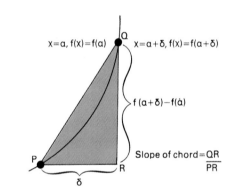

We then let δ get very close to zero so that the chord PQ becomes the tangent at P. The derivative of $f(x)$ at $x = a$ is the limiting value of the slope of the chord as δ approaches zero. The process of obtaining the derivative of $f(x)$ is called differentiation, and its reverse (namely, finding a function whose derivative is a given function) is called integration. Integration can be used to find the area under a given curve or, in more complex cases, areas and volumes of given surfaces and solids. Calculus has many applications, such as in the sciences and all areas of engineering.

One particularly interesting function is the exponential function, $f(x) = e^x$. Here, e is a real number whose value is slightly in excess of 2.7. This function has the property that its derivative is equal to itself. It is also related to the trigonometric functions mentioned above. In particular,

$$\sin x = (e^{ix} - e^{-ix})/2 \text{ and } \cos x = (e^{ix} + e^{-ix})/2$$

where i is the square root of –1. The exponential function can be represented by the infinite series

$$e^x = 1 + x/1! + x^2/2! + x^3/3!...$$

where for any number n, $n!$ (factorial n) denotes the product of all numbers up to and including n. For example, $4! = 4 \times 3 \times 2 \times 1 = 24$.

Related to the exponential function is the logarithmic function $\ln(x)$, which satisfies

$$x = e^{\ln(x)}$$

so that the exponential and logarithmic functions are inverses of each other. Logarithms were widely used to perform long multiplication calculations before the advent of computers and calculators, because they can be used to reduce the process of multiplication to the much simpler one of addition.

Algebra

Elementary algebra consists of manipulating quantities expressed in symbols rather than numbers themselves. For example, the equation

$$x^2 - y^2 = (x - y)(x + y)$$

remains true whichever values are used to replace the symbols x and y. Here, the parentheses on the right denote that $x - y$ and $x + y$ are multiplied. Often an equation for an unknown quantity, say x, is given, and x must be found. For example, consider the quadratic equation

$$x^2 + 4x + 3 = 0$$

It is called a quadratic equation because it involves the term x^2 but no higher powers of x. In this case, the left hand side factors so that

$$(x + 1)(x + 3) = 0$$

Now two numbers can give a product of zero only if one or both of them are zero. Thus, the above equation has two roots (or solutions). They are $x + 1 = 0$ and/or $x + 3 = 0$. In other words, $x = -1$ or $x = -3$.

The general form of a quadratic equation is

$$ax^2 + bx + c = 0$$

where a, b, and c are real numbers. The general rule for the solution is

$$x = [-b \pm \sqrt{(b^2 - 4ac)}]/2a$$

Rules are known for solving equations involving up to the fourth power of x.

More formally, algebra is the study of certain abstract mathematical structures. An example of such a structure is a group. A group is simply a set in which any two elements can be joined together (multiplied) to form another element of the set. There are very carefully specified rules that this joining together must satisfy. These rules are called axioms, and all theorems about groups are derived from these axioms without making any further assumptions. An example of a group is provided by cutting out an equilateral triangle from cardboard and coloring the three corners (on both sides) red, blue, and yellow. Lay the triangle flat on a table as shown in (a) the diagram below, with the red corner at the top. Suppose g represents the action of rotation of the triangle through 120 degrees clockwise (b) so that g replaces the red corner with the blue, the yellow corner with the red, and the blue corner with the yellow.

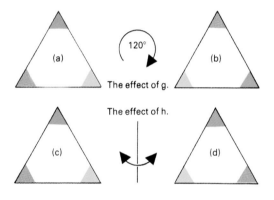

The effect of g.

The effect of h.

We can think of $g^2 = g \times g$ as performing g and then g again. In this way, $g^3 = g \times g \times g$ brings the triangle back to its original position, and we write $g^3 = 1$, where 1 denotes the identity element that leaves the triangle alone. Now let h be the action that turns the triangle over so that the two bottom corners are interchanged. Clearly $h^2 = 1$. If we perform g and then h, we find the triangle has its blue corner at the top, its red corner at the bottom left, and its yellow corner at the bottom right. Note that we get a different result if we perform h and then g. In other words, gh and hg are not the same.

Geometry

Geometry is largely the study of relationships in space and was the principal component of Greek mathematics. The Greeks studied lines and circles in the plane, three-dimensional geometry, and the shapes (parabolas, ellipses, and hyperbolas) made by cutting circular cones with planes. These

EGYPTIAN	BABYLONIAN	GREEK	ROMAN	MAYAN	WEST ARABIC	HINDU
I	▼	A	I	•	I	₹
II	▼▼	B	II	••	2	२
III	▼▼▼	Γ	III	•••	ⱬ	३
IIII	▼▼▼▼	Δ	IIII	••••	௴	୫
III / II	▼▼▼ / ▼▼	E	V	—	٩	५
III / III	▼▼▼ / ▼▼▼	F	VI	•̄	6	६
IIII / III	▼▼▼▼ / ▼▼▼	Z	VII	••	7	౨
IIII / IIII	▼▼▼▼ / ▼▼▼▼	H	VIII	•••	8	८
III / III	▼▼▼▼▼ / ▼▼▼▼	Θ	IX	••••	9	९
∩	◄	I	X	═	I•	१०

◀ The origins of counting and number systems are lost in antiquity, although it is known that as long as 4,000 years ago the Babylonians used an arithmetic based on the number 60, unlike modern arithmetic in which the number 10 is basic. This chart shows the numerals for 1 to 10 used by other civilizations.

shapes are called conic sections and arise in celestial mechanics, the study of the motion of planets.

Early geometry was based on the axioms of Euclid. These axioms were meant to be self-evident, but in later years, their truth was questioned, leading to non-Euclidean geometries.

Projective geometry deals partly with those properties of shapes that remain unchanged when projected onto another plane so that, for example, whether or not a point lies on a line is important, but distances between points are not. If we draw any two lines in a plane and mark three separate points (A^1, A^2, A^3) and (B^1, B^2, B^3) on each (see diagram), we can draw pairs of lines joining pairs of these points.

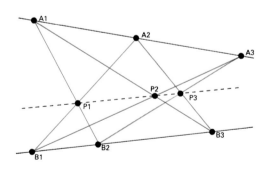

The points P^1, P^2, and P^3 where these pairs of points intersect always lie on a straight line no matter where the original points (A^1, A^2, A^3) and (B^1, B^2, B^3) were.

Topology

Topology is often called "rubber sheet geometry" because it deals with properties of shapes and surfaces that remain unchanged when they are con-

tinuously deformed. For example, a solid sphere and a solid cone are the same topologically, for we could mold a modeling clay sphere into a cube without making holes or breaking the material in any way. However, a solid sphere and a solid cube with a hole drilled through it are not topologically equivalent.

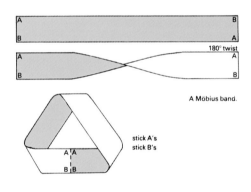

A Möbius band.

Many fascinating models having unusual topological properties can be made. For example, a Möbius band can be made by sticking together the ends of a strip of paper, having given a 180-degree turn (or half-twist) to one end first (see above).

This band has the property that it has only one surface and one edge. A pencil line drawn along the length of the strip returns to its starting point having covered both sides of the paper without the pencil leaving it. Cutting along this line produces a band with two full twists.

SEE ALSO: BINARY SYSTEM • CALCULATOR • CHAOS THEORY • COMPUTER • LOGIC • NUMBER THEORY

Matter, Properties of

Matter is the stuff of which all substances in the Universe consist, from earthbound objects and beings to planets, stars, and interstellar gas and dust. The most familiar states of matter are solid, liquid, and gas. A fourth state of matter—plasma—is a form of hot gas that consists of ions and electrons. A plasma emits light as a consequence of electronic transitions in its ions, as is evident in the plasma formed in lightning strokes and in discharge lamps such as neon tubes.

Solids, liquids, and gases defined

Solids, liquids, and gases are distinguished by their different tendencies to maintain their shapes and volumes. At a given temperature and pressure, a sample of solid occupies a constant volume and has a fixed physical form.

Liquids and gases belong to a larger class of substances called fluids, which are substances that conform to the shapes of their containers to a greater or lesser extent. A liquid maintains its volume while adopting the shape of the bottom of its container in a gravitational field; a gas, on the other hand, expands indefinitely to fill its container. A true gas keeps its gaseous properties at all volumes and can be liquefied only by cooling below a given temperature; a vapor is a gaseous substance that can be liquefied by reducing its volume per unit mass below a given threshold.

In some cases, the distinction between liquid and solid states is obscured. Pitch, for example, is a viscous liquid mixture of hydrocarbons that appears to be solid under most conditions but that yields in a fluid manner under persistent high pressure. Furthermore, pitch flows under the pull of gravity, but at such a rate that its deformation may become obvious only after months or years.

Solids, liquids, and gases consist of atoms, molecules (chemically bonded groups of atoms), or ions (charged species derived from atoms and molecules by the addition or removal of electrons). The balance of attractive and repulsive forces between these species is what determines the bulk properties of matter.

One bulk property is density, which is a measure of the closeness of packing of matter. The density of solids and liquids is much greater than that of vapors or gases because the atoms, molecules, or ions are much closer together in the solids or liquids, the so-called condensed states of matter.

Solids

In the solid state, atoms, ions, or molecules are attracted to one another by electrostatic forces—attractions between permanent or transient charges of opposite signs. In the case of crystals, these forces result in highly ordered structures in which the separations and orientations of component atoms, ions, or molecules repeat in a regular manner. The smallest collection of particles that represents such a structure is called its unit cell and is characteristic of a given compound. In the case of common salt (sodium chloride, NaCl), the unit cell is a cube of alternating sodium cations (Na^+) and chloride anions (Cl^-). A crystal of sodium chloride, which consists of a vast number of unit cells, also has the form of a cube.

▼ This water boatman, a member of the family of *Corixidae* species, uses the surface tension of water to support itself on the surface of a pond. The surface tension of a liquid is a result of the attraction between constituent molecules, notably strong in the case of water.

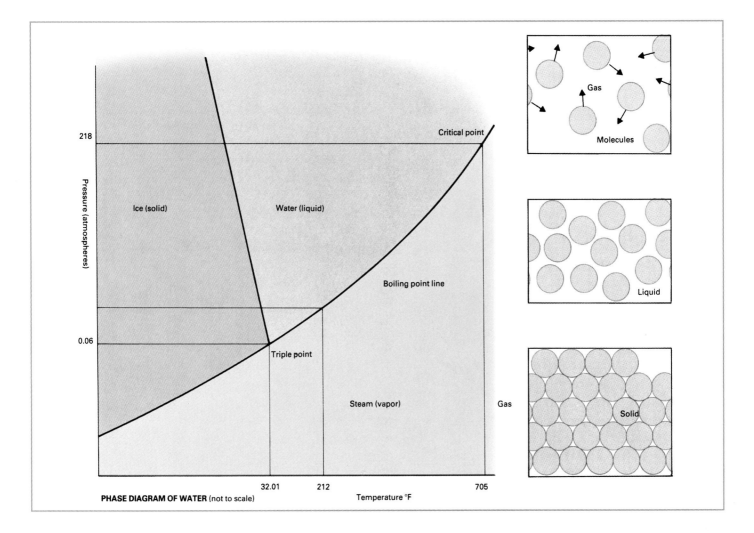

PHASE DIAGRAM OF WATER (not to scale)

Pressure (atmospheres)

218

0.06

Ice (solid)

Water (liquid)

Critical point

Boiling point line

Triple point

Steam (vapor)

Gas

32.01   212   705

Temperature °F

Gas

Molecules

Liquid

Solid

▲ The phase diagram of water at left indicates the regions of stability of ice (top left), steam (bottom right), and liquid water (top right). The lines indicate how the transition temperatures between these states vary with temperature, and the intersection marked "triple point" indicates the unique combination of temperature and pressure in which the three phases of water can coexist. The diagrams at right show the packing of molecules in the gaseous (top), liquid (center), and solid (bottom) states of matter.

Not all solid structures are as highly ordered as crystals. In glass, which is slightly impure silicon dioxide (SiO_2), each silicon atom is surrounded by a tetrahedron of oxygen atoms. The silicon atom is attached to the oxygen atoms by covalent chemical bonds, and the regularity of this arrangement gives glass the property of short-range order. Adjacent SiO_4 tetrahedra share oxygen atoms through Si–O–Si linkages, whose bond angles are approximately 120 degrees. This angle allows each SiO_4 tetrahedron to assume various orientations relative to its neighbors, creating long-range disorder in the structure. This combination of short-range order and long-range disorder is characteristic of glasses and other types of ceramic materials.

Allotropy

Some substances—notably chemical elements—exist in a variety of solid forms that have different structures. This property is called allotropy, and the different solid forms are called allotropes.

Carbon, for example, has two well defined allotropes: diamond and graphite. In diamond, each carbon atom is surrounded by a tetrahedron of four similar atoms. These atoms are surrounded by their own tetrahedra of carbon atoms, and so on throughout the crystal. The bonds between carbon atoms are covalent, so a perfect diamond crystal is effectively a single molecule.

In graphite, each carbon atom is directly bonded to three similar carbon atoms that form a triangle. As such, graphite consists of flat sheets of interlinked hexagons of carbon atoms. A third allotrope of carbon has been recognized in recent years: buckminsterfullerene (C_{60}), which consists of near-spherical molecules in which carbon atoms are linked in hexagons and pentagons.

Electrical properties of solids

Conducting solids all possess electrons that are free to move and thereby carry charge in a current. In metals, the free electrons are those that form the delocalized bonding system that spreads through the metallic crystal structure. When a voltage is applied across a region, electrons start to flee from negative to positive under the influence of the applied electrical field.

A few nonmetals also possess electrons that can conduct electricity in an electrical field. Graphite is such a substance: one of the four bonding electrons of each carbon atom takes part in a delocalized bonding system that spreads through the sheet of atoms of which that carbon atom forms part. The electrons in this system are able to conduct electricity; the other three bonding electrons of each carbon atom are occupied in localized bonds with adjacent atoms and are unable to move through the molecule.

The electrons of insulating solids are all held tightly within bonds, atoms, or ions and are therefore unable to move. Semiconductors, such as silicon and gallium arsenide, have few electrons available to carry current when pure. The conductivities of such materials can be readily improved by adding traces of appropriate impurities, which increase the number of available charge carriers—electrons or electron vacancies.

Magnetic properties of solids

The magnetism of certain solids originates from the magnetic dipoles that electrons have as a result of their quantum-mechanical spin. In general, electrons form pairs in which their spins are opposed, so the magnetic dipole of the pair is zero. However, some elements—notably cobalt, iron, and nickel—have unpaired electrons that can align with the magnetic fields of their counterparts in neighboring atoms. This effect can result in powerful magnetic fields.

Thermal and elastic properties

The time-averaged positions of particles—atoms, ions, or molecules—in a solid are determined principally by balances between attractive and repulsive forces that act between them. The particles are not static in those positions, however, since they possess thermal energy that makes them vibrate around their average positions.

As temperature increases, so does the thermal energy of the particles, causing the particles to vibrate more vigorously and increasing their average spacings—the effect is the basis of the thermal expansion of solids.

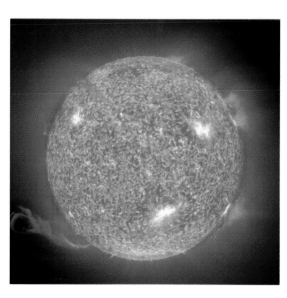

▶ The Sun consists mainly of hydrogen and helium in the form of plasma, a gas in which atoms have been split into positive ions and electrons. Under the immense pressures near the core of the Sun, this plasma undergoes nuclear fusion reactions that produce the Sun's heat.

The spacings between particles in a solid are also influenced by external pressure. A compressive force will reduce the average spacings, while a tensile (stretching) force will increase the average spacings. In either case, removal of the external force allows the particles to return to their normal positions for a given temperature, so the solid returns to its original dimensions. This phenomenon is the basis of the elasticity of solids.

Liquids

A liquid owes its fluidity to the fact that its cohesive forces—the forces that attract its particles to one another—are too weak to hold the particles in a fixed structure. Hence, the particles in a liquid can pass one another with various degrees of ease. The cohesive forces in a liquid are nevertheless sufficient to prevent rapid vaporization.

Like solids, liquids tend to expand with increasing temperature, because the greater thermal motion at higher temperatures reduces the influence of the cohesive forces. Water is an exception, however, since it expands with decreasing temperature below 39°F (4°C). In this case, reduced thermal motion allows hydrogen bonds to form between molecules, and these bonds hold the molecules in relative orientations that do not allow the closest possible packing of molecules. When it freezes (at 32°F, 0°C), water in the form of ice occupies a greater volume than the liquid from which it formed. This expansion on freezing causes ice to have a density of 0.92 relative to that of liquid water so that, at the freezing point, ice floats on water.

Surface tension

The surface tension of a liquid is a measure of its tendency to form droplets. Surface tension is directly related to the strength of the cohesive forces at work within a liquid. When a liquid comes into contact with a solid, its behavior depends on the balance between these cohesive forces and the adhesive forces that attract the liquid to the surface of the solid.

When water is placed on clean glass, the attraction between the water molecules and the glass (the adhesive force) is greater than the cohesive force. Hence, the water covers the surface of the glass with ease. In a vertical glass tube, the surface of the water curves upward near the glass so as to increase the contact area between glass and water. This curvature is called a meniscus.

If water is placed on greasy glass, the attraction between water molecules and the grease molecules on the surface of the glass is weaker than the cohesive force within the water. As a result, water forms into droplets so as to minimize the contact area between water and grease. The effect can be reversed by adding a small amount of detergent, which reduces the surface tension of water and allows it to wet a greasy surface.

Gases

In the gaseous state, thermal energy overwhelms the attractive forces between atoms or molecules. Therefore, under most conditions, they can be thought of as independent fast-moving particles whose separations are so great that their physical size is negligible in comparison.

This model, called the ideal gas approximation, is used as a basis for calculating the properties of gases. For example, the pressure exerted by a gas on the walls of its container is calculated from the average momentum of the particles and the frequency of their collisions with the container walls. These quantities depend on temperature and the number of particles in the container. The equation that connects temperature (T, in Kelvin), pressure (p), volume (V), and particle number (n) is the ideal gas law—$pV = nRT$—where R is the universal gas constant.

At extremes of high pressure and low temperature, the interactions between particles are no longer negligible, and gases deviate from ideal-gas behavior. Below a threshold temperature, called the critical temperature (T_c), compression can cause a gas to liquefy as the attractive forces become sufficient for liquid to form.

Phases and phase changes

A phase is a physically distinct form of matter. Water and steam would be the two phases in a boiling kettle, for example, and diamond and graphite would be two phases in a mixture of carbon allotropes. A change of phase—from one state or allotrope to another—can be brought about by either temperature or pressure. The importance of both these conditions is shown by the fact that water boils at 212°F (100°C) at sea level but at lower temperatures as altitude increases and atmospheric pressure decreases. At any particular pressure, however, the boiling point and melting point of pure substances are constant, as are the transition temperatures for changes between other types of phases.

The relationships between transition temperatures and pressure are conveniently shown in phase diagrams. In such diagrams, lines show the conditions under which two phases can coexist with stability, and intersections show where three or more phases can coexist. The regions between lines indicate conditions under which one phase is stable relative to all others. However, it is possible for unstable phases to persist when their mecha-

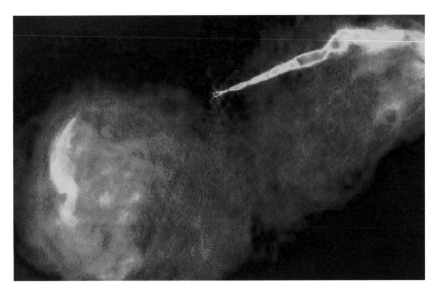

nism of phase transition is slow. Phase diagrams of carbon show that diamond should change into graphite under normal conditions, for example, but the change is so slow that the transformation of diamonds into graphite is never seen.

Phase changes are accompanied by a change in the energy and entropy (disorder) of a system. The transition of water into steam, for example, requires an energy input to overcome the cohesive forces in liquid water. The resulting steam has greater entropy than water, since its molecules are more sparsely and randomly distributed.

Other states of matter

Certain substances possess states in which they exhibit exotic behavior. For example, some organic compounds whose molecules are rodlike exist as liquid crystals under certain conditions—they possess some of the order present in solid crystals while maintaining the ability to flow. Helium-II is a form of liquid helium that can exist only at temperatures less than 2 K—3.6°F (2°C) above absolute zero—and is superfluid. Helium-II has zero viscosity (reluctance to flow) and can escape from an open container by flowing up the inside walls and down the outside.

All stars, and much of the matter between stars, consist of plasma, which for many purposes can be treated as an electrically conducting gas. Plasmas have been produced in the laboratory—notably for fusion experiments—but are difficult to control because of their high temperatures.

An estimated 90 percent of the Universe consists of dark matter, so called because it emits no light. Some scientists believe that at least part of this matter exists in as yet unknown states.

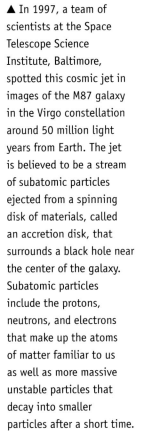

▲ In 1997, a team of scientists at the Space Telescope Science Institute, Baltimore, spotted this cosmic jet in images of the M87 galaxy in the Virgo constellation around 50 million light years from Earth. The jet is believed to be a stream of subatomic particles ejected from a spinning disk of materials, called an accretion disk, that surrounds a black hole near the center of the galaxy. Subatomic particles include the protons, neutrons, and electrons that make up the atoms of matter familiar to us as well as more massive unstable particles that decay into smaller particles after a short time.

SEE ALSO: Energy, mass, and weight • Gas laws • Liquid crystal

Mechanical Engineering

Mechanical engineering can be regarded as the core subject in engineering, as it finds a place in many related areas, from civil engineering to aerospace engineering, and even in electronics, in the manufacture and assembly of parts. Consequently, mechanical engineering is found in all industries and affects the manufacture of almost every type of product or process, from the kitchen toaster to space vehicles.

Mechanical engineering developed rapidly after the invention of the steam engine toward the end of the 18th century. The application of steam power to many different industrial processes required an understanding of mechanics that resulted in an increasingly scientific approach to the design of machines. Today, different areas of mechanical engineering are highly specialized, requiring extensive training and scientific knowledge. Mechanical engineers must have a thorough knowledge of a broad range of subjects, including thermodynamics, fluid flow, the properties of materials, and vibration. The engineer must be able to coordinate these various aspects of design to create a machine that is energy efficient, easy to maintain, and economical to manufacture. Speed of development has also accelerated, resulting in the rapid production of new products.

The different branches of mechanical engineering include the design of machines for producing power from fuels such as oil and coal as well as wind and water; the design of machines for manufacturing goods; the development of weapons; and the use of engineering to control the environment, with, for example, air conditioning and ventilation systems.

Materials

Developments in materials science have always been at the heart of engineering processes. Among recent developments are shape-memory alloys,

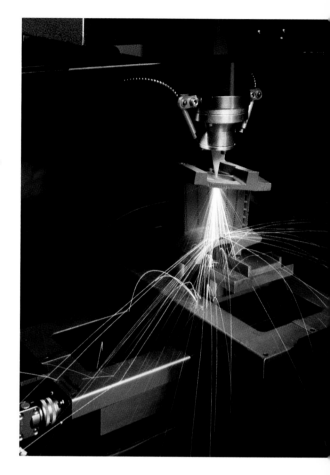

▶ An industrial laser drilling a nozzle guide vane. The Nd:YAG (neodynium–yttrium–aluminum garnet) laser can make 200 holes a second and can cut through stainless steel up to 3 in. (7.5 cm) thick.

which have a mechanical memory built into them, triggered by a change in temperature. Based on materials such as iron, nickel, copper, and titanium, the shape-change properties of such alloys can be used to make permanent joints and fixings, taking the place of welding or other conventional joints. Scientists at Goodyear Aerospace Corporation have developed an antenna for small spacecraft based on a nickel–titanium material called Nitinol. The antenna expands from a ball with a diameter of only 2 in. (5 cm) to an antenna with a diameter of 10 in. (25 cm). This change occurs only when the temperature of the ball has increased to 170.6°F (77°C).

Superplastic forming has been known as a principle for many years, but its practical use has awaited the arrival of specially developed alloys. These alloys, when heated to between 878 and 968°F (470–520°C), will stretch to many times their original length under low pressure. Cheap one-sided molds with air pressure applied to the other side allow complex shapes to be made from thin alloy sheets. This process is ideal for manufacturing aircraft panels.

Also being developed are "smart" materials that incorporate sensors through which instructions can be sent to "tell" the material to behave a

◀ Although prototype trains using magnetic levitation (maglev) have been made since the 1960s, the practical use of these systems has only become a commercial possibility since the late 1990s.

certain way. Alternatively, sensors can feed information to a control station to relay back data about temperature, pressure, stress, or other parameters. The final stage will be to combine these two with a controller to produce "intelligent" materials that can respond to events as they occur.

Mechanical engineers also use piezoelectric materials, such as lead zirconate titanate (PZT), that produce an electric current when a pressure is applied to them or, conversely, change shape when an an electric current is passed through them. Such materials have been used in automobile design for shock absorber systems.

Metal cutting

Besides the many long-established methods of cutting metals, such as turning, milling, grinding, sawing, and drilling, several new methods have been developed recently. Among these are plasma cutting, laser cutting, spark machining, and abrasive water jets.

Plasma-arc cutting uses a gas stream, which is heated in a tungsten arc to such a high temperature that it becomes ionized and can conduct electricity. It can cut almost any type of metal product. Additional heat may be added by passing a current through the plasma and into the metal being cut. This technique is particularly useful in cutting metals that cannot be flame cut, such as aluminum, brass, and stainless steel.

Lasers provide a powerful concentrated source of energy that can be controlled and guided to cut materials used in engineering. They are becoming an everyday shop-floor tool; they can cut out parts faster and, more important, with better quality than conventional methods. Lasers are also used to cut materials that are difficult to machine by other means; they can weld without distorting the part and can mark, engrave, heat treat, and even cut through ceramics.

Spark machining, also known as electrodischarge machining (EDM), uses the energy from a spark created

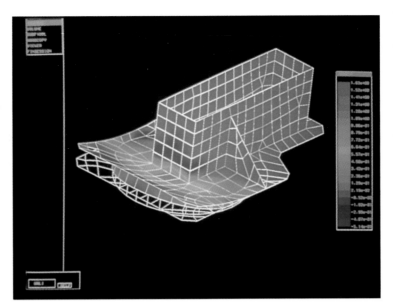

▲ A 3-D image used in computer-aided design (CAD). This drawing was produced using a finite element analysis program, which handles tasks too complex to be carried out using conventional design methods.

▼ Traditionally, cars have been crushed for low-grade scrap at the end of their lives. BMW pioneered the recyclable car—all parts shown in green can be easily removed and recycled, while those colored blue are already recycled.

between an electrode—the tool—and the workpiece by applying a voltage between them to erode or burn out the metal to the required shape. It is often employed in very precise work, usually computer controlled, such as making the die molds for intricate plastic parts.

Water-jet cutting is more recent than the other methods and incorporates a fine abrasive material in a high-pressure jet of water directed at the part being cut. The jet is the carrier for the abrasive and provides the source of energy to give a clean cut through thick metal plates. Because of the cooling effect of the water, there is no heat distortion; this process is also fume, dust, and noise free.

All of these newer techniques expand the possibilities for mechanical engineers to design and construct machines and devices in ways that would previously have been extremely difficult or prohibitively expensive.

Railroads

Rail transportation has remained fundamentally unchanged from the first steam-hauled locomotives: they still consist of railcars and wagons running with wheels on rails driven by an engine, be it steam, diesel, or electric motor. There have been attempts to build tracked vehicles on the principle of the hovercraft or air-cushion vehicle, but no service based on this method is yet in operation.

Since the 1960s, a completely different principle, based on magnetic levitation, has been under development in several parts of the world. This system uses the fact that opposite poles of a magnet repel or force each other apart. Powerful electromagnets lift the cars about ⅜ in. (9 mm) above the track. A linear electric motor propels the cars, giving a quiet vibration-free means of transportation. Since there is no direct contact between the vehicle and the track, the system is virtually frictionless.

The world's first maglev system was installed in 1984 on a track about three-quarters of a mile (1 km) long running between the exhibition center and the airport at Birmingham, England. It is still running, though it is essentially a prototype slow-speed system. More recently, a major demonstration unit was built in Germany, and another in Japan. The first practical application of a fast maglev train will be on a system to be built in China linking the city of Shanghai with its airport. Scheduled to be completed by 2003, this maglev link will cover the 19-mile (30 km) distance in under 10 minutes. This system may eventually be extended to link Shanghai with Beijing, a distance of 800 miles (1,280 km). There are also possible plans for maglev trains in the United States. Suggestions have been proposed for links between Baltimore and Washington D.C. and Pittsburgh and its eastern suburbs.

Electromagnetic technology has also been used in bearings to reduce friction. They have applications in machine tools, centrifuges, compressors, pumps, and mechanical handling. Transportation systems and bearings have always been limited by friction between their sliding and rolling surfaces. Frictionless systems have therefore always been an aim of engineering.

Computers in engineering

The computer has invaded mechanical engineering as with most other aspects of science and technology. The advent of the computer has been the biggest change experienced by mechanical engineers in the last 20 years.

Its influence begins at the design stage, where the drawing board has largely been replaced by a keyboard and a screen. Drawings are made directly on-screen, appearing in color and in three dimensions. Images can be expanded, contracted, altered, and rotated and parts analyzed for strength, behavior, and performance under load without ever printing a drawing or cutting metal.

Highly technical computer programs are available to carry out finite element analysis, a technique for analyzing structures too complex to work out by conventional methods. Following the computer-aided design (CAD) stage, the design is transferred electronically to computer-aided manufacture (CAM) to be made in computer-controlled machines. Even the factory administration methods for ordering, scheduling, assembly, inspection, and testing are now controlled by the microchip.

There are few purely mechanical engineering products or processes left that do not have a computer or programmable logic controller (PLC) as part of the finished product. Many domestic products and most cars now have at least one computer built in. So far has this process gone

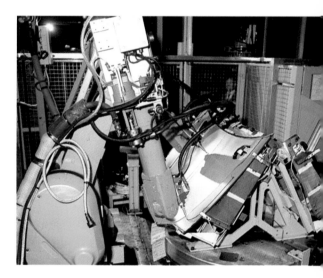

▶ A robot in a car factory lays glue beads on car hoods. Robots play an increasing role in automating mechanical engineering projects.

that electronic engineers work with mechanical engineers from the beginning of the design process to ensure that the most is made of the new technology. This partnership had led to the development of a discipline called mechatronics, fusing mechanical and electronic engineering.

Marine engineering

Traditionally, marine engineering progress is relatively slow compared with that in aerospace and computers. As methods of powering ships and boats, steam engines slowly gave way to turbines and then to diesel propulsion. Now there are electrically driven ships in which a large diesel engine or gas turbine drives a generator acting as a power station to provide all the power needs of the vessel electrically, including the ship's main propulsion. The engines of some large cruise liners are constructed this way, driven by a cyclo-converter-controlled AC system, which needs no costly reducing gears.

Water-jet propulsion has been used for high-speed light craft for some time, but large, fast, car and passenger ferries driven by 20,000-horse-power (15,000 kW) engines driving water jets are now also common. Water is drawn from beneath the vessel to an inboard pump and discharged astern to drive the ship forward. Guide vanes at the rear can deflect the jet to aid steering. These ships have good fuel economy at speed, are maneuverable, and have shallow draft, and the impellers are protected from floating debris.

Fast displacement catamarans are designed to operate on trips up to 150 nautical miles (285 km), making them suitable for most ferry crossings worldwide. They are built with a central buoyancy hull below the cross deck in case the side hulls are punctured. In 1998, a high-speed catamaran called *CatLink V* broke the transatlantic speed record, averaging 41.2 knots (100 km/h).

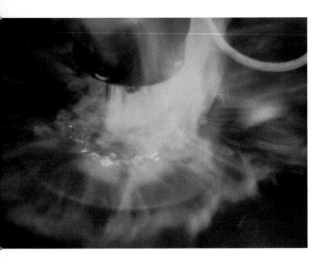

◀ During spark-erosion metal cutting the workpiece is submerged in a dielectric fluid inside which the process takes place.

The design of submarines for marine exploration has required mechanical engineers to create designs that can cope with the extreme pressures that exist far below sea level, as well as creating unpiloted robot submersibles that are capable of reaching depths of over 20,000 ft. (6,000 m).

The need for large military submarines that are able to remain below the surface for long periods of time and that do not require frequent refuelling has led to the development of nuclear reactors as power systems.

Robots

Robots now perform many tasks previously done only by humans, from simple, repetitive actions to those that are highly complex, and some that no person could achieve. They are able to perform such tasks as cutting, welding, screwing, assembling, and spraying. The largest use today of robots is found in the automobile construction industry, but they are also used in space, in medicine for highly accurate work, and in nuclear power installations where it is unsafe for humans to go.

Current developments include a walking robot created by Honda in Japan. Many mobile robots use wheels to move around, but wheels tend to restrict them to single floors. Honda's humanoid robot research project endeavors to create robots that can function in more human-like ways, and thus enable them to climb stairs, turn in place, and navigate their way around a building without a system of guides.

Recycling and the automobile

The automobile is a complex combination of a vast number of parts made from many different materials and combinations of materials. Although steel may make up some 70 percent of the materials of a car, it is not necessarily easy to recover, because most of it is either painted or coated with some noncorrosive metal. Also, in automobile manufacture, different types of steel

are used for different parts of the car, such as the fenders, frame, body, and engine.

Deliberate design for dismantling is already a reality; partly to gain a "green" image for their products, several companies have embarked on schemes to recycle parts of their cars. One way is to make parts in simple, modular, snap-fit construction so that they can be easily stripped down for reuse. This method produces economies in labor, which is the main cost of the recycling operation. BMW in Germany is already reprocessing many of the parts in its cars.

Plastics are obvious items for recycling, as they are easy to shred, melt, and form into new parts, but they must be sorted into the correct grades, and thus, the material must be easily identified. Often, plastic materials degrade in the process and must be reused for less demanding applications. The next stage in progress toward full recycling is to design parts so that they can be used again in a new vehicle.

Prototypes

When a new part has been designed, either on a drawing board or a computer, the next stage is usually to make a sample, called a prototype, so that it can be visualized and tested with the other parts in the machine. With intricate components and difficult shapes, this step can be a very time consuming and expensive process. As a result, a part may have to be accepted as good enough because it would take too long to go through the process again with a changed design.

The technique of rapid modeling can help designers check their designs quickly and make changes if necessary. One way is to connect the computer that contains the design to the machine tool directly and make the part without a skilled operator, who needs to work from drawings.

A faster technique for producing prototypes, called stereolithography, or three-dimensional modeling, has led to the development of rapid prototyping (RP). This technique involves ultraviolet-sensitive coatings used in the printing industry. The computer-aided design (CAD) model, which exists only inside the computer, breaks the design down into a large number of thin slices, which are then recreated by building up successive layers of light-sensitive liquid plastic to form the three-dimensional part. Each layer is rapidly solidified or cured before the next layer is laid on top.

▼ Many techniques may be used for welding. Here, welding is achieved using cheap and efficient microwaves to create a controllable plasma beam that heats the metal to melting point.

SEE ALSO: COMPUTER • MARINE PROPULSION • MASS PRODUCTION • MATERIALS SCIENCE • METAL CUTTING AND JOINING • RAILROAD SYSTEM • ROBOTICS

Medicine

Medicine, the study of the prevention and treatment of diseases of the human body, has been practiced since prehistoric times, when humans learned to differentiate between substances that caused harm and those that had beneficial effects. Early remedies were based on plants and herbs and used for common ailments, such as colds and constipation. More serious illnesses were viewed in a very different light; magic, supernatural forces, and evil spirits working on the soul were held responsible for the ills of the body and necessitated incantations, magic charms, and appeasement of angry gods to bring about recovery of the patient.

By the time of the Greek physician Hippocrates, often called the father of medicine, disease was increasingly being seen as a natural rather than a supernatural phenomenon. He studied the effects of food, occupation, and climate on illness and advocated dietary changes rather than drugs as treatments. The use of medicines, however, was the cornerstone of Arabian medicine throughout the Middle Ages, and many of the discoveries made by Middle Eastern physicians of the time are still in use today. It was also during this period that the first European hospitals were set up in monasteries and convents.

The Renaissance saw the advent of detailed investigations into the anatomy and physiology of the human body when prohibitions on dissection began to be lifted. Improved surgical techniques, together with new understanding about the nature of chemical elements, did much to encourage new thinking on the spread and treatment of diseases. One of the most significant discoveries was made in 1628 by an English physician, William Harvey, who described the circulation of the blood around the body. Another was the invention of the microscope, which enabled the Dutch microscopist Antonie van Leeuwenhoek to view bacteria for the first time.

Throughout the 19th century, medicine made rapid advances, particularly in the understanding of physiological processes, such as the role of the pancreas and how blood vessels expand and contract. Diagnostic techniques were further improved with the discovery of X rays by the German physicist Wilhelm Röntgen and the isolation of radium by Pierre and Marie Curie in France. Tropical medicine made a breakthrough at the end of the 19th century with the identification of the mosquito as a vector for the transmission of a number of diseases, including malaria, yellow fever, and elephantiasis.

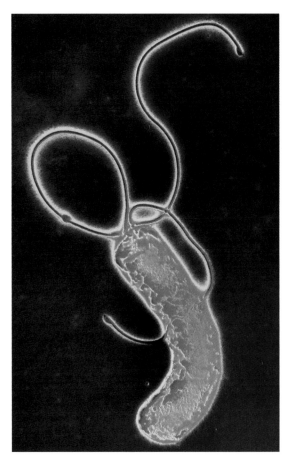

◀ An artificially colored electron micrograph of the bacterium *Helicobacter pylori*, which has been linked with the formation of stomach ulcers. Eighty percent of ulcer sufferers found to be harboring this bacteria in their digestive tract can be treated successfully with antibiotic therapy.

Asepsis and anesthetics

Key to halting the spread of disease was the establishment of the germ theory, which arose through the work of the French chemist Louis Pasteur and a German doctor, Robert Koch. Pasteur was the first to prove that the microbes seen by van Leeuwenhoek were living organisms and that some of them were responsible for causing illness. He further proved that killing certain microbes would prevent the spread of specific diseases. Pasteur's discoveries were backed up by Koch, who invented a method for determining which bacteria caused a particular disease through his work on the anthrax bacillus. As a result of this pioneering work, the agents responsible for a whole host of infectious illnesses, including cholera, leprosy, plague, tetanus, tuberculosis, and pneumonia, were discovered.

The recognition of microscopic organisms as the source of disease prompted an English surgeon, Joseph Lister, to consider methods of keeping wounds clean after surgery. He used carbolic acid, which proved to be a powerful disinfectant. However, preventing germs from reaching the wounds in the first place, a process known as aseptic surgery, soon became standard practice. Surgeons began to dress in operating gowns, gloves, and masks, rather than their outdoor clothes, and washed their hands and the area of the body to be operated on before surgery.

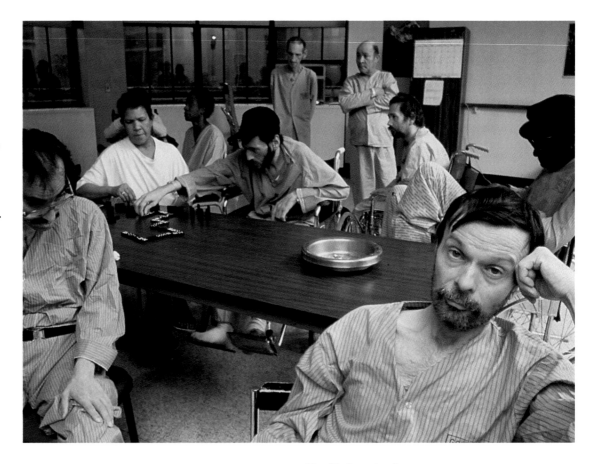

The prospect of surgery for the patient was also much improved by the introduction of effective anesthetics. Early attempts to reduce pain involved the use of opium or alcohol, but these simply dulled the pain, and the patient remained conscious of what was going on. The advent of ether and chloroform revolutionized surgical procedures, enabling doctors to perform increasingly complex operations while the patient remained mercifully unaware of the proceedings.

20th century medicine

The pace of developments in medical understanding and technology accelerated considerably during the 20th century. Chemotherapy was instigated as a means of treating infectious diseases by a German bacteriologist, Paul Erlich, who used an arsenic compound called salvarsan to treat syphilis. Antibiotics were discovered accidentally in 1928 by a British bacteriologist, Alexander Fleming, who noticed an unusual mold growing on a culture dish that appeared to be killing the bacteria surrounding it. Fleming grew the mold as a pure culture and isolated the active ingedient, which became known as penicillin. Together with the discovery of sulfa drugs in the 1930s, antibiotics have proved to be highly successful medicines for treating many common ailments afflicting man. Science is constantly having to stay one step ahead, however, because of the development of antibiotic-resistant superbugs.

Medicine today

General medicine, as practiced by family practitioners, is undergoing its most profound change in many years, as is general hospital medicine. New drugs and diagnostic agents mean that diseases such as peptic ulcers and diabetes can be treated by family physicians. New technology is also allowing family physicians to perform an increasing number of tests and procedures at office level. As a result, many community medical practices now have the facilities once found only in hospitals.

Diagnosis is the first stage in determining the ailment afflicting the patient. Despite all the tools now available to the physician, the symptoms the patient presents may indicate a number of diseases, so each possibility must be eliminated before treatment begins. For example, a stomach ache may be a symptom of an ulcer, a hiatus hernia, a kidney stone, or simply indigestion. A pain in a particular part of the body could be an indirect effect of a disease in a different organ or bodily function. An added drawback is that not all the symptoms of a disease will appear at the start of an illness, and it may take repeated examinations, tests, and trial therapies before the disease shows its true nature. Another delay in diagnosis can arise because the family physician has not come across the disease during his or her career. Smallpox, once a common killer around the world, has been eradicated by vaccination, and doctors graduating at the end of the 20th century will almost certainly never see a case of the disease except in a medical textbook.

Once the physician has physically examined and questioned the patient, he or she will either start the patient on a course of treatment or refer the patient to a specialist at a hospital for further testing and assessment of the condition.

Primary care physicians now recognize that some patients have physical symptoms that may be caused by states of mind, including anxiety and phobias. Such symptoms are particularly common in people who drive themselves too hard (a common modern day problem) and are unsympathetic to psychological symptoms. These physical symptoms include fatigue, irritability, palpitations, gut symptoms (including irritable bowel), breathlessness, increased sensations of hot and cold, visual disturbances, and headache.

In the early 1980s, a British survey showed that 15 to 30 percent of patients seen by hospital specialists have no physical cause for their symptoms. Since the 1990s, this number has declined as family physicians have become more skilled at reassuring these patients that they have no organic disease and helping them develop strategies for coping with their symptoms.

Steps forward

The 1980s saw the development of a number of new vaccines, of which the most important was for hepatitis B. Hepatitis B is a serious disease in Western society, and chronic infection often leads to liver cancer. In developing countries, it is the most common cause of liver cancer. This disease has led doctors to understand the importance of treating chronic hepatitis B infection, even in patients with few or no symptoms. They are now treated with a course of daily interferon injections, often lasting four to six months.

Arthritis remains a serious cause of ill health. Osteoarthritis, which should properly be called osteoarthrosis, is known from skeletons to have existed since ancient times. It remains difficult to treat, other than by the replacement of hips and knees by artificial joints in those who are severely affected. There are two forms of inflammatory arthritis: rheumatoid and ankylosing spondylitis. Both of these are autoimmune diseases in which the body reacts against itself. Treatments using monoclonal antibodies are showing promise. Both these diseases have been known for only 200 to 300 years (as can be seen by examining ancient skeletons), and both seem to be declining in incidence for unknown reasons.

Suicide, which in the 1960s was the most common cause of death in young adults, has declined considerably and continues to do so. Part of this is because there are now widespread counseling services, including telephone helplines, and part because barbiturates are now rarely prescribed for insomnia. They have been replaced by benzodiazepines, which are not fatal in overdose, but have themselves caused addiction problems.

The arrival of AIDS

The end of the 20th century saw a change in the types of disease known throughout most of history. Since the introduction of antibiotics in the 1940s, the Western world has been able to forget that acute infections can kill healthy children and adults. By 1950, the one common fatal infectious disease left was poliomyelitis. After that was conquered by vaccines invented in 1956, there were three decades when it was unusual for anyone in the West to die from an infection. Then AIDS arrived. It had been festering relatively unnoticed in Africa for some years under the name slim disease, so named because patients lost weight from it. It is caused by a slow virus that destroys the killer T-cells of the immune system. For many years, the only licensed treatment was zidovudine (AZT), but massive research programs have led to the development of new drug combinations that have been shown to slow the onset of full-blown AIDS, while the search continues for a vaccine.

In the late 1980s, French and American workers separately showed that AIDS was caused by a virus, which the French called LAV (lymphadenopathy virus) and the Americans called HLTV (human T-cell leukemia virus). In 1989, both agreed to call the virus HIV (human immunodeficiency virus), and a reliable test was developed. Meanwhile the only preventive measure is to ensure that the body fluids of infected people do not enter the bodies of uninfected people; in practical terms prevention means safe sex, antibody testing of blood donations, and sensible pre-

◀ A community health worker (foreground) with a vaccination cold pack treats a family of Somalian nomads. Vaccination against common diseases such as measles, polio, and diphtheria has done much to improve the life expectancy of children in developing countries.

cautions when handling bodily fluids of patients. However, the virus is far less infectious than the hepatitis virus, which requires far more stringent precautions. History suggests that epidemics of sexually transmitted diseases will be contained not by frightening people into careful behavior, but by developing effective drugs and vaccines.

Developing-country health problems

Developing countries have all these problems and more. The city-dwelling middle classes have much the same health needs as their Western counterparts; cities are also home to many unemployed, homeless, and vagrant people, and drink and drug problems abound in them. In rural areas, there is also primary poverty, where people do not have enough to eat. Many countries, especially in Africa, produce sufficient food, but it is often unequally distributed and poorly stored so that it becomes unusable or harmful; repeated food poisoning is a common reason for malnutrition. Infant mortality in rural areas has been lowered owing to education about infant nutrition, particularly the advantages of breast feeding rather than using formula milk, and to better treatment of acute diarrhea, a common condition in poverty-stricken areas.

There are also financial limitations to health care, even in the wealthiest societies. Moreover, increasing expectations lead to increasing litigation, which adds to the overall costs and, arguably, makes doctors overly cautious about entering certain specialities such as obstetrics and gynecology.

Fringe medicine

There are patients who are unwilling to accept that their symptoms could possibly arise from within themselves, and various branches of fringe medicine, calling themselves by names such as "nutritional medicine," "clinical ecology," or "environmental medicine," have sprung up as a result. Despite lack of recognition from the orthodox medical professionals, they tend to have a cult following. They often diagnose diseases that have headline value, such as chronic Epstein-Barr syndrome, candida hypersensitivity syndrome, multiple chemical sensitivities, total allergy syndrome, and myalgic encephalomyelitis (ME, or chronic fatigue syndrome).

There is also a growing trend for "alternative" treatments, some of which have been found to relieve symptoms without recourse to conventional drug therapies. The Chinese art of acupuncture has been practiced for centuries in treating a wide range of conditions, including disorders of the respiratory, digestive, and nervous systems. Chiropractic and osteopathy use manipulation to treat problems involving the skeleton and musculature.

Hypnotherapy is another treatment that has been used to combat emotional illnesses, phobias, and bad habits by putting people into trances and using the power of suggestion to control their fears. One of the most successful uses of hypnosis is as an alternative to anesthetic—it is often used in dentistry and has even been used in major surgery to control pain, the patient remaining conscious throughout the operation. Other treatments finding favor include reflexology, naturopathy, homeopathy, and herbalism.

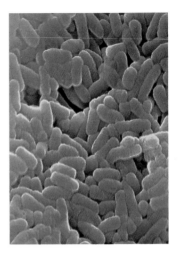

▲ Tuberculosis, once considered to be all but conquered, made a dramatic comeback in the 1990s as a result of patients not completing their course of drug therapy, thus allowing the bacteria to become resistant to antibiotics. The bacterium is spread by coughing or sneezing by carriers who may not even show any symptoms.

FACT FILE

■ Despite enormous strides in medicine in recent years, many developing-country health problems can be alleviated by low-tech remedies. For example, World Health Organization initiatives have taught people oral rehydration therapy as a treatment for diarrhea, which kills more children in developing countries than any other disease. Adding a spoonful of sugar and a pinch of salt to a liter of water is simple, cheap, and saves lives that might otherwise have been lost through dehydration.

■ An increase in vaccines has also reduced disease, and at comparatively little cost. However, many vaccines deteriorate rapidly in warm temperatures and rely on the "cold chain"—transportation in insulated containers from one town's refrigerator to the next. Improvements here could save much wasted effort. Four-fifths of the world's children are now immunized against measles, tetanus, polio, diphtheria, whooping cough, and tuberculosis—compared with only one-fifth in 1981.

SEE ALSO: Bones and fracture treatment • Cancer treatment • Electronics in medicine • Epidemiology • Gerontology • Immunology • Microsurgery • Obstetrics and gynecology • Pediatrics • Psychiatry • Sports medicine • Surgery • Transplant

Mercury

The alchemists of the Middle Ages recognized mercury not as a metal, but as the metallic essence of all metals, imparting to them their characteristic luster, density, thermal conductivity, and malleability. This quality gave mercury the name quicksilver and the Latin name *hydrargyrum*, meaning "liquid silver." It is also from this Latin name that we obtain the chemical symbol for mercury, Hg. Alchemists considered the other basic component of metals to be sulfur, which accounted for the changes that metals underwent on heating. It was not until Braune succeeded in freezing mercury—it solidifies at –38°F (–39°C)—one cold night in St. Petersburg, Russia, in the winter of 1759 that mercury was generally accepted to be a metal in its own right. Mercury boils at about 357°C (675°F) and is chemically related to the metals cadmium and zinc, members of the same group of the periodic table.

Occurrence

Mercury is sometimes found as native globules among outcrops of its ore, so its discovery must be credited to prehistoric times. Apart from the famous Almadén mine in Spain—which has been worked continuously since before the time of Christ—and the Yugoslav Idrija mine, mercury is found in Peru and extensively throughout the western United States, with mines in Nevada, Idaho, Arizona, Oregon, Alaska, and California.

Because mercury occurs in highly concentrated deposits, it is not regarded as a rare metal, although it ranks only around 67th in the natural abundance of elements in Earth's crust, making it less common than platinum or uranium.

Extraction

Mercury is most commonly found in the form of mercuric sulfide (HgS) in the ore cinnabar. Mercury is usually won from its ore by roasting in the presence of air and condensing the mercury vapor produced:

$$HgS \; + \; O_2 \; \rightarrow \; Hg \; + \; SO_2$$

cinnabar   oxygen   mercury   sulfur dioxide

It is possible to roast fairly coarse ore in a vertical shaft furnace. Finer ores, however, inhibit the air flow through the furnace, and for this reason, designs have been introduced in which the ore powder moves gradually down the shaft, falling progressively from one to another of a series of ledges inclined at 45 degrees to each other. It is modern practice to crush all the ore to

a fine powder and roast it either in a multihearth mechanical furnace, where it is moved from one hearth to the next lower one by rotating rakes, or in a rotary kiln, which is a long cylinder with its rotation axis inclined at a few degrees from the horizontal. When fine ores are roasted, considerable dust is carried over into the flue by the furnace gases. The dust is removed before it reaches the mercury condensing tubes, which would otherwise become clogged. The mercury collected from the condensers is separated from the soot by filtration, and the soot, which contains some mercury compounds, is treated with lime so as to recover the metal. Finally, the metal can be purified by vacuum distillation.

Uses of mercury

The mercury barometer was invented by the Italian physicist Evangelista Torricelli in 1643, and the thermometer by the German physicist Gabriel Daniel Fahrenheit in 1714.

Alloys based on mercury are called amalgams. The best-known use of an amalgam is in dental fillings, made by mixing mercury with an alloy composed of 69.4 percent silver, 3.6 percent copper, 0.8 percent zinc, and 26.2 percent tin. The filling sets as interdiffusion occurs between the liquid and solid phases. The ability of mercury to form amalgams is also made use of in the extraction of gold and silver, although some metals, such as iron and platinum, will not form amalgams with this element. Mercury is also used as

▲ Mercury, or quicksilver, is the only metal that is liquid at room temperature. The metal has a surface tension that is so high that small droplets can form almost perfect spheres. Highly toxic to humans, mercury is used in electrical apparatus, catalytic processes, poisons, and dental amalgam.

the cathode in cells that produce chlorine by the electrolysis of brine. The sodium liberated at the cathode immediately forms an amalgam and can subsequently be recovered as caustic soda. An amalgam of mercury with the metal thallium has a lower melting point, –76°F (–60°C), than mercury itself and is therefore used to make low-temperature thermometers. Mercury batteries have a higher power and a longer life than conventional batteries and are used in applications where size must be kept to a minimum. The anode in such batteries is an amalgam of mercury and zinc, and the cathode is formed of mercuric oxide, HgO, mixed with about 5 percent graphite. Mercury is also used in electric lamps to provide ultraviolet light and is used to make the pigment vermillion.

Mercury compounds are used to a limited extent in industry and medicine. Mercuric sulfate, $HgSO_4$, is a catalyst in the production of acetaldehyde from acetylene and water, and a complex salt of copper, mercury, and iodine, $Cu_2(HgI_4)$, which changes color on heating, is used as a temperature indicator. In addition, mercury is used in a variety of processes, such as the production of caustic soda and chlorine through electrolysis, and its high electrical conductivity has led to its use in electrical equipment.

Toxicity

Mercury, particularly mercury vapor, and most of its compounds are poisonous, and it is now generally accepted that in environmental terms, mercury is a danger. Grain treated with phenyl-mercuric acetate almost wiped out Sweden's yellow bunting population; the compound was withdrawn in 1960. Treated grain has also acci-

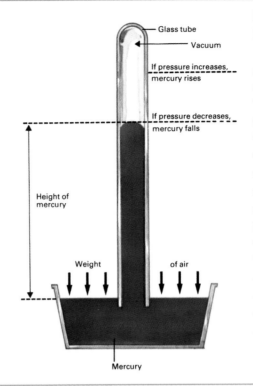

MERCURY BAROMETER

Glass tube

Vacuum

If pressure increases, mercury rises

If pressure decreases, mercury falls

Height of mercury

Weight   of air

Mercury

Atmospheric pressure is measured by a barometer. This diagram shows how the height of the column in a mercury barometer varies with the pressure of the air. Barometers are used to forecast weather, and since atmospheric pressure also changes with height above sea level, barometers may also be used to measure altitude. Standard atmospheric pressure at sea level is usually given as 760 mm of mercury.

dentally been used as food. In Minamata, in Japan, industrial waste containing mercury compounds caused heavy-metal poisoning of seawater, polluting fish and sea life that was then eaten by local inhabitants, resulting in severe illnesses such as loss of sight and hearing, mental retardation, and paralysis, as well as affecting unborn children, resulting in severe birth defects.

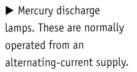

▶ Mercury discharge lamps. These are normally operated from an alternating-current supply.

FACT FILE

■ *Daedalus, the character in Greek mythology famed for inventing wings and then flying too close to the sun, was also renowned for building moving statues. He employed the weight and mobility of mercury to act as a counterweight, causing movements in the limbs and eyes of his creations.*

■ *As mercury prices have risen over the years along with industrial demand, it has become economic to seek it out in old mine dumps and tailing piles. Manufacturers even find it worthwhile to process the soil around sites where mercury was recovered from processing ore in earlier days.*

 SEE ALSO: BAROMETER • BATTERY • METAL • THERMOMETRY

Metabolism

Metabolism is the name given to all the chemical reactions, both constructive and destructive, that occur in living organisms. Metabolism is a huge field, encompassing many areas of biochemistry. Constructive reactions produce macromolecules used by organisms as the materials for growth and as stores of energy. Destructive reactions extract energy from the environment by breaking down particular molecules. The net effect of metabolic processes is an overall uptake of energy from sources outside the organism.

Individual reactions involved in metabolism are often very simple, perhaps only breaking or forming a set of chemical bonds. These simple reactions form a step in a metabolic pathway, a highly defined series of chemical reactions. Each chemical reaction in metabolism is catalyzed by an enzyme, and the reactions in any particular cell need hundreds of different enzymes.

Energy

The source of energy for all living organisms is, ultimately, sunlight. Green plants and a number of very simple microorganisms use light directly in a process called photosynthesis, in which simple substances like carbon dioxide (CO_2), water (H_2O), and ammonia (NH_3) are changed into larger molecules, such as glucose, that can be used by the cells in the organism.

Living things, such as animals, that do not use photosynthesis directly often use the products of photosynthesis (vegetable material) as food or eat other organisms that live on vegetable material.

The chemical components of food are mainly proteins, carbohydrates, and lipids (fats). They are broken down into simpler building blocks from which cellular materials can be built—causing growth—and provide the energy needed for many of the chemical reactions of metabolism.

The major carrier of energy in living cells, no matter how the cell obtained the energy, is a compound called adenosine triphosphate (ATP). ATP undergoes a chemical change when it passes on its energy to other molecules, losing either one or two of its phosphate groups. ATP then becomes either adenosine diphosphate (ADP) or adenosine monophosphate (AMP). Using either light energy or chemical energy, the phosphate groups can be regained, making ATP again. Two other important energy-carrying molecules in respiration are nicotinamide adenine dinucleotide NAD^+, which with the addition of a hydride ion, H^-, becomes NADH, and flavin adenine nucleotide FAD, which with the addition of H_2, becomes $FADH_2$.

Catabolism

Catabolism is the name given to the processes by which large molecules in food are broken down during digestion into smaller ones, so releasing energy. Breaking down food first involves converting large protein molecules into strings of about 20 amino acids; carbohydrates are converted into sugars, and lipids are converted into fatty acids and glycerol. Only a very small amount of energy, about 0.5 percent, is obtained from food in this first phase of catabolism. The amount is unimportant because, as it is produced as heat, it cannot be used by the cell.

The second phase involves partially oxidizing the products from phase one—oxidation is the process of removing electrons. This phase, which

▼ Athletes are able to rapidly metabolize food to produce molecules of adenosine triphosphate, ATP, used by muscles to provide energy.

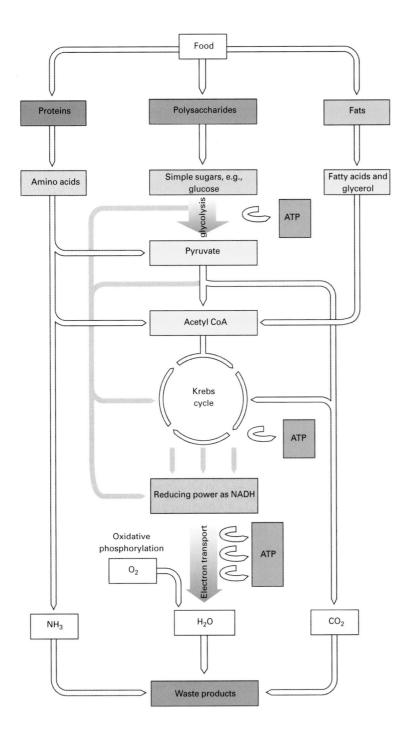

releases energy for the cell. Releasing carbon dioxide and water is the end point of catabolism.

Simultaneous oxidations in which hydrogen atoms and electrons are removed from a number of intermediate compounds, such as NADH and $FADH_2$, formed during the cycle generate ATP from ADP and inorganic phosphate. Collectively, these reactions are called oxidative phosphorylation and terminal respiration.

Glycolysis

Glucose is the most important source of energy for cellular processes. During digestion, polysaccharides, usually glycogen and starch, are hydrolyzed by digestive enzymes. After passing from the gut into the bloodstream and then into cells in the liver as well as other tissues, the glucose enters the fermentation phase of its catabolism, known as glycolysis.

First, glucose reacts with ATP to form glucose-6-phosphate and ADP. This process is called phosphorylation and requires two enzymes—a hexokinase and a glucokinase. The glucose-6-phosphate is then catalyzed by phosphoglucoisomerase to form fructose-6-phosphate.

Adding ATP to fructose-6-phosphate produces fructose-1,6-diphosphate, which is then split into two smaller molecules—dihydroxyacetonephosphate and glyceraldehyde-3-phosphate; these compounds are also known as triose phosphates, and the enzyme, triose phosphate isomerase. This completes stage one of glycolysis.

Stage two reverses the uptake of ATP and starts ATP production. Glyceraldehyde-3-phosphate is oxidized, producing 1,3-diphosphoglycerate, which is a high-energy compound, making this step one of the most important in glycolysis. The next step releases ATP by reacting 1,3-diphosphoglycerate with ADP. Aside from the ATP produced by the reaction, the other product is 3-phosphoglycerate. At this stage, all the ATP that was taken up in the first stage of glycolysis has been liberated once more.

Glycolysis continues with a reaction that is catalyzed by phosphoglyceromutase and converts 3-phosphoglycerate into 2-phosphoglycerate. The 2-phosphoglycerate then becomes phosphoenolpyruvate (PEP) and water. ADP is then added to PEP, producing pyruvate and ATP. As this reaction occurs twice for every molecule of glucose that started glycolysis, the net gain is two molecules of ATP. At this stage, no further glucose can enter the glucolic pathway until oxidation of some by-products of glycolysis has taken place. The exact details of this last stage of glycolysis vary from organism to organism, but once oxidation has taken place, glycolysis can continue.

takes place in the cytoplasm of the cell, results in five possible end products. They are acetyl coenzyme A with two carbon atoms, oxaloacetate with four carbon atoms, oxoglutarate with five carbon atoms, carbon dioxide, and water. The most important process of phase two is glycolysis, which is the splitting of the sugar glucose to produce ATP.

Phase three further oxidizes the multicarbon atom products of phase two. The Krebs cycle—also known as the citric acid cycle or tricarboxylic acid (TCA) cycle—takes care of this final stage of oxidation. On each turn of the Krebs cycle, citrate is formed from oxaloacetate and acetyl coenzyme A. Then oxaloacetate is reformed along with two molecules of carbon dioxide. This process

▲ Flow diagram showing the three phases of metabolism. Adenosine triphosphate (ATP)—the body's main source of usable energy—is created during all three states of metabolism, but most ATP is produced from the nicotinamide adenine dinucleotide (NADH) produced during the Krebs cycle.

The details of the glucolic pathway give some idea of the complexity of the metabolic processes, but glycolysis is just one process in a range of processes of similar complexity. For example, the phosphogluconate pathway, which is a variation on the glucolic pathway, has more steps.

Similarly, other sugars can be catabolyzed. Larger carbohydrates are split into components that are intermediates of one of the main metabolic pathways. From there, the intermediates can easily be dealt with. Other metabolic pathways deal with fatty acids and proteins.

Krebs cycle

Following glycolysis, the resulting pyruvate passes into one of the mitochondria—one of the cell organelles—where it is converted to acetyl coenzyme A (acetyl CoA). This can then enter the Krebs cycle, which is the part of metabolism that is ultimately responsible for most energy production. Acetyl CoA passes through a series of enzyme-catalyzed transformations that result in the production of NADH and $FADH_2$ as well as CO_2, H_2O, and one molecule of ATP. First, the acetyl CoA, in combination with oxaloacetate, is converted to citrate and then isocitrate, which is in turn converted to α–ketoglutarate, and in the process, NADH and CO_2 are produced. The α–ketoglutarate is changed to succinate and releases NADH, ATP, and CO_2. The succinate then becomes fumarate, and this time, $FADH_2$ is created. Fumarate becomes malate, which is made into oxaloacetate and more NADH. The oxaloacetate then reenters the Krebs cycle, and the whole process repeats.

Oxidative phosphorylation

Oxidative phosphorylation is the final process of respiration, the one in which NADH and $FADH_2$, produced in the Krebs cycle, are used to make ATP. This complex process releases a great deal of chemical energy by using the electrons and protons that constitute the hydrogens in NADH and $FADH_2$. The electrons are held on the hydrogen ions and are easily split from the single hydrogen proton. Each electron then passes down a chain of carrier molecules—the electron-transport chain—that occur on the cristae, the internal folded membranes of the mitochondria. The protons remain in the aqueous solution within the mitochondria. At the end of the electron transport chain, an oxygen molecule (O_2) picks up four of these electrons and two of the protons that are in aqueous solution to form two molecules of water. As the electrons pass down the chain, they release energy that is used to pump protons out across one of the mitochondria's inner membranes into an intermembrane space, thus creating an electrochemical proton gradient across the membrane. The protons pass back into the mitochondria by diffusion and thereby provide energy for the enzyme ATPase to add a phosphate to ADP, thus forming ATP. ATP at this stage produces between 32 and 34 molecules, giving a total at the end of all stages of respiration of between 36 and 38 molecules. Once created, the ATP passes from the mitochondria to the rest of the cell, where it may be used as the source of energy for nearly all of the organism's processes. A typical cell may contain as many as 10^9 molecules of ATP in solution.

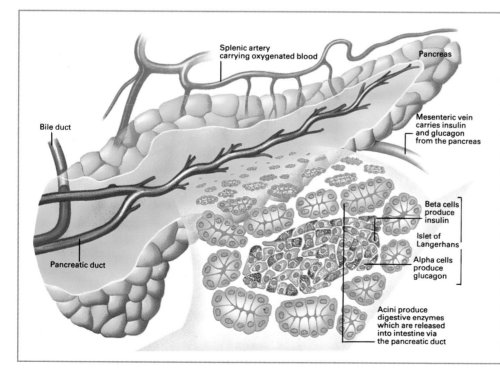

Bile duct

Pancreatic duct

Splenic artery carrying oxygenated blood

Pancreas

Mesenteric vein carries insulin and glucagon from the pancreas

Beta cells produce insulin

Islet of Langerhans

Alpha cells produce glucagon

Acini produce digestive enzymes which are released into intestine via the pancreatic duct

HOW INSULIN IS MADE BY THE BODY

The hormones insulin and glucagon are produced in the Islets of Langerhans— a cluster of hormone-producing cells in the pancreas. They enter the bloodstream via the mesenteric vein and balance the body's sugar level by opposing the effects of hormones, such as cortisone and adrenalin, that raise the level of sugar in the blood. The insulin exerts its influence by allowing sugar to pass from the bloodstream into the body's cells to be used to provide energy. The disease diabetes mellitus is caused by insufficient production of insulin or reduced sensitivity to insulin.

Anabolism

Anabolism is a similar but opposite series of reactions to catabolism. Where catabolism releases energy from molecules, anabolism stores it in them. Therefore, anabolic pathways construct building blocks of macromolecules, such as proteins, carbohydrates, and fats, from simpler components. Anabolism is also known as biosynthesis.

Anabolism and catabolism are not achieved through the same paths. The process of taking one set of large molecules and catabolizing them is not reversible by anabolizing the products.

Anabolism happens in two main stages. Stage one takes intermediate compounds from catabolic pathways and forms relatively small products, which are precursors of macromolecules. Stage two sees these precursors being knitted together to make macromolecules such as proteins, nucleic acids (DNA, RNA), lipids, and polysaccharides. ATP is used up in both stages because these processes are energy-hungry. Anabolism needs high levels of ATP and correspondingly low levels of ADP and AMP.

Stage one varies between different organisms, but once the macromolecular precursors have been formed, anabolism proceeds along a smaller number of recognized routes, according to the nature of the final products. In stage one, simple sugars are formed by glyconeogenesis, which may be thought of as being something like a reversal of glycolysis. Glycerol, fatty acids, and some other compounds (ultimately forming lipids) are built up from another biosynthesis pathway, and yet more pathways yield amino acids (ultimately forming proteins) and purine and pyrimidine nucleotides (ultimately forming RNA and DNA). The synthesis of the macromolecules themselves follows. Again, different types of reaction pathways occur according to the substances being produced.

Controlling metabolism

In most cases, catabolic pathways are regulated by the balance between ATP, ADP, and AMP in the cell. These three compounds react with specific regulatory sites on pacemaker enzymes without which ATP could not be produced.

Anabolic pathways are inhibited by the presence of ADP or AMP. The existence of these two compounds in any quantity in a cell can be seen as a signal that there is a low level of energy in that cell. Pacemaker enzymes usually have a role to play at the start of an anabolic pathway. The existence of quantities of specific substances that react with specific sites on pacemaker enzymes acts as a negative feedback system. If there is at any time an excess of a particular substance or substances, the pacemaker enzymes will initiate a pathway to dispose of them. Thus, a cell will only synthesize as much of a substance as it needs.

A second control mechanism regulates the rate of synthesis of pacemaker enzymes. This coarser kind of metabolic control is most important in microorganisms and has been found to have very little effect in animals.

Each of the main metabolic pathways has its own regulatory mechanism. In the case of glycolysis, phosphofructokinase is the most important control site of the pathway. High levels of ATP inhibit phosphofructokinase, and so the rate of glycolysis depends on the level of ATP, which is judged by the ATP/AMP ratio.

In the Krebs cycle, two parts of the cycle are tightly coupled—coupling is called respiratory control because of the role oxygen plays in the cycle. The effect is that the rate of the cycle matches the need for ATP. An excess of ATP inhibits the activities of three enzymes involved in the cycle—citrate synthetase, isocitrate dehydrogenase, and alphaketoglutarate dehydrogenase.

The rates of glycolysis and glyconeogenesis vary inversely with one another. Therefore, when activity in one pathway is high, the other is low, and vice versa. AMP inhibits part of the glyconeogenesis pathway but has the opposite effect on the glycolysis pathway because of the way it interacts with enzymes involved in the pathways.

FACT FILE

- Some mammals, such as squirrels and hedgehogs, are able to dramatically reduce their rate of metabolism and enter a state of hibernation. It is done during winter when food supplies are reduced. The hibernating animal lowers its temperature to almost 32°F (0°C) and uses fat reserves built up over the warmer months as a source of energy.

- Tibetan monks are able to raise the temperature of certain parts of their bodies during meditation. It appears to be done without raising metabolic rate—increased metabolism would require an increase in food, and the monks live on a sparse monastic diet. It is thought this temporary temperature rise is due to vasodilation—the engorging with blood of the blood vessels in the skin.

 SEE ALSO: BIOCHEMISTRY • CELL BIOLOGY • ENZYME • HORMONE • NUTRITION AND FOOD SCIENCE • PHOTOSYNTHESIS

Metal

Although metals constitute a very small percentage of the masses of either the Universe or Earth, they have had a disproportionate importance in human development. About 97 percent of the Universe (by mass) is composed of hydrogen and helium, the next most common elements being oxygen, iron, nitrogen, and carbon. As Earth formed, the vast majority of hydrogen and helium and a substantial proportion of carbon, nitrogen, and oxygen were lost to space, as their atoms were not heavy enough to be retained by Earth's gravitational field. The primeval Earth was therefore mainly iron with other elements more or less present as impurities. During the gradual cooling that took place over many millions of years, the lighter and more reactive elements combined with oxygen and sulfur to form a slag, which floated on the surface of the molten iron core. In time, the slag solidified to form Earth's crust on which we live. The most abundant metal in Earth's crust is aluminum, followed by iron, calcium, sodium, and magnesium. Other metals such as copper, silver, gold, and uranium, although less common, are concentrated in specific areas where workable deposits allow the mining of these technologically important elements. In most cases, the metals occur in combination with other elements as ores.

Exploitation of metals

The first metals to be exploited were not those present in most abundance but those that could be formed most easily from their ores. Indeed, some metals, such as gold, copper and iron, which sometimes occur naturally in elemental form, were probably first beaten into useful or decorative shapes before 5000 B.C.E. The systematic winning of metal by decomposition of the ores by heating marked the Bronze and Iron Ages (5000 and 3000 B.C.E., respectively). The criterion determining the historical order in which metals were discovered and exploited has been in direct proportion to the ease with which they can be separated from their ores.

▲ Forging a platinum ingot from a 99 percent pure metal, using a pneumatic hammer. Platinum is the world's most precious metal, and a key raw material for science and industry.

◀ Novelty items die cast from zinc. The atomic structure and chemical bonding of metals contributes to their ability to be shaped into useful items for domestic and engineering purposes.

In the case of copper, silver, mercury, and lead, the oxides, which constitute the ores, can be easily reduced to the metal by heating in a wood fire. The production of the alloy bronze by simultaneously melting copper and tin and the development of the more difficult skill of iron smelting using charcoal or coke to aid in the reduction process provided materials suitable for the manufacture of tools and weapons that literally transformed human fortunes.

Further developments did not occur until the industrial revolution, when the invention of the blast furnace allowed substantial reduction of the carbon content of iron to produce iron and steel in large quantities suitable for industrial use. The extraction of the lighter and more abundant metals aluminum, magnesium, and calcium was not achieved until the 19th century, because their ores are too stable to be reduced by charcoal or coke.

Their extraction on a commercial scale was made possible by the availability of electric power. Around 1850, the British chemist and physicist Michael Faraday and the German chemist Robert Bunsen independently developed an electrolytic method of extracting magnesium from its chloride. In the 1850s, aluminum was a rare and precious metal; it was not until an American chemist, Charles M. Hall, and a French chemist, Paul-Louis-Toussaint Héroult, developed methods of extracting aluminum from its ore bauxite—by dissolving the oxide in a flux of sodium aluminum fluoride prior to electrolysis—that aluminum could be produced in large quantities. Today, aluminum ranks second only to iron in quantity of production. Pure calcium metal is also obtained by electrolysis from molten calcium chloride.

Characteristics of metals

Metals are characterized by a series of common features. They are good conductors of both heat and electricity, but the conductivity decreases with increasing temperature, contrasting with ionic or covalent compounds, which have poor conductivities when solid but become more conductive with increasing temperature. Metals are generally strong and ductile, making them particularly suitable for a wide range of applications from engineering structures to cooking containers, and they can be formed into very intricate shapes by a variety of processes, such as pressing, casting, and powder metallurgy. They form mixtures with other metals with a wide range of proportions of the elements, rather than compounds with strict atomic ratios, allowing optimum compositions to be easily identified for specific properties.

These characteristics are a direct consequence of the atomic structure and nature of binding of atoms in metals. In general, the atoms of metals have weakly bound electrons in their outer shells. Metals usually have crystalline structures with close-packed atoms that have no directional bonding; the outer-shell electrons are shared by the crystal lattice as an electron cloud rather than being associated with an individual atom. The very high mobility of the electron cloud is responsible for the ease with which electricity and heat can be conducted. The high opacity and luster associated with metals are due to the absorption and reemission of light by the electron cloud.

The high ductility of metals results from the nondirectional character of the crystal structure. Faults in the stacking sequence of atoms allow deformation of the metal to occur at much lower stresses than is required for fracture of the metal. The dislocation progressively moves through the crystal to give a small displacement. This property allows very large deformations to be achieved in wire drawing, sheet rolling, and stamping.

In many applications, the fracturing of metals is eventually associated with the highly disordered structure at the junctions between crystals. Single-crystal components can sometimes be produced with improved properties.

Metallic artifacts can be shaped by a variety of procedures. In particular, the metals often melt at relatively low temperatures and do not volatilize, making them particularly suitable for casting into shaped molds or for joining other materials in processes like soldering, brazing, and welding.

SEE ALSO: Alloy • Casting • Chemical bonding and valency • Conduction, electrical • Electrolysis • Iron and steel • Metal cutting and joining • Metalworking • Sheet metal

Metal Cutting and Joining

◀ A pneumatic precision riveter being used to anchor an aircraft windshield to the body. Rivets used in aircraft construction are made of a light alloy to keep the weight of the airplane as low as possible.

Metals are used widely in the manufacture of durable equipment and machinery, but fabrication of these items usually involves the cutting and joining of pieces of sheet metal. A wide variety of techniques have evolved to deal with the different strengths and hardnesses of metals and the temporary or permanent nature of the bond required.

Flame cutting

Flame cutting is a process commonly used in industry for cutting or shaping metals, usually iron or steel. It is extensively used for shaping the large plates used in shipbuilding and boiler making and is widely used elsewhere in industry. Plates as thin as ⅛ in. (3 mm) or as thick as 5 ft. (1.2 m) can be flame cut on a regular basis. An oxyacetylene torch is a common example of a flame-cutting tool, though it can also be used for welding, depending on how much oxygen is supplied to the flame.

For metal to be flame cut, it must first be heated and maintained at its ignition point, that is, the temperature at which it will burn in a jet of pure oxygen, the cutting stream, to form its oxide. This heating is carried out by a preheating flame consisting of a flammable fuel gas burning in a supply of oxygen, known as the heating oxygen. The oxide, or slag, which must have a lower melting point than that of the metal from which it is formed, is blown away by the force of the cutting stream. This process exposes the metal under-neath to the cutting stream, and it is burned in turn and blown away as slag. The burning produces heat, which helps the process to continue.

When the cutting stream has made a hole or nick right through the metal to be cut, the cutting torch is moved, moving the cutting stream through the metal and elongating the hole or nick into a cut. As the metal is cut, a strip—known as the kerf—is removed, the width of the kerf varying with the thickness of the metal being cut.

Flame cutting torches

The essential functions of a flame cutting torch—which may be handheld or machine guided—are to mix the heating oxygen with the fuel gas (usually propane or acetylene but sometimes hydrogen) to produce a flammable mixture that can be burned in the preheating flame and to direct the cutting stream onto the area that has been heated by the preheating flame.

A common design of torch consists of an injector, a mixing chamber, and a series of narrow holes, or jets. The injector introduces the preheating oxygen supply to the fuel gas, with which it is then thoroughly mixed by expanding it into the mixing chamber. Finally, the mixture is passed out through the heating jets, which are usually arranged in a ring around the cutting jet. The high-pressure cutting oxygen is then forced out of the cutting jet.

Flame cutting can be carried out underwater with an additional air feed to form an air bubble around the cutting tip. This bubble helps to stabilize the preheat flame and keeps water away from the flame.

Powder cutting

If a metal has an oxide with a higher melting point than itself, such as is the case for stainless steels, the oxide (slag) produced tends to clog the cut. It may still be possible to cut the metal by modification of the simple flame-cutting process. One approach is to feed a flux into the oxygen stream. The flux (sodium carbonate and bicarbonate) reacts with the oxide to convert it to a fluid slag, which can be blown clear. Alternatively, fine iron powder or wire can be fed into the cutting zone, where it burns to increase the temperature, thus helping to keep the oxides clear.

Plasma cutting

In plasma cutting, a gas is forced through the gap between an electrode and an outer nozzle between which an electric arc, the nontransferred arc, is passing. This gas, which may be any of several mixtures, of which the most common are argon–hydrogen, argon–nitrogen, and air, is ionized by the nontransferred arc—that is, its constituent elements are broken into electrically charged particles known as ions. This ionized gas, or plasma, is very hot, around 5430°F (3000°C), and is capable of melting the metal at which it is directed. Often, additional heat is introduced to the metal being cut (the workpiece) by passing a current from the electrode to the workpiece through the plasma, which conducts electricity readily. This current is the transferred arc. Plasma cutting is particularly useful for cutting stainless steel and other metals that cannot be flame cut, such as aluminum and brass.

Flame cutting machines

A number of machines are used to guide a flame cutting torch around a complex shape or profile. They range from a small tractor with an electric motor and a simple speed control, for straight line cuts along portable rails or hand steering around simple shapes, up to large computer-controlled machines that are capable of cutting complex shapes over areas of 66 ft. (20 m) by 165 ft. (49 m), or more. A very popular system of guidance is photoelectric profiling, in which two photoelectric cells measure the reflected light from a line drawing of the item to be cut and emit electronic signals to the drive motor so that they are kept on each side of the line as the machine moves around the drawing. One or more flame cutting torches

▼ Using flame cutting machines on a production line in an automobile factory. The welding or flame cutting torches, either held in the hand or guided by a machine, are used to direct the cutting stream of the flame onto precisely the area where it is needed.

are mechanically linked to the photoelectric head so that they cut the same shape as the drawing. Normally, two, three, or four torches are used at one time, but on some large machines, as many as 26 may be used.

Brazing

Brazing is one of the three main methods of joining metals together, the other two being soldering and welding. Each is carried out at different temperatures: soldering at 356 to 590°F (180–310°C), brazing at 1020 to 2012°F (550–1100°C), and welding at about 1830 to 6330°F (1000–3500°C). Brazing can be regarded as a form of soldering using a high-melting-point solder.

In brazing and soldering, two metal components are joined together by melting a third piece of metal, called the filler metal, in the gap between them. The filler metal must melt at a lower temperature than the two base metals and be formulated so as to flow uniformly over both metal surfaces while molten. A flux is generally added to cleanse the two surfaces of oxides or other unwanted impurities that would interfere with the joining process. In welding, the two base metal surfaces actually fuse together, a process that does not occur in either soldering or brazing, where the two metals are fused to the filler metal but not to each other. A brazed joint is stronger than a soldered one.

Filler metals

The most common brazing filler metals are alloys of copper and zinc. They are forms of brass, and it is from the word brass that the name brazing is derived. Other common filler metals are made from copper alloyed with silver, zinc, and sometimes cadmium; and aluminum–silicon alloys for joining aluminum. Using suitable fillers and fluxes, even such metals as palladium, titanium, and beryllium alloys, which are used in the aerospace and electronics industries, can be brazed.

Many brazing processes can be carried out automatically, but where a craftsperson is involved, the work area must be well ventilated, because some of the filler metals and the fluxes used give off harmful fumes when heated. Fluxes contain such ingredients as borax, boric acid, chlorides, fluorides, and phosphorus. In one process, brazing tungsten to copper using a silver alloy filler, a flux containing the highly poisonous sodium cyanide is used. In all cases, the correct flux helps the filler metal to flow completely over the two metal surfaces and removes oxides and other undesirable impurities. The fluxes are very corrosive, and care must be taken to remove any residue around a joint.

Brazing methods

The filler metal is applied to the joint in one of several ways, depending on the base metals to be joined and the physical nature of the joint involved. Heat may be applied at the same time as the filler metal or after it has been placed between the base metals. An example of the first method is in the making of brass instruments such as trumpets and trombones. The various tubes that make up the instruments are brazed together with a copper–zinc filler and borax flux. The bell of the instrument is made from a flat sheet of brass cut to the required shape and formed into a crude cone. The join of the cone is brazed by a craftsperson using a flame torch, and this section is then brazed to the tube assembly. Another craftsperson hammers the joint until it is completely smooth so that when the final polishing takes place, the brazed joint is undetectable.

For mass-produced brazed items, the filler metal is packed between the parts to be joined, and the assembly is passed through a furnace whose temperature is carefully controlled so as to be above the melting point of the filler and below that of the base metals. This technique is used to manufacture bicycle frames, valve assemblies, and hydraulic equipment. In one method, two steel components are fitted loosely together with a piece of copper foil between them. The assembly is passed through an induction furnace to melt the foil, and the molten copper is drawn by capillary action to fill the joint completely. The furnace is filled with hydrogen to avoid any undesirable oxidation of the copper or the steel components.

Other methods of brazing used for mass production include the dip process, in which the parts to be joined are dipped into a bath of molten filler metal, and electric resistance heating, where an electric current is passed directly through the prepared assembly to melt the filler metal. The heating may also be produced by a carbon arc arrangement or in an induction furnace, where the assembly is heated by the electric currents created in it by the energy from powerful electromagnetic coils placed around the furnace.

Soldering

Soldering is a technique for joining metals using a metal bonding alloy (solder), which is applied in a molten form and has a melting point significantly below that of the metals being joined. The joint has to be properly fitted before soldering because the solder is drawn between the joint surfaces by capillary action. Soft soldering is the most common form, using alloys with melting points up to 800°F (430°C). Soldering is a convenient way of making joints that do not require high mechanical

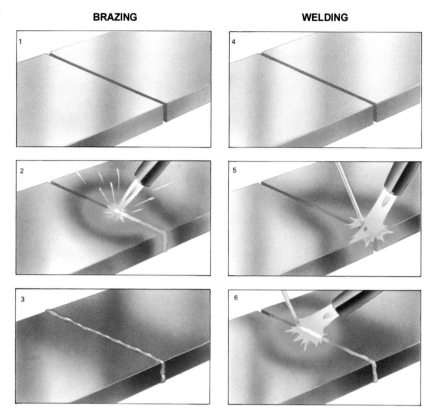

BRAZING   **WELDING**

strength and has the advantage that the joints can be readily unmade—for example, to permit the replacement of components.

To make a solder joint, the joint surfaces are cleaned, flux is applied to remove surface oxide coatings, and the parts are assembled. Heat and the solder are applied with the work surfaces being heated sufficiently to reach the melting point of the solder. The molten solder is drawn into the joint and the workpiece allowed to cool before any excess solder and flux residue is cleaned off. The molten solder wets the metal surfaces to give a continuous coating with a solid bond.

Solders

There is a wide variety of soft solders with a range of properties that can be matched to specific applications. The solidus temperature of a solder is the highest temperature at which it is completely solid, and the liquidus temperature is the one at which it is completely liquid.

The most common solders are alloys of tin and lead, with lead contents ranging from 80 percent to 30 percent. These solders have a common solidus temperature of 361°F (183°C), but the liquidus temperature varies considerably. General purpose solders with tin contents of 35 to 50 percent have liquidus temperatures of around 450°F (232°C). Fine solder, with a tin content of 60 percent, has a liquidus of 374°F (190°C) and is used where overheating could cause damage, as in elec-

▲ To braze two pieces of metal together, the surfaces are cleaned (1) and packed with a brazing metal—the filler. A flame torch is then applied (2) to the join to fuse the filler into the gap (3). For welding, the surfaces should be prepared similarly (4). Next, a rod of filler metal is heated (5) with the join, melting the rod and join so that they fuse together (6).

◀ Close-up view of a microplasma welder. This type of welder is very powerful, the arc and jet of gas being intense enough to push a hole through a piece of steel 0.25 in. (6 mm) thick.

tric connections. These solders are not suitable for use at temperatures much over 250°F (120°C) because the mechanical strength falls off rapidly as the solidus is approached.

Solders such as the tin–antimony–lead alloys have higher working temperatures of up to 392°F (200°C), and solders such as tin–silver–lead can be used at even higher temperatures. Fusible alloys containing bismuth have much lower solidus and liquidus temperatures and are used for special applications. The availability of a range of solders with different solidus temperatures allows complex assemblies to be built up—the first joints being made with the higher temperature solders so that they do not melt when heat is applied to make subsequent joints.

Fluxes

Most metals form oxides when exposed to the air (especially when heated), and fluxes are used to remove the oxide film and prevent reoxidation until the solder has wetted the surface. Corrosive fluxes such as acids and salts have a strong action but have to be thoroughly cleaned from the finished joint by washing to prevent subsequent corrosion. Noncorrosive fluxes such as rosins and tallows have a weaker fluxing action but are generally used for electric joints and where the cleaning of the completed joint is not possible.

Equipment

In hand-soldering operations, heat is applied with a soldering iron, generally with a copper bit, which also acts as a reservoir to hold molten solder and carry it to the work. Soldering irons may be heated with gas flames or electrically, the latter method being the most common for general use. A thermostatic control may be used to maintain a constant temperature.

Gas flames can be used to provide direct heating of bulky workpieces, while blowpipes are used to divert fine gas flames for delicate work. Where complete assemblies have to be soldered, oven or hot-plate heating is used. In such cases, the solder is often applied as preforms, which are fitted to the joint during assembly and melt when the workpiece reaches the appropriate temperature.

In dip soldering, the joints are dipped into a bath of molten solder that heats and wets them so that the solder is drawn into the joint by capillary action. It is particularly suitable where a large number of joints have to be made together, as with automobile radiators and food cans. Dipping may be carried out automatically or manually. A similar process—used for electronic assemblies, such as printed circuit boards—is flow soldering, where the assembly is passed over a standing wave of molten solder, the limited contact being sufficient to make the joints without undue heating of the components.

Welding

Welding is a process used to join metals, but the technique can be applied to other materials, such as plastics. Most welds are achieved by fusion, a process in which the materials being joined are melted at and around the joint between them. An autogenous fusion weld is one in which no filler metal is added—most welds today are done with filler metal, and most of the resultant weld is composed of this added material. Some of the more recent processes, however, perform autogenous welds and have no need for filler materials. There are also welds employing, for example, pressure rather than fusion, and others employing a mixture of the two. The essential feature of a fusion-welding process is a heat source. It may be in the form of a flame from an oxyacetylene torch or an electric arc.

Gas welding

In oxyacetylene and similar welding processes, the main source of heat is supplied by the combustion of acetylene or other fuel gas with oxygen. Both gases are supplied from cylinders and fed into a torch through flow regulators. The flame produced after ignition has a peak temperature of about 5430°F (3000°C), which is adequate to melt steels and many other metals.

Arc welding

An arc is arranged to run between an electrode in a welding torch and the workpiece that is to be welded. The electrode is usually of negative polarity—the cathode—so electrons move to the workpiece, the anode. Tremendous heat is generated in the arc, which may have a temperature of 27,000 to 36,000°F (15,000–20,000°C), and more heat is released at the anode. The arc can be made to run in an atmosphere of an inert gas, such as argon, to prevent oxidation of the metal, and the process is known as inert-gas tungsten-arc welding. There are many variants of the gas shielded welding process, involving such techniques as wire feeding, the provision of fluxes, constricted higher-temperature arcs, and the use of noninert gases.

The most common of all arc-welding processes is metal-arc welding. This process is carried out manually and involves the transfer of metal. The electrode is a metal rod (the filler wire) surrounded by a flux. The rod is clamped in a holder and connected to an electricity supply (AC or DC). The welder then touches the inner rod momentarily against the workpiece, so drawing an arc. The flux on the outside then comes into play; it acts partly as an ionizer when AC is used and helps to reignite the arc each half cycle and also provides the shielding medium to prevent the formation of oxides and nitrides. The flux has also been used to influence the composition and properties of the weld metal.

Plasma welding

Plasma welding is an extension of inert-gas tungsten-arc welding: it has similarities in that it uses a nonconsumable tungsten electrode and an inert shielding gas flowing through a torch. In plasma welding, however, a small-diameter nozzle is placed just beneath the electrode. It has the effect of heavily constricting the arc, and increasing its temperature and also the velocity of the gas. The power used in plasma welding can be much higher (about 10 kW) than in inert-gas arc welding (about 1 kW), and the arc can be much more constricted, so the effect of this power intensity on the workpiece is dramatic. In essence, the arc and jet are sufficiently intense to push a hole through a workpiece of up to 0.25 in. (6 mm) steel.

Electron-beam welding

Electron-beam welding is a nonarc process of high power intensity, and one in which the keyhole welding technique is used. The electron beam is generated by the emission of the electrons from a cathode at a high negative potential with respect to an anode, with the whole system enclosed in a chamber kept at a high vacuum—about 10^{-5} mm of mercury. The electrons move toward the anode at high velocity; a hole in the anode permits the electrons to pass straight through. The electron beam may then be focused by means of an electrostatic lens in a manner similar to that of a cathode-ray tube.

▼ In gas welding (top left), the heat source is produced by burning a mixture of oxygen and acetylene. In submerged-arc welding (top right), the arc is submerged beneath the flux. In plasma-arc welding (bottom left), the gas flows through a constricted nozzle surrounding the arc. Laser welding (bottom right) relies on the heat that is produced by a concentrated light beam.

In these electron-beam guns, a fine beam—0.004 to 0.02 in. (0.1–0.5 mm) diameter is the normal range—is generated with power usually of about 10 kW but often up to 100 kW. Power intensity at the point where the beam hits the surface is considerable; the process produces the keyhole effect with deep and narrow welds that are less distorted than normal welds, where the width of the weld is often greater than the depth.

Laser welding

Special welds can be performed using solid-state ruby lasers that give short pulses of red light with peak powers of tens of megawatts. Ruby lasers have been used for small welding applications, usually involving microminiature components for which the total heat requirement is small.

More recently, a powerful type of gas laser has been developed (the carbon dioxide laser), which produces a continuous beam of radiation. It produces an output beam of up to 20 kW continuously at a wavelength of 10.6 μm. However,

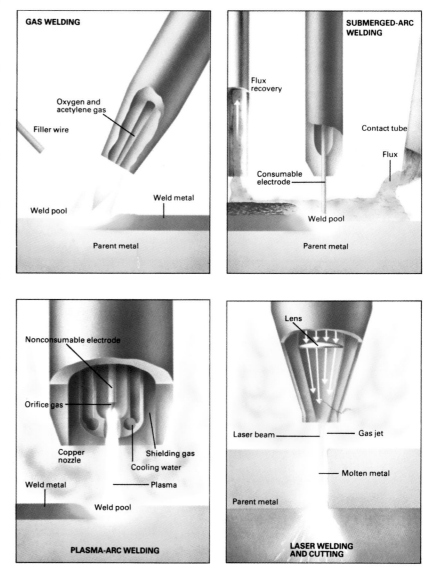

because the beam is in the microwave wavelength, it cannot be seen, and a tracer beam from a helium–neon laser has to be superimposed on the main beam. Another problem is that, at this wavelength, most metals that need to be joined are reflectors and act as mirrors, so the power needed has to be very high to vaporize the surface of the metal. Though more widely used for cutting than joining metals, carbon dioxide lasers may prove useful in welding in impossible positions, such as inside a nuclear reactor, by using a focusing mirror. These lasers can weld steel 0.5 in. (12.7 mm) thick at 4ft. (1.3 m) per minute.

Pressure welding

Pressure welding includes most of the welding processes that do not rely on fusion alone, the most important of which is resistance welding. It can be defined as any process in which the heat for fusion is produced by the current flowing through the resistance of contact between two materials. Pressure is applied to obtain good contact. No filler material or shielding gas is used, but the weld is usually done in discrete spots because of the heavy current supply (up to 50,000 amps) required.

In friction welding, heat is generated by friction between two rubbing surfaces. It is commonly used for joining two tubes—one is rotated at very high speed, and at a predetermined point, the other is pressed against it. In explosive welding, a similar action occurs but the process is more rapid. The only heat supplied is that from the mechanical forces of the impact. Ultrasonic waves are also used for welding. The high-frequency sound waves cause rapid frictional movement, which acts parallel to the interfaces to be joined, creating some localized heating. With metals, it causes breakdown of the oxide film; the clean surfaces presented are then free to diffuse.

Riveting

Riveting is another method of joining together parts of a structure. A rivet consists of a formed head and a cylindrical body or shank. Rivets are usually made of mild steel or, for aircraft construction, a light alloy. Bridges, roofs, cranes, steel-framed buildings, and other such constructions are built from sections secured together by means of rivets. Holes are drilled through two adjacent surfaces, the rivet is inserted, and the shank end of the rivet is hammered flat.

Types of rivets

The head of the rivet may be round (a snap head), flat (pan head), or countersunk. Snap heads are usually used in machine riveting, while pan heads

are hand hammered in enclosed spaces. Countersunk rivets are used on ships and aircraft to result in a flush surface for decreased resistance against wind or water. The shank of the rivet may be solid or tubular; the part of the shank immediately underneath the head may be tapered to provide a more gradual cross-sectional transition to the rivet head, affording greater resistance against failure.

The part of the rivet farthest from the head is called the tail; this is the part that will be hammered or swaged by the riveter, while the head is held by the riveter's mate in a dolly serving as an anvil. Tubular rivets have the tail splayed into a countersunk hole, or the tail is made to bulge into a barrel shape. Some tubular rivets contain small explosive charges, which are set off by heat or a detonating device that forms the rivet head by expansion of the hollow tail. The hammering may be done by hand or by pneumatic tool.

Squeeze riveting displaces the metal by means of constant pressure rather than repeated blows. Squeeze riveting is also used with tubular rivets with a mandrel; a hand tool pulls the mandrel through the hollow center to form the opposite head before snapping the mandrel off and releasing the tool. Solid steel rivets of up to 1.2 in. (35 mm) diameter can be headed by a combination of squeezing and radial spinning of the tail end. The tool moves in an orbit and applies a line of pressure from the center outward, displacing some metal with each turn.

In construction work, rivets are driven home hot. When they cool, they shrink lengthwise, providing a tight joint, but they also shrink away from the walls of the hole, producing an air space for possible leakage. On certain kinds of work such as water tanks and steam boilers, the rivet heads and plate joints must be carefully finished using a caulking tool to avoid leaks. This tool resembles a cold chisel and is used in a similar way, except the purpose is to displace metal around edges rather than to cut it. A caulking tool of equal thickness to that of the plate is called a fullering tool.

▲ Soldering electrical connections. The solder is melted against the hot iron and makes a contact that is easy to undo if repairs are needed.

| **SEE ALSO:** | ALLOY • ELECTROCHEMICAL MACHINING • IRON AND STEEL • LASER AND MASER • LEAD • METAL • METALWORKING • TIN |

Metal Detector

◄ A metal detector being used to search bread rolls for metal objects. The automatic reject system in the foreground discards any rolls that have been contaminated by a piece of metal.

Metals have one important property possessed by no other elements that enables them to be readily distinguished with suitably sensitive apparatus—this property is their high electric conductivity. By generating an alternating magnetic field in the vicinity of a metal object, electric currents are induced in the object, thus distorting the original field. By detecting this distortion, the metallic object can be located. In recent years, metal detectors have become increasingly popular with amateur treasure hunters, but they serve more important functions in places such as airports where they are used for the detection of concealed weapons, in industry to detect metal contamination, and by builders, who may use small handheld metal detectors to avoid drilling or hammering through electric wiring or metal water pipes.

One particular class of metals—the ferromagnetic materials—can also be detected using a different technique. Ferromagnetic materials have a high permeability, that is, they offer less resistance to the flow of magnetic flux through them than any other material. A magnetic field, such as Earth's magnetic field, generates lines of flux, which will take the path of least resistance and therefore concentrate in the vicinity of any ferromagnetic materials, causing a distortion of the general magnetic field, which can be detected. Devices operating on this principle are known as magnetic search units.

Balanced-coil units

Balanced-coil search units have two identical search coils, each with a primary and secondary winding. The primary windings are driven in series by an alternating current and so generate an alternating magnetic field. With the two coils placed over a nonmetallic medium, the voltages induced in the secondary windings by this alternating field will be identical. In this situation, when the two secondaries are connected in opposition, there is no signal. A metallic object, such as a coin, will, however, produce an induced magnetic field that interacts more strongly with the secondary to which it is closest. A net signal (the difference between the signals in the two coils) is then produced, which, when amplified and displayed, indicates the presence of a metallic object.

The problem with this type of unit and the others that operate on the principle of magnetic induction is that, when used over earth, variations in the rock or soil's conductivity can affect the readings. Such detectors tend to be useful only over small distances in the order of 6 in. (15 cm).

Heterodyne unit

The heterodyne search unit also uses the principle of induced magnetism but consists of two coils with only one winding in each. They are separately connected to two oscillator circuits in which they form the inductive components. The two oscillators are initially adjusted to have the same frequency so that the two coils produce an alternating magnetic field at that one frequency. A metal object placed close to one of the coils changes the inductance of that coil and therefore also the frequency of oscillation of that circuit. By mixing the signals from the two circuits, a beat frequency is generated. This frequency can be reproduced through earphones, thus enabling the operator to locate the object. This type of detector can be very sensitive, but again, variations in earth conductivity can affect the results, and it is difficult to obtain sufficiently stable oscillators.

Field search unit

The field search unit operates similarly to the balanced-coil unit. It employs a loop of wire driven by a static high-power oscillator that can generate an operating field over an area the size of a tennis court. Such a device, since it reacts to variations in earth conductivity as it does to the presence of metal, has an interesting archaeological use. If the detector readings of an archaeological site are plotted on a map, the outline of a building often becomes apparent from the variations in conductivity.

Pulse magnetization units

Pulse magnetization units rely on the fact that a magnetic field takes a finite time to propagate through air or earth—in fact, the speed of propagation is the same as that for electromagnetic radiation, that is, the speed of light. Such units operate as magnetic radar units. A short high-power pulse is generated in a search coil, and after the pulse is cut off, the unit goes from a transmit mode to a receive mode. If there is a metallic object within the field, this object generates its own magnetic field by the process of induced magnetism, and it is detected a finite time after the transmitted pulse. Such units can be very effective, but again, there are limitations owing to conductivity of the soil and rock structures below ground.

Magnetic search units

Iron, steel, and other ferromagnetic materials are much easier to detect using a magnetic search unit. It will find a 1 in. (2.5 cm) nail at a distance of about 24 in. (60 cm) or a car at 60 ft. (18 m).

All objects on Earth are in Earth's magnetic field. Where there are no ferromagnetic objects, this field can be considered as constant in strength and uniform—that is, in the same direction. Any ferromagnetic object will, however, distort Earth's field because the lines of flux will take the path of least resistance and be concentrated in the vicinity of the object. To detect this distortion in Earth's

◄ An archaeologist using a metal detector to search the site of the ancient city of Petra in Jordan for artifacts. Metal detectors will react to variations in the conductivity of earth as well as to the presence of metal, so they are extremely useful tools to the archaeologist.

field, a magnetometer is used. This is capable of detecting the difference in magnetic field strength at two points and is sensitive to field differences on the order of $\frac{1}{100,000}$ part of Earth's field.

In practice, two magnetometer probes are used. These are fixed in a tube about 12 in. (30 cm) apart and carefully aligned along the same axis. Being largely independent of the qualities of the earth over which it is used, such search units are extremely useful for archaeologists even where nonmetallic objects are sought, because they are often found alongside metallic objects such as coins. Having identified a site, the less powerful inductive units can be used.

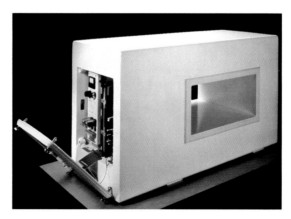

◄ A Goring Kerr metal detector showing a typical housing and electronic control unit. Systems such as these are used by industry to detect metal contamination.

SEE ALSO:	Conduction, electrical • Magnetism • Magnetometer • Meter, electrical • Security system

Metalworking

Metals have been worked to make them more suitable for mankind's purposes for thousands of years. Simple processes, such as heating a metal or mixing a metal with another metal (alloying) can completely alter its basic properties, making them harder, more malleable, or more flexible. There are six basic processes through which metals are shaped to suit the multitude of purposes they are used for in today's metal-hungry world.

Heat treatment

The expression *heat treatment* covers a wide range of procedures by which metals and alloys are heated and cooled to change their properties. Essentially, there are four main methods: annealing, tempering, normalizing, and hardening, all of which allow the material to be more readily processed or to give an improved performance in use.

The properties of a metal depends on its crystalline structure, which accounts for the characteristic grains. The addition of alloying elements to a pure metal modifies the crystal structure and thus the properties of the metal. This effect is based on the fact that the alloying elements dissolve in the parent metal at high temperature to give a solid solution, but they tend to precipitate out at lower temperatures and so distort the structure. The controlled adjustment of such distortions is the basis of heat treatment.

Heat treatment can alter the properties of steel—essentially an alloy of carbon and iron. The process can best be explained by consideration of the different crystal structures adopted by iron as it is heated. At room temperature, the iron crystals have a body-centered arrangement, with one atom at the center of an imaginary cube and other atoms at the cube corners. When the iron is heated to a temperature over 1663°F (906°C), the structure changes to face-centered cubic, with the iron atoms positioned at the corners of an imaginary cube and in the middle of the faces of the cube.

The face-centered cubic structure is such that carbon atoms—which are smaller than the iron atoms—can fit between the iron atoms to give a solid solution of carbon in iron. This solution is known as austenite. As austenite is cooled below the transformation temperature of just over 1650°F (900°C), it starts to change to the body-centered form, but this structure is such that the carbon will not fit into the iron crystals, so the crystals are of virtually pure iron, known as ferrite. Carbon from the austenite is precipitated out of the solid solution, so the rest of the austenite becomes richer in carbon.

As the carbon content of the austenite increases, the temperature at which it changes into ferrite gradually reduces until the concentration of carbon reaches approximately 0.85 percent. This is the eutectoid composition, with the lowest transformation temperature at 1337°F (725°C). Any alloys that start with a carbon content of more than 0.85 percent have higher transformation temperatures, and iron carbide, or cementite, is formed until the eutectoid composition is reached. When the eutectoid alloy changes phase, it converts into pearlite, which is a mechanical mixture made up of alternating laminations of ferrite and cementite.

These changes are based on the assumption that the cooling is slow enough to allow the carbon to come out of solution in the iron. If the hot steel is cooled rapidly, this is not the case, and the carbon is effectively frozen into the ferrite, distorting the crystal structure to give a very hard structure known as martensite.

In addition to the crystal structure, the properties of all metals are also dependent on their grain structure, with the grain size being dependent on the cooling rate. A rapid rate of cooling produces a finer grain than slow cooling.

Annealing and normalizing

The purpose of annealing is to remove internal stresses caused by the working of the metal or by uneven cooling, leaving the metal soft for further working or machining. With mild (low carbon) steels, full annealing is achieved by heating the steel to convert it to austenite (the exact temperature used depends on the steel composition) and slow cooling to give ferrite and pearlite. Finer control over the structure formed is given by isothermal annealing, where the metal is first

◀ A cable-making machine. Lengths of insulated wire are placed on two drums, which in turn are each placed on a wheel. As the wheel goes around, the wire is pulled down, turned, and shaped around the cables, so completing them.

Surface hardening

Many components require a combination of a hard, wear-resistant surface coupled with overall toughness—a combination that cannot always be achieved by simple heat treatment of carbon or alloy steels. There are two main methods of surface hardening. In the first (flame and induction hardening), the surface of the component is rapidly heated to a temperature of about 1380°F (750°C)—the exact temperature depends on the metal composition—and then rapidly cooled with water jets. The rapid heating and cooling means that only the surface skin or case of the object is converted to martensite; the main body of the item remains in its original condition.

The other method of case hardening involves immersing the object in a suitable medium so that its surface can take up carbon or nitrogen to give a harder structure. Carburizing is a common example of this method of treatment, the medium being a powdered material rich in carbon (such as a mixture of charcoal and barium carbonate) or carbon-rich gas. The depth of the hardened case depends on the soaking time but for heavy-duty parts—such as automobile transmissions—the thickness is around 0.004 in. (1 mm).

Nonferrous alloys

A variety of heat treatments are also used for nonferrous alloys, the basic principles being much the same as for steel. The most common process is annealing, used to restore softness following cold working, but hardening techniques are also employed. For example, alloys such as copper–aluminum (aluminum bronze), copper–chrome and copper–beryllium (beryllium bronze) can be precipitation hardened, with the alloying element acting in a similar manner to the carbon in steel.

Equipment

Heat treatment processes are normally carried out in specially designed furnaces. These may be of the continuous type, with the work passing through different temperature zones, or of the batch type. The atmosphere in the furnace is normally controlled to minimize the risk of oxidation or chemical attack. Liquid baths of molten salts or lead are also used for heating purposes, and especially for soaking at a set temperature. Molten salt baths are also used in some case-hardening processes, with the salt acting as both a heating and a carburizing medium.

Forging

Forging is the shaping of metal objects by means of hammers or presses. The metal to be forged is heated until it attains a plastic state; that is, a state

heated to give austenite and then held at an intermediate temperature to allow the complete transformation to pearlite before cooling.

Normalizing is similar to full annealing, but the cooling is allowed to take place in still air and so is faster, resulting in a finer grain structure. The main aim is to get a uniform, fine-grain structure and even distribution of the carbides.

Hardening and tempering

Rapid cooling of steel from the austenite region results in a hard, martensitic structure and is achieved by quenching. Normally, this is achieved by plunging the heated metal into a tank containing the quenching liquid; different liquids are used to give different cooling rates. Oil gives a less rapid cooling than water, which is itself slower than brine. The depth of hardening achieved by quenching depends on the hardening ability of the steel. It can be altered by the addition of alloying elements, such as manganese, chromium, nickel, and molybdenum.

Because the martensite is brittle, it is normal practice to temper hardened items to regain toughness and ductility, though this is normally at the expense of some of the hardness. The tempering operation involves reheating and holding at a set temperature (soaking) to allow the structure to stabilize. Typical components subjected to hardening and tempering range from bolts, springs, and wrenches to engine crankshafts and gun barrels.

▲ After recovery from the ore, metals are supplied in bulk or processed to form alloys, also in bulk form. The bulk metals are further processed into useable forms, such as sheet metal, as here. Aluminum is shaped at room temperature by the cold-rolling metal process, during which the aluminum hardens into foil of accurate dimensions and a high-quality finish. The foil has a high polish to prevent abrasion during rolling and unrolling of the rolls.

in which it can be shaped by hammering. The advantage of forging compared with other means of shaping metal is that the grain pattern and therefore the strength of the metal is rearranged in an appropriate direction to ensure the finished product can withstand stresses. Gear blanks, connecting rods, and other forged parts are therefore stronger than they would be if they were machined from cold stock.

There are several types of forging process, depending on the type of object to be forged. They include drop forging, press forging, upset forging, and roll forging.

Drop forging

Hammer forging is used to forge relatively flat, simple shapes that must sometimes be machined by conventional methods to their final dimensions. Only flat dies are used. The anvil is the lower part of the machine, on which the piece to be forged is placed; the hammer or ram is raised and dropped between vertical guides by steam, air, or mechanical methods. Steam or pneumatic installations can be designed so the steam or air can be diverted and used as a cushion to control the force of the blow. The size of the hammer is about 50 lbs. per cross-sectional inch (3.5 kg/cm^2), and the total weight of the hammer can vary from 200 lbs. (91 kg) to 50 tons (45 tonnes).

Die forging is similar to hammer forging except that the hot billet is shaped by dies as it is struck. The machinery has to be more precise: for example, there has to be a way to adjust the guides to compensate for wear and thus ensure that the upper die and the lower die always meet accurately.

Almost any object can be die forged as long as it can be removed from the die. One of the most commonly forged parts is the connecting rod for the internal combustion engine. This part takes a lot of stress during use; hot forging it means the grain pattern of the metal is arranged to ensure the greatest possible endurance of these stresses.

Forging machines used to form smaller parts in mass production can undertake over 300 blows a minute; the pressure of the blow in drop forging can range from 500 up to 50,000 psi (3.4 x 10^6–3.4 x 10^8 N/m^2).

Press forging

In a hydraulic press, nearly all the force exerted is absorbed in the work, rather than some being absorbed by the machine. Press forging is used for large ingots weighing up to 250 tons (225 tonnes), using pressures of up to 25 tons per sq. in. (3.9 x 10^8 N/m^2). Crankshafts of 50 tons (45 tonnes) and 16 in. (40 cm) naval guns are examples of objects that have been press forged.

Upset forging

A heavy machine stud or bolt with a large head is the type of object produced by upsetting, the head being the upset part. A bar or rod of stock is clamped by two gripper dies that are semicircular in cross-section; at one end, the dies have been machined to the diameter of the larger part of the forging. The ram, or header, enters this end of the die and "upsets" the end of the piece in several steps until it is shortened and fills the larger dimension of the die. This process lends itself especially well to automation; the machine can insert the bar up to an adjustable stop, cut it off at the correct length, and index through the upsetting steps.

Roll forging

Straight or tapered pieces with reduced sections are produced using this method. The hot stock is squeezed between the rollers, which are machined to produce the desired shape. Cable bolts and carpenter's chisels are among the objects that are produced in this way.

Casting

Casting is a process in which a fluid is poured into a mold and allowed to solidify in the shape of the cavity within the mold. The commercial production of high-quality, often intricately shaped castings required by industry, such as components for hydraulic pumps and engine blocks, demands expertise of a high order. Casting is a versatile metal-shaping process because it enables intricate three-dimensional shapes to be made in a single operation.

Die casting

Die casting is a mass-production technique in which molten metal is forced into a mold (or die) under high pressure and then allowed to solidify. In the related process of permanent mold casting (also known as die casting in Europe), the metal is poured into the mold and flows to fill it under the action of gravity. Owing to the cost of the mold, the gravity process is more expensive than sand casting but gives components with better mechanical proper-

▼ In hammer forging, the top half of the die is attached to the hammer—called the tup—and the bottom half to the anvil. When the tup is released, it falls under gravity (or it may be power assisted) and strikes the metal, causing it to flow into the shape of the die. To form a hollow blocker from which pipes are extruded, an ingot is first deformed, then formed into a billet of larger diameter before being punched and trimmed. (1) The ingot is positioned on station. (2) Ingot is deformed and descaled. (3) Billet is placed in blocking pot. (4) Diameter is increased. (5) Punch is positioned. (6) Blocker is punched. (7) At the trim station. (8) Blocker is trimmed. (9) Ready for extrusion.

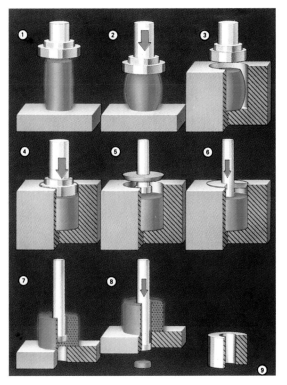

ties and a finer finish. However, this process is less expensive than pressure die casting, which involves the use of a die casting machine.

Die-casting machines

Die-casting machines have to perform three main functions: to inject molten metal into the die under high pressure to fill it completely, to hold the parts of the die together to resist the internal pressure of the molten metal (this can require a holding force of several thousand tons), and to eject the finished casting when it has solidified. The casting pressure used depends on the metal, varying from around 500 lbs. per sq. in. (35 kg/cm^2) for aluminum to over 20,000 lbs. per sq. in. (1400 kg/cm^2) for brass.

Molds

The dies (molds) are complex units that are normally made from heat-treated steel. They have to be designed so that the molten metal will rapidly flow to all parts of the mold, and so that the air is allowed to escape freely, to ensure there are no air pockets in the finished product. The mold, designed to allow the cast pieces to be pushed out, is made in two main parts that are clamped together in the die-casting machine. Movable sections can be included in order to form holes in the piece. The speed at which the molten metal sets in the mold can be increased by cooling the mold using water.

Alloys

The alloys most commonly used for die casting are zinc- and aluminum-based. Much of the output of zinc-based alloys is used for pressure die casting. A particular advantage of zinc alloys is that they are very suitable for chrome plating. Aluminum-based alloys offer a good combination of lightness, strength, and corrosion resistance. Other alloys are used for specific applications.

Drawing

Drawing is a term that can be applied to two main groups of processes, typified by wire drawing and deep drawing. Metal products that are deep drawn include cartridge casings for bullets, shallow cans for food such as sardines or anchovies, and some varieties of beverage can.

Wire, bar, and tube drawing

Drawing processes reduce the cross-sectional area of a length of metal by pulling it through a hole in a drawplate smaller than the material entering it. This method of reduction has been known since pre-Christian times and, with the use of modern techniques, is capable of producing almost all metals and alloys in the form of wire.

The process usually starts with hot-rolled or extruded rod or bar metal, which must be prepared by treatment with suitable chemicals, such as dilute sulfuric acid, to render its surface free of oxide, scale, or other unwanted impurities. Steel

▲ Nickel-alloy parts for gas-turbine engines in airplanes are moved into an oven for annealing.

may be coated with zinc phosphate to provide a suitable base for lubrication, and hard metals that are difficult to draw may be coated with softer metals to facilitate the process. The workpiece is then reduced in stages by passing it through a series of dies, each having an orifice smaller than the previous one, until the required size is attained. The greater the reduction imposed in a given pass, the larger is the required drawing force. The permissible reduction in each pass is therefore limited by the strength of the emergent wire and does not often exceed 30 percent. Thus, a great many passes and dies are required to produce fine wire. For continuous operation, lengths of rods are welded together before drawing.

As the drawing process proceeds, the workpiece hardens and becomes more resistant to further deformation. It may be necessary to anneal the wire so that its ductility—its ability to be drawn—is restored. Drawing is important in the production of tubes and seamless pipes. It is possible to produce very fine tubes for medical and other purposes, such as inoculation of flies for research into tropical diseases or the insemination of queen bees.

Deep drawing

Deep drawing is a method of shaping sheet in which a flat sheet of metal is squeezed between a male punch and a female die to give a deep, hollow shape, as distinct from pressing. As the punch progressively penetrates the die, taking the blank with it, the undrawn part of the blank must be prevented from wrinkling, usually by applying a load to the edges. The whole operation makes very severe demands on the material being drawn, and materials differ widely in their suitability for this type of working. Materials considered suitable for deep drawing are usually soft and ductile and contain only small amounts of alloying elements. One example of a product that is made using this process is the sardine tin.

Rolling

Rolling is a process used to convert cast metals into semifinished and finished products. About 90 percent of steel production, for example, is rolled. In principle, the process is simple: a pair of cylindrical rollers made of iron or steel rotate in opposite directions with a gap between them that is smaller than the cross section of the piece to be rolled. The workpiece is entered into the gap, and as it passes between the rolls, it is squeezed, and its cross section is reduced. Because the working volume remains constant, the result of one pass through the rolls is a lengthening of the workpiece and a precise reduction and

shaping of the cross section. Rolling may be carried out either hot or cold. Hot rolling is the most common process, especially for the initial working of cast ingots, for which the lower rolling forces required give lower costs. Cold rolling is carried out at room temperature (though with some metals, such as lead, this is high enough for hot working) and has the effect of hardening the metal. This strain hardening can increase the strength of the finished product, but where further working is required, the metal is annealed to restore it to a soft condition. Cold working can produce a much better surface finish than hot working and more accurate finished dimensions.

Flat rolling

Rolling mills for processing metal ingots are known as blooming or slabbing mills. Generally, blooms are square in cross section, with a thickness of 6 in. (15 cm) or more, but slabs have a rectangular shape. Blooms are further rolled to give billets, which are then processed into sections, such as rails, angles, and channels.

Section rolling

For a section-rolled product, grooves of the appropriate profile must be cut into the rolls. Each pair of rolls is provided with a number of grooves of decreasing area and progressively varying shape, depending on the complexity of the required product. The distance between the rolls is normally kept constant, with the necessary reduction being accomplished by passing the workpiece successively through progressively smaller grooves. The direction of movement in this process is reversed for each pass.

Tubular products

Seamless tubes are manufactured by opening out the center of an ingot or billet in a piercing mill and then working the resulting shell to produce the correct diameter and wall thickness. Rotary piercing may be carried out in a Mannesmann mill, which consists of a pair of rolls with their axes angled to each other and rotating in the same direction. The action of the rolls rotates and deforms the workpiece as it is passed between them and causes a crack to open along the central axis. As the crack opens, the workpiece is forced onto a pointed plug that opens up the crack and shapes the hole, and the resulting tube is fed onto a mandrel that carries the plug.

 SEE ALSO: Alloy • Casting • Iron and steel • Metal • Metal cutting and joining • Sheet metal • Surface treatments

Meteor

A meteor is the streak of light seen in the night sky when a small particle of interplanetary dust burns up high in Earth's atmosphere. Meteors are also known as shooting stars, although they are not stars in any sense. On a clear night, away from city lights, most people are able to pick out about ten meteors per hour with the naked eye.

Any piece of debris from space that reaches Earth's surface is called a meteorite. Astronomers call particles that are less dense than about a millionth of a gram micrometeorites. There remains one further confusing word: meteoroid, the collective name for all meteoritic material in the Solar System. Most of the mass of the meteoroid cloud that orbits the Sun is made up of particles with masses in the range one-ten-millionth of a gram to one-thousandth of a gram.

Meteoroids enter Earth's atmosphere at speeds between 6 and 46 miles per second (11 and 75 km/s). Slow impacts occur when Earth in its orbit just catches up with a particle. Fast impacts occur when Earth hits a particle head on. The number of meteors per hour therefore peaks at about 4 A.M., when an observer is on the leading side of Earth, that is, the side plowing into the cosmic dust cloud.

Over 2,300 meteorites have been recovered from the surface of Earth, and around 16 are added to the list each year. About 3,300 are estimated to make it to the surface without burning up, giving some idea of how difficult they are to find. The majority fall in oceans, deserts, and other uninhabited regions and are, therefore, lost.

The first documented meteorite was one that fell near Ensiheim, Alsace, in 1492. However, it was not until 1803 that meteorites were accepted by the scientific community as debris from space.

Types of meteorite

There are three main types of meteorite: stony meteorites, iron meteorites, and stony-iron meteorites. Iron meteorites contain, on average, 90 percent iron and 10 percent nickel and have a density of about 7.8 grams per cubic centimeter. Stony meteorites, on the other hand, have a density of about 3.4 grams per cubic centimeter. Their composition is roughly 40 percent oxygen, 20 percent silicon, 15 percent magnesium, and 15 percent iron, with no other single element accounting for more than 2 percent.

Stony meteorites are further divided into chondrites and achondrites. Chondrites are the most abundant meteoroids found in the Solar System, accounting for some 85 percent of all meteoroids. They are distinguished from achondrites because they contain small solid globules of silicate material known as chondrules. Chondrules are near-spherical bodies ranging in size from 0.008 to 0.16 in. (0.2–4 mm) and are usually composed of a mixture of olivine, $(Mg,Fe)_2SiO_4$, and pyroxene, $(Mg,Fe)SiO_3$, but they can also be made of glass.

The appearance of chondrules strongly suggests that they formed as free droplets in a molten liquid that solidified. However, astronomers are not sure where this happened. One possibility, though, is that chondrules are the crystallized droplets of rock melted in the collision of minor planets, or asteroids.

The most intriguing chondrites are the carbonaceous chondrites. They are very rare indeed; only about 30 have ever been found. Carbonaceous chondrites contain some of the organic, or carbon-based, compounds that are the basis of life. Among the compounds that have been found are high-molecular-weight paraffins and long-chain aromatic hydrocarbons like tar, fatty acids, and porphyrins, the building blocks of both chlorophyll and hemoglobin. It would seem then that carbonaceous chondrites are tentative evidence that life may exist beyond Earth. However, carbonaceous chondrites are porous and crumbly and are almost certainly contaminated with terrestrial microorganisms as they fall through the atmosphere and as they lie on Earth's surface before collection.

The third type of meteorite is the stony-iron meteorite. Stony irons comprise a relatively small group of meteorites and contain equal amounts of nickel, iron, and silicates. About 1 percent of all meteorites seen to hit the ground are stony irons compared with about 6 percent for irons and 93 percent stony meteorites. Astronomers believe that meteoroids exist in about these proportions out in space.

◄ Meteor Crater, Arizona, was blasted out by an iron meteorite, 200 ft. (61 m) in diameter that ran into Earth some 6,000 years ago.

The material of meteorites is quite different from any rocks found in the crust of Earth. Most meteorites are believed to be fragments chipped off asteroids, or minor planets, when they collide with each other. Most asteroids orbit in the asteroid belt between the orbits of Mars and Jupiter and are usually between 0.6 and 620 miles (1–1,000 km) in diameter. The carbonaceous chondrites, however, are thought to have a different origin. They are thought to be fragments broken from the nuclei of comets. Comets are icy bodies, a few miles across, that are melted by the heat of the Sun when they plunge into the inner Solar System.

The ages of meteorites have been determined by the technique of radioactive dating. The oldest meteorite is 4.7 billion years old, older than any rock found on Earth or on the Moon. Meteorites therefore constitute the oldest material in the Solar System and must have solidified shortly after the nebula that formed the Sun and planets collapsed.

Meteor showers

Sometimes Earth is treated to a meteor shower, when the rate of meteors goes up considerably, which occurs when Earth passes through a meteor stream. Meteor streams consist of dust particles driven from a comet. They therefore follow quite closely the orbit of a comet, but as time goes by, they may drift away, and eventually, when the comet has broken up, they may be all that remains. A meteor stream may contain anywhere between one million and ten billion tons of dust.

The Orionids, for example, is a fairly active stream that appears in October and is associated with Halley's comet. Meteor streams are named for the constellation from which they appear to come. In fact, they appear to emanate from a single point within a constellation. The point is known as the radiant of the meteor shower. Meteor streams tend to dissipate in time and become less and less noteworthy.

When Earth intersects a new meteor shower close to the comet that spawned it—a meteor storm, a meteor shower with an enormous rate of arrival—may result. The most famous was the Leonid storm of November 12 and 13, 1833, when the rate exceeded 10,000 visual meteors per hour. Single observers reported seeing 20 a second.

The largest meteorite found, the 60-ton (54 tonne) Hoba West, came to light in 1920. It lies partially exposed at the site of its discovery near Grootfontein in Namibia. The Hoba West belongs to a rare class of nickel-rich iron meteorites. The largest meteorite in a museum, though, is the 36½-ton (33 tonne) Ahnighito

meteorite in the American Museum of Natural History in New York. It was found in Cape York, Greenland, in 1894. Until its discovery, it had provided the only source of iron for the Inuit people living in the Cape York area.

Most meteorites, though, fragment on entry. For this reason, the largest stony meteorite is rather meager. Weighing in at 1 ton (0.9 tonne), it

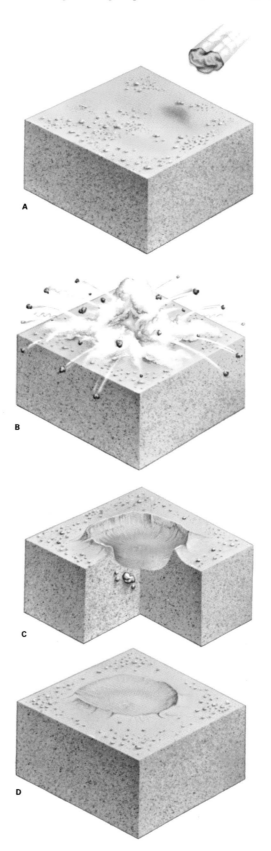

◀ A reconstructed view of the collision that created Meteor Crater in Arizona. (A) The fiery meteor speeds toward the desert. (B) It collides, sending up a cloud of dust. (C) After collision, the meteorite breaks up. Some pieces lie buried deep under the crater; others scatter over the surrounding desert. (D) After many thousands of years, the crater attains its present shape. The sharp rim is worn and rounded by continual erosion.

is a fragment of the Norton County meteorite that fell in Kansas in 1948. Carbonaceous chondrites tend to break into smaller pieces because they are so crumbly. For this reason, the largest carbonaceous chondrite recovered is barely more than 66 lbs. (30 kg). It is part of the Allende meteorite that fell in Mexico in 1969, scattering 5 tons (4.5 tonnes) of material over a large area.

Craters

Undoubtedly, Earth has been hit by large meteorites in the past. If, as is usually assumed, Earth formed near to the Moon, then it must have suffered a similar bombardment. But while the Moon is heavily cratered, with many of the craters visible with the naked eye or binoculars, wind and water and volcanic activity on the face of Earth have erased most evidence of large craters.

The most famous large meteorite crater on Earth is the Arizona meteorite crater. The crater is 4,200 ft. (1,280 m) across and 590 ft. (180 m) deep. It was formed when a 250,000-ton (227,000 tonne) meteorite, about 230 ft. (70 m) in diameter, struck Earth around 6,000 years ago. The impact speed is judged to have been about 37,000 mph (60,000 km/h). The meteorite almost completely vaporized on impact, leaving only a few hundred tons of material scattered over an area of over 30 sq. miles (80 km^2).

More recently, on the morning of June 30, 1908, Earth was struck by a large piece of space debris. A gigantic explosion occurred in the basin of the Podkamennaya Tunguska River in central Siberia. Trees were destroyed or flattened like matchwood over a region 50 miles (80 km) across, and eyewitnesses up to 300 miles (500 km) away reported seeing a blinding light in the cloudless sky. The explosion was heard thousands of miles away, and sensitive microbarographs, which detect small air pressure changes, recorded the shock wave as it circled the world twice. No remnant of the body that caused this explosion was ever found, despite scientific expeditions soon after the Tunguska event and in the years since. The body of the meteorite simply vaporized.

Astronomers can deduce that the body disintegrated in an explosion at a height of 5.2 miles (8.5 km). They can only guess what it was—probably a small comet or a very fragile asteroid.

Prehistoric evidence

All across the globe are lakes and depressions whose shapes suggest they may have been prehistoric impact craters. A number have been identified in Canada, of which good examples are the Clearwater Lakes near Hudson Bay, two roughly circular lakes, side by side. The largest one is nearly 18 miles (30 km) across. That there are two craters so close together is very interesting because it implies that the two meteoroids were traveling through space as a pair. Even larger craters have been tentatively identified, but erosion over many hundreds of millions of years has disguised them very well.

A topic receiving much serious scientific attention in the last few years is that of meteorites and mass extinctions. Evidence has been found in rocks from about 60 million years ago suggesting that a very large meteorite struck Earth and brought to an abrupt end the reign of dinosaurs. Rocks from this period contain unusually high concentrations of iridium, an element common in meteorites. The huge quantity of dust pumped into the atmosphere by such an impact could have drastically cooled the planet by reflecting back heat from the Sun. Dinosaurs, being cold-blooded reptiles, would have been least able to survive the drop in temperature.

Tektites

Tektites are small meteorites, usually only a few inches in size, that look like pieces of very dark green or black glass. The largest ever found weighed 7 lbs. (3.2 kg). Unlike other meteorites, they are not found evenly spread throughout the world. Analysis has shown that tektites contain a variety of minerals. Those found in the Philippines, for example, contain small amounts of nickel and iron-based minerals. These minerals are similar to those found in the type of meteorites called siderites. Other tektites found in Australasia (australites) show signs of having been heated very strongly, not once, as would happen on entering Earth's atmosphere, but twice. This discovery could be interpreted as evidence that the tektites, having been formed in some hot environment out in space, entered Earth's atmosphere, undergoing a second heating—this time from friction with the air molecules in the atmosphere.

▼ The world's largest known meteorite, still lying where it fell during prehistoric times near Grootfontein, Namibia. It is a giant piece of iron that weighs well over 60 tons (54 tonnes).

Theories for the origin of tektites

There has been much speculation and disagreement among scientists regarding the origin of tektites. One suggestion was that tektites were simply the remnants of some gigantic meteor, which on entering our atmosphere, broke up, leaving the fragments we find today. But, if this were the case, then their ages should be very widely spread, as meteors are known to have arrived at quite a high rate throughout Earth's history. The oldest tektites, however, are only about 35 million years old (the bediasites from Texas), while the australites are less than one million years. Other theories concerning tektites have focused on their superficial resemblance to obsidian, a mineral produced by volcanoes. It was thought that volcanoes may have provided the initial heating through which tektites appear to have gone and that massive volcanic explosions hurled molten material up through the atmosphere, where it solidified while continuing its ascent. This material was not able to leave Earth's gravitational field, and so it slowed down, stopped, and fell back to Earth, undergoing the characteristic reentry heating. Tektites, however, are unlike any known terrestrial volcanic material,

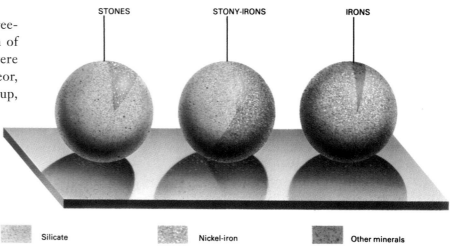

STONES STONY-IRONS IRONS

Silicate   Nickel-iron   Other minerals

so the explosions that created them must have involved some very peculiar mixing of the available materials. In addition, scientists have shown that it would be difficult for solidifying tektites to reach the very high velocities needed to escape the atmosphere without breaking up under the aerodynamic stress.

Another suggestion was that tektites came from volcanic explosions on the Moon blasting the tektites to Earth. It is possible that the right kind of material could be produced in such an explosion. The Moon, however, is thought to have been geologically dead for several billion years, too long to produce the tektites on Earth.

Scientists now commonly agree that tektites were formed when huge meteors entered Earth's atmosphere, striking Earth's crust with devastating force and sending material up into the atmosphere high enough for friction heating to occur as the material fell back. Therefore, they would expect to find both a very large impact crater and nearby tektitelike objects that did not get high enough in the atmosphere to undergo the second heating. One example is a 9-mile (15 km) wide impact crater, the Zhamanshin crater, in southern Siberia. Black glassy tektitelike objects have been found scattered near the southeastern part of it. Chemical analysis shows that the material around the crater bears a strong resemblance to the Australasian tektites. The Zhamanshin crater was produced by a colossal meteor that plunged to Earth about 700,000 years ago, traveling in a northwesterly direction and crashing in a remote part of Siberia. The heat created by the impact generated a vast plume of material, some of which traveled out of the atmosphere to reenter and land again in Australasia as small glassy tektites.

▲ Tiny pieces from meteoroids often stray into the atmosphere as shooting stars. If they do not completely burn up, they land as meteorites. There are three main types, corresponding to the meteoroids from which they originated.

FACT FILE

■ In 1979, a clay layer rich in the metal iridium was discovered at Gubbio in Italy. Such high concentrations, rare on Earth, normally are found in some meteorites. This discovery led to the theory that the clay layer, subsequently found elsewhere on Earth, could be the result of a giant meteor impact from which the dust blocked sunlight for years, eventually causing the extinction of the dinosaurs.

■ In Chihuahua, Mexico, archaeologists discovered an iron meteorite wrapped in a linen cloth; it had been buried in a temple by the Montezuma Indians. The Indians revered the meteorite as a sacred object.

■ In 1957, a rocket carrying artificial meteors was fired by scientists to an altitude of 50 miles (80 km) above New Mexico, and the meteors were released. The trajectories of the fragments were monitored; they fell at 9 miles (15 km) per second and vaporized after 3,300 ft. (1,000 m).

SEE ALSO: CARBON • GEOLOGY • PLANETARY SCIENCE • SOLAR SYSTEM • TELESCOPE, SPACE

Meteorology

Meteorology is the study of weather and climate and encompasses the whole range of atmospheric science. The atmosphere is an envelope of air some 620 miles (1,000 km) deep, held by gravity to Earth, with which it mostly rotates.

Air is a mixture of gases, about 78 percent nitrogen, 21 percent oxygen, and traces of other gases with a variable amount of water vapor. If it were not for water, there would be no clouds and no visible weather. Radiation from the Sun provides the energy necessary for motion within the atmosphere. The weather that affects us occurs in the lowest 7 miles (12 km) or so of the atmosphere in a region called the troposphere. In this region, the temperature decreases with height by about 11°F per 100 ft. (30 m), up to the tropopause. Above this boundary is the stratosphere, where the temperature is nearly constant or increases with height. It is the troposphere that attracts the most attention from meteorologists.

◀ Launching a radiosonde. This device, which is carried up into the air by a balloon, measures air pressure, temperature, and humidity in the lower atmosphere. The information is radioed back to a ground station. Wind speed and direction can be deduced by tracking the device's reflector.

Atmospheric energy

Some of the energy radiating from the Sun reaches Earth and its envelope of air as virtually parallel rays. Earth is approximately spherical, and the radiation reaching the surface is more concentrated in equatorial regions than toward the poles. If there were no atmosphere or oceans, the tropics would become continually hotter and the poles colder. The excess energy in the tropics drives air and ocean currents that, in simple terms, transfer heat energy toward the poles and draw cooler air at lower levels toward the tropics. The uneven heating of the surface, and hence the air, leads to unequal air pressures. The forces due to pressure differences cause the air to move.

The uneven distribution of sea and land, with irregular mountain ranges and friction at low levels, all contribute to complex interacting forces that move the air in complex patterns. The air moves at speeds varying from calm to well over 100 knots (170 ft., or 50 m, per second), often in ribbons of wind called jet streams in the upper troposphere. The atmosphere not only acts as a heat distribution system but also filters out some of the radiation that is harmful to life.

Water

In the atmosphere, water is a very important constituent that takes three forms: invisible gas (water vapor), liquid (cloud droplets, fog, drizzle, rain, and so on), and solid (ice—most usually, minute crystals but also as snowflakes or hailstones). The change of state from gas to liquid to solid releases latent heat into the atmosphere. Energy in the form of latent heat is absorbed during the reverse changes. The cycle of events starts with water evaporating from the oceans, lakes, and other wet surfaces, with the Sun providing the energy (latent heat) needed to convert liquid water to vapor. The invisible vapor in the moist air rises into the atmosphere and is transported by the wind. Later, it condenses as droplets or ice crystals to form clouds, releasing latent heat in the process. Droplets and crystals combine, often with further condensation, to form rain or snow that precipitates to Earth and ultimately replenishes the oceans and other surface water. The complex motion of the atmosphere means that both moisture and heat are transferred around the globe. As the temperature of air increases, its capacity to absorb water vapor increases more rapidly, hence the vigor of clouds and rain is generally greater in tropical regions.

Observing the weather

A surface observation normally comprises details of the wind speed and direction, the atmospheric pressure and its changes over three hours, air temperature, dew point (indicating humidity), visibility, types of clouds and their height and coverage, and the weather phenomena prevailing at the time (for example, snow, rain, sandstorm, fog, thunderstorm, and so on). Observations are made regularly every three or six hours but may be half-hourly at some airports. They are broadcast over national and global communication circuits.

International standards of quality, frequency, and distribution are agreed through the World Meteorological Organization (WMO), which includes virtually every country. At the agreed times, data are collected at many national and international centers from over 7,000 land stations, over 1,000 merchant ships, and hundreds of automatic weather stations and buoys. A complex, high-speed communications network is necessary to handle this information. This network is largely computer controlled, using some of the most powerful computers in the world.

The global observing network is both inadequate and too irregular to give a comprehensive picture of the weather. However, some of the gaps are filled by information from satellites.

The first meteorological polar orbiting satellite was launched in April 1960 and viewed the atmosphere from about 430 miles (700 km) above Earth; its successors still provide vital information. Continuous monitoring of the weather is also available from geostationary satellites orbiting some 22,000 miles (36,000 km) above the equator. Both types of satellite provide pictures at visible and infrared wavelengths and allow forecasters to study cloud distributions, often within half an hour of the scan. Information can also be derived from these scans about wind, temperature, humidity, and clouds.

Even more important are results from new Doppler radars, which operate just like the radar guns that police use to catch speeding drivers. These radars can map the distinctive echoes of air motions inside clouds or in the early stages of tornadoes and can provide detail of the distribution of rain and snow with a precision not possible from a network of direct observations. Radars can be calibrated to show, almost in real time, the intensity of the precipitation falling and the accumulation of rainfall, and they can also detect microbursts—invisible intense downdrafts, which sometimes cause airplanes to crash.

Predicting weather

Weather forecasting is an important part of meteorology. Employing complex mathematical models of the atmosphere, meteorologists can successfully predict the path and severity of hurricanes and other large-scale weather events. They are beginning to understand many important processes, such as the buildup of electrical charges in thunderclouds, which leads to lightning. Yet, predicting the weather several days or weeks ahead has proved much more difficult.

A new branch of mathematics, chaos theory, has shown the reasons for this difficulty. The theory proves that it is impossible to predict accurately the exact state of the atmosphere at any one place for more than a limited time into the future.

Even the slightest inaccuracy in our knowledge of all the billions of tiny factors that could affect the weather will very rapidly lead to huge inaccuracy in predictions. The atmosphere is extremely sensitive to small fluctuations in its initial conditions and therefore the weather will never be the same from year to year.

▼ This diagram shows the behavior of warm and cold fronts near a depression center. When the warm and cold air masses meet in this spot, the warm moist air is cooled as it rises over the colder air, creating clouds and rainfall.

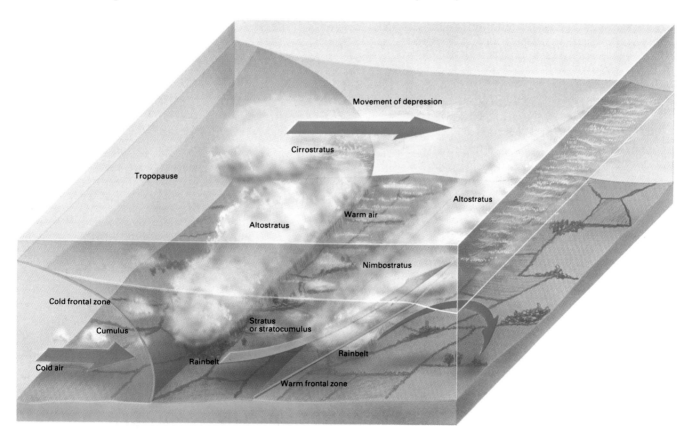

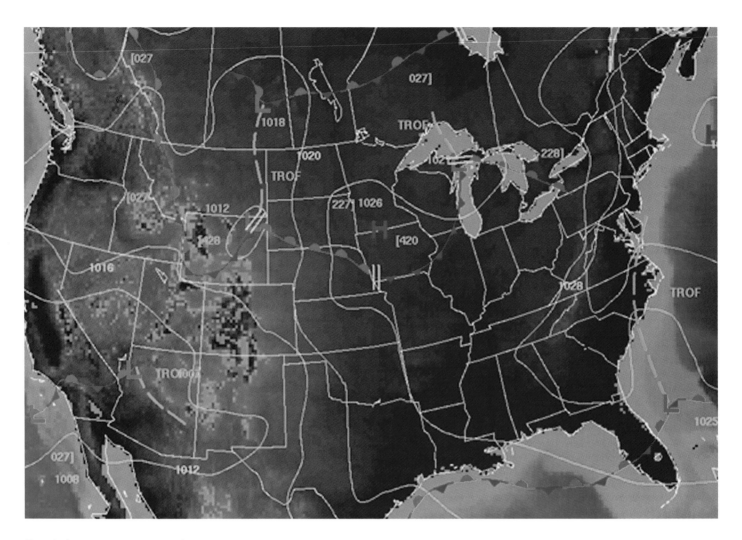

Studying current weather

One way in which meteorologists have tackled this fundamental limitation regarding the accuracy of their medium-term predictions is by improved "nowcasting"—determining exactly what is happening right now.

An example often seen on TV is the radar map of rainfall, which covers an area hundreds of miles across. Much of the weather is governed by conditions high in the atmosphere. Although instrument-carrying balloons (radiosondes) are released simultaneously twice a day at a few hundred sites around the world, they provide insufficient data for really accurate modeling. Satellites have the advantage of orbiting well above the atmosphere and can carry instruments that measure conditions between the orbit and Earth's surface.

In addition, the National Oceanic and Atmospheric Administration (NOAA) uses a system called Nexrad (next generation radar) that employs Doppler radar. Radar devices continuously measure wind speeds and directions and produce images that are updated every 5 to 10 minutes, depending on whether the radio is operating on clean-air mode (during dry weather) or on precipitation mode (during wet weather). The radar emits short intermittent pulses that over the

▲ A weather map of the United States. The red semicircles on the bars indicate warm fronts, while the blue triangles indicate cold fronts. Lines showing a mixture of these two symbols represent stationary fronts. The letters "H" and "L" indicate areas of high and low pressure, respectively, while the yellow lines connect areas with the same atmospheric pressure. The word TROF refers to troughs, elongated areas of low atmospheric pressure.

period of one hour add up to a total of only seven seconds of transmission time—the rest of the hour is spent listening for return signals. The information obtained from radar helps meteorologists to produce accurate models of local conditions, resulting in improved national weather forecasts and the ability to provide advance warning for potentially harmful weather events, such as tornadoes.

Charting the weather

In order to forecast the weather, an initial picture is required of the state of the atmosphere. The surface and upper-air observations, data from ships, aircraft, and satellites, are plotted on charts at specific times to provide this picture. Charts for various levels in the troposphere can be plotted by hand for small areas, but major centers studying global weather now produce plotted versions using computers. In fact, the machines are programmed not only to plot the charts but also to analyze the distribution of the weather data and to incorporate them in numerical forecasting programs. Such forecasting is possible because the air obeys the laws of physics, which can be expressed as mathematical equations that the computer solves, at least to a reasonable approximation.

Surface charts

Perhaps the best-known analysis is the surface chart showing the distribution of atmospheric pressure and the related fronts together with the surface observations. Patterns of pressure distribution become apparent when lines are drawn joining places with equal mean-sea-level pressure. These lines, called isobars, were introduced in the 1860s and are analogous to the contours on a topographical map, and it is not surprising that some of the same descriptive terms are used. Troughs are like valleys—an elongated area of low values—ridges are an extension of high pressure, and a col is an area of little or no pressure gradient between other high and low values. Most important, however, are the enclosed centers of low pressure called depressions and those of high pressure called anticyclones.

The movement of the air, that is the wind, depends on the force due to the pressure differences or pressure gradient; the closer the isobars, the tighter the gradient and the stronger the wind. However, the air does not flow directly from high to low pressure but is deflected by the Coriolis force, which arises from Earth's spin and flows nearly parallel to the isobars. The direction of the wind may be related to the isobaric pattern by remembering Buys Ballot's law, which states that if you stand with your back to the wind in the Northern Hemisphere, low pressure is to your left. On a weather chart, one sees that in the Northern Hemisphere, the wind blows counterclockwise around a depression and clockwise around an anticyclone. The rule is reversed in the Southern Hemisphere, where, with your back to the wind, low pressure is on your right. The weather associated with these pressure systems results from the related vertical motion of the air.

Extensive cloud, and perhaps rain, is generated by rising air in the troposphere over a depression, and the quiet, often fine conditions in an anticyclone are due to air subsiding or sinking. To study the troposphere above the surface, charts of wind and temperature are plotted at several different levels to build up a three-dimensional picture of the atmosphere. Throughout the atmosphere, winds obey Buys Ballot's law, and the equations describing the physical processes have to be solved in a three-dimensional framework. Other data from the upper-air observations of radiosondes are plotted as vertical profiles of the temperature and dew point.

Air masses

Another feature that is apparent on surface weather charts is that, although the weather varies from place to place, a similar type of weather may affect a whole region at any one time, because there are large areas of the world where the surface changes little: the oceans, the polar ice caps, and the major deserts and continental plains. Over some of these regions, the atmosphere may nearly stagnate, and large masses of air acquire temperature and humidity characteristics that change little across the region. From time to time, imbalance in the atmosphere causes a distinctive air mass to move from its source region to other parts of the globe. Although the original

▼ The development of an anvil-shaped cumulonimbus cloud. The cumulonimbus shape develops when rising hot, moist air condenses at condensation level. As this air condenses, water droplets form, and some fall as rain. As the cloud grows, the lighter droplets are held in the updraft until they reach the ice-crystal level, when they freeze. At this point, the cloud flattens out into the familiar anvil shape, becoming relatively even and smooth instead of lumpy in appearance.

A scientist working at computer terminals in the European Center for Medium-Range Weather Forecasting at Reading in the United Kingdom. Staff here prepare weather forecasts for 18 European meteorological services.

characteristics may be recognizable, the moving airstream becomes modified by the nature of the surface under its track.

Airstreams

The airstreams affecting northwest Europe, for example, generally originate from a polar or tropical source, crossing a maritime or continental track. One of the commonest is tropical maritime, originating as warm, moist air in the semipermanent anticyclone that exists over the central tropical North Atlantic. As the air moves north or northeast over cooler seas, the lower layers are cooled and the moisture condenses to form a fog or extensive low cloud. Sometimes drizzle or even rain may develop if the air is cooled further by some process such as lifting over hills, for example. The air usually feels mild and humid in winter and warm and muggy in summer. Polar maritime starts life as cold, clear air with low humidity levels. Moving southeast over the North Atlantic, the air is warmed from below and acquires moisture from the sea but picks up little dust or haze. On reaching Britain, polar maritime is usually fresh and clear, with patches of cumulus cloud often giving showers, especially over the northwestern parts of the country. In winter, the track may be more from the north and is therefore cold, and the showers are of snow.

Tropical continental airstreams start over desert regions like the Sahara and are very hot and dry with dust and haze suspended in the air. Passage northwestward cools the lower layer so that temperature increases with height—this is called a temperature inversion because usually the temperature decreases with altitude. The inversion traps the haze and dust, more of which is picked up over the continental track. This airstream is uncommon in winter but can give a heat wave in summer.

Polar continental air is particularly dry since there is little surface water on the great plains of northern Asia, where the airmass originates, or its European track. In summer, this airstream is very warm, dry, and hazy, but in winter it is bitterly cold and dry and may be very hazy and smoky. Snow showers can develop over the North Sea if part of the track is long enough. These distinctive airstreams are sometimes easy to recognize, but very often, the tracks follow a roundabout route and the air is modified considerably, making it difficult to identify its origin.

Fronts

Fluids, including gases, of different densities do not mix easily. Air masses cover wide areas and have fairly uniform characteristic temperature, and humidity and hence density. At the boundaries between air masses there are marked changes, the main bulk of the air masses not mixing, except along a narrow sloping layer. At these boundary zones, the cooler, denser air mass undercuts the warmer air, forcing it to rise and produce clouds. The belts of clouds, and often rain associated with them, are called fronts, marking the advance of a moving air mass. They are called warm fronts if the surface air is replaced by warmer conditions and cold fronts when cold replaces warm. When a cold front overtakes a warm front, the warmer, lighter air mass is lifted as a wedge above the surface, and the resulting complex front is called an occlusion. Frontal systems are usually associated with depressions and are responsible for major areas of wind, rain, and clouds.

Clouds

Water is an important variable constituent of the troposphere. All clouds comprise minute water droplets or ice crystals and are therefore visible, their form giving some indication of the processes in the atmosphere producing the clouds. Although the appearance of clouds is variable, they may be classified according to a plan introduced by the British meteorologist Luke Howard in 1803. He proposed three main classes: stratus (layered), cumulus (heaped), and cirrus (wispy). By international agreement, these terms are now combined with many others to describe the shape, height, and depth of the clouds in the sky. The World Meteorological Organization gives three categories of height of cloud base above Earth's surface; values are quoted for temperature regions. High clouds between 16,500 and 45,000 ft. (5–13 km) are cirrus, cirrocumulus, or cirrostratus and are normally composed of ice crystals. Medium-level clouds between 6,500 and 23,000 ft. (2–7 km) are called altocumulus, altostratus (often extending to cirrus levels), and nimbostratus (which usually extends to both higher and lower levels). Clouds based below 6,500 ft. (2 km) are stratocumulus, stratus (which may contact the surface), cumulus, and cumulonimbus. Cumulus may extend to medium levels, and cumulonimbus always towers up to high levels with a fibrous top of cirrus. Nimbus, or the prefix *nimbo*, describes clouds deep enough to produce rain or snow.

Cloud-forming processes

Steam, fog, and clouds are all formed when invisible water vapor is cooled sufficiently to condense into droplets or ice crystals. At any given temperature there is a maximum amount of water vapor that the air can hold; the air is then said to be saturated. The dew point is defined as the temperature to which the air must be cooled for it to become saturated. Hence, when air is saturated, the temperature and the dew point are the same, and when the temperature is above the dew point, the air is unsaturated. If the air is cooled below the dew point, without condensation taking place, it is said to be supersaturated; this phenomenon can occur in very clean air, but normally, microscopic particles of salt or dust are present in the atmosphere and these encourage condensation.

By far, the most important mechanism that cools the air is ascent. As air rises to levels of lower pressure, it expands and in the process uses up internal energy (heat), so its temperature falls. In unsaturated air, the temperature falls by about 5.4°F per 1,000 ft. (1°C per 100 m). Once the air is saturated, further cooling causes condensation of the water vapor. Once condensation is occurring, the rising air cools more slowly because of the release of latent heat. The rate at which a rising air mass then cools depends on the pressure and temperature but may be only half the cooling rate of dry air. If the rising air does not mix with its surroundings, it will cool at about 3°F per 1,000 ft. (0.5°C per 100 m) while condensation takes place.

The most direct lifting and cooling occurs when air is forced to rise over hills or mountains. In very moist air, only small hills may be necessary to produce very low clouds (stratus) with extensive hill fog. Fog also forms over land when the ground cools at night and the air in contact with the surface is cooled below its dew point. Sea fog forms when moist air moves over progressively cooler sea.

Accurate forecasting

Many experts believe the most accurate predictions of the weather are made by the European Centre for Medium-Range Weather Forecasts in Reading, in the United Kingdom. The meteorologists there use three Fujitsu computer systems, which contain thousands of microchips that can process millions of pieces of information simultaneously.

The forecasters use what is called the Monte Carlo method, which introduces random variations into the simulation. The computer produces many forecasts per day with these slightly altered starting points. When several forecasts agree, they indicate that the modeling is stable to small fluctuations and that the actual weather will probably match the forecast.

A typical global model incorporates about one million data points—measurements of pressure, temperature, wind speed, humidity, and so on, made at sea level and at various levels in the atmosphere. Using this information, the computer is able to calculate the weather for several days in advance.

Upper-atmosphere studies

Aeronomy is the study of Earth's upper atmosphere and combines both aspects of meteorology and astronomy. The atmosphere's upper limit may be considered to lie at an altitude of about 60 miles (100 km), where the number of particles is a millionth of that at sea level. Even so, it can have dramatic effects—the outer atmosphere expands at times of increased sunspot activity, causing drag on low-orbiting satellites and sometimes bringing them to Earth prematurely.

To determine humidity and temperature information at these heights, meteorologists need instruments at the altitude in question. Special lightweight ghost balloons have been used in experiments. They maintain a constant height; some have made several circuits of the globe over the Antarctic Ocean.

◀ A NASA ER-2 high-altitude research plane being readied for a flight to study the ozone layer. Proposed plane designs will be unmanned and may stay aloft for as long as a year.

SEE ALSO: AIR • CLIMATOLOGY • HURRICANE AND TORNADO • RAIN AND RAINFALL • SATELLITE, ARTIFICIAL • THUNDERSTORM

Meter, Electrical

There are four types of electrical meter, and each measures a different property of electrical current. They are the ammeter, galvanometer, voltmeter, and watt meter.

Ammeter

An ammeter measures electric current, the unit of which is the ampere (A). For small currents, such as in most electronic circuits, the milliampere (mA) and microampere (μA) are used.

The principle on which ammeters work is that current passing along a wire creates a magnetic field around it, the strength of which is proportional to the current. The force of the field around the wire moves a pointer over a scale by an amount depending on the size of the current.

There are three basic types of ammeter: moving coil, moving iron (or moving magnet), and digital. The moving-coil type has a linear scale—its divisions are equally spaced—whereas the moving-magnet ammeter has a nonlinear scale. The moving-coil ammeter has three basic components: a permanent magnet, an electromagnet and pointer assembly, and a helical spring. The electromagnet comprises a flat, rectangular coil formed on a cylin-

drical soft iron core, on which the pointer is secured. This assembly constitutes the moving coil of the instrument, and it is pivoted, usually on jeweled bearings, so that the coil lies at right angles to the permanent magnet's field.

The current to be measured is passed through the coil, producing a magnetic field in opposition to that of the permanent magnet. The reaction between the two fields causes the coil and pointer to rotate over the scale. The rotation assembly is held in check by the spring. Without the spring, the assembly would rotate until the two magnets no longer opposed each other. It resists the rotation and restores the pointer to the zero current position when the current is switched off. Every position on the ammeter's scale corresponds to a particular force and hence to a particular current. In this form, the ammeter measures direct current (DC), but with the addition of rectifiers, they can be made to measure alternating current (AC).

Galvanometer

Galvanometers are instruments for measuring extremely small currents and belong to the same family as ammeters and voltmeters. They contain a moving element that is moved or deflected by the current to be measured and the means for detecting and measuring this movement. The deflection

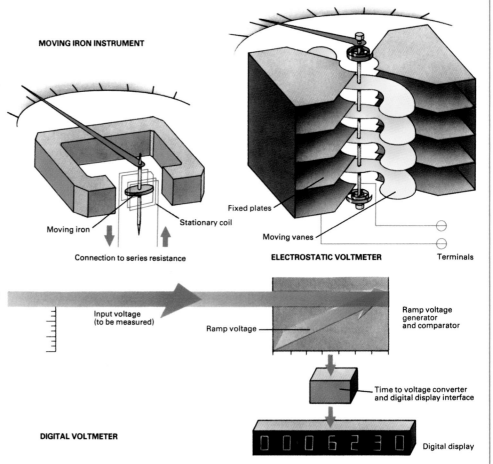

VOLTMETERS

There are a number of different types of voltmeter. Moving-iron (and moving-coil) voltmeters actually measure current. The electrostatic voltmeter works on the principle that unlike charges attract. With a voltage applied, the moving vanes are drawn in so as to be closer to the fixed plates. This type draws no current.

The digital voltmeter shown here has a comparator circuit with a ramp voltage generator. Unlike other types of voltmeter, a digital voltmeter (DVM) depends on the use of electronic circuits. The basic principle of the DVM is the comparison of the measured voltage with the instrument's own accurate reference voltage and the use of the resulting difference to drive a digital display. These voltmeters are capable of providing a higher level of accuracy, sensitivity, and resolution than conventional voltmeters.

MOVING IRON INSTRUMENT

Moving iron

Stationary coil

Connection to series resistance

Fixed plates

Moving vanes

ELECTROSTATIC VOLTMETER

Terminals

Input voltage
(to be measured)

Ramp voltage

Ramp voltage generator and comparator

Time to voltage converter and digital display interface

DIGITAL VOLTMETER

0 0 0 6 2 3 0

Digital display

is achieved by the interaction between an electromagnet and a magnet. There are two possible ways of arranging these two components: as either a moving-magnet or a moving-coil system.

Moving-magnet galvanometers use a permanent magnet pivoted or suspended between the poles of a horseshoe electromagnet. When a current flows in the wires of the electromagnet, a magnetic field is set up between its horseshoe poles that produces a turning force on the permanent magnet and turns it against the return force of a fine spring or suspension ribbon.

In moving-coil galvanometers, the electromagnet is suspended or pivoted between the poles of a horseshoe-shaped permanent magnet. The electromagnet consists of a coil of fine copper wire wrapped on a light rectangular aluminum frame within which is a soft iron core. This core concentrates the field of the permanent magnet and makes it radial in character.

Current flowing through the coil produces a magnetic field that interacts with the uniform radial field of the permanent magnet to produce a turning force.

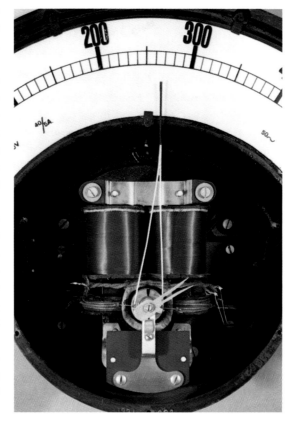

◀ In an induction type of watt meter, an aluminum cylinder is pivoted between a pair of coils. Current passed through the coils induces magnetic flux in the cylinder, thus actuating the meter.

Voltmeter

A voltmeter measures electric potential difference or voltage. There are four common types of voltmeter—moving coil, moving iron, electrostatic, and digital or electronic. The first two types—moving coil and moving iron—make use of ammeters with additional electric resistance. An ammeter is turned into a voltmeter by including a large resistance in series. As long as the total resistance of the voltmeter is very much greater than the resistance across which the voltage is being measured, the current drawn will be negligible. Changing the scale on the ammeter to read in volts then allows it to act as a voltmeter, although it must be stressed that at all times the device is actually measuring current. Electrostatic voltmeters provide a reading of voltage without drawing an electric current by using the mechanical force exerted between two bodies that are at different electric potentials.

Watt meter

The watt meter is an instrument for the measurement of electric power. Power is the rate of doing work and is usually measured in watts or kilowatts. The watt meter should not be confused with the watt-hour meter, which measures energy—the power used in a certain time. The power in a circuit is measured as a combined measurement of the current flowing in and the voltage value across the load. This measurement is then indicated by a pointer against a scale. The most important type

of watt meter is the dynamometer, which in general construction can be compared with the moving-coil ammeter. In the dynamometer watt meter, however, the permanent magnet of the moving-coil ammeter is replaced by an electromagnet in the form of a fixed pair of coils, located one on each side of the moving coil.

The voltage across the load is applied to the pivoted moving coil. The current in the load is passed through the two fixed coils connected in series. These two coils are arranged so that their resultant magnetic fields produce, in the area of the moving coil, an effectively uniform field.

As a result of the voltage applied to the moving coil, a low current flows that is proportional to the voltage, and this current produces a magnetic field about the coil. The field now reacts with the field produced by the current in the two fixed coils so as to cause a force between the fixed and moving coils, causing the pivoted coil, and therefore the pointer, to turn.

The coil continues to move until it is brought to equilibrium by the opposing torque of the control springs. This static deflection is indicated by the pointer, attached to the moving coil, against a calibrated scale and is proportional to the product of the current and voltage in the load.

SEE ALSO: Conduction, electrical • Electricity • Electromagnetism • Induction • Integrated circuit • Rectifier • Resistor • Semiconductor

Meter, Electricity

Electricity meters are used by electricity providers to measure the amount of electricity used by customers so that the customers can be accurately billed. Electricity meters are also used by industry to estimate electricity demand so that peak-hour usage can be planned. To avoid over- or undercharging customers, the meter must be tested to ensure that it gives correct readings. Testing is done using portable meters that give highly accurate readings for the number of watts used per hour.

During the latter part of the 19th century, most electricity supplies were direct current (DC), and so the majority of electricity meters were DC instruments. The British electrical engineer Sebastian Ziani de Ferranti pioneered a mercury motor ampere-hour meter, and a similar type developed by Hookham was a true watt-hour meter. Thompson's commutator motor meter, Wright's electrolytic meter, and the Aron clock meter also enjoyed fairly widespread usage.

Ampere-hour meters depend only on the amount of current being consumed, and registration in watt hours or kilowatt hours (kWh or units) assumes a constant nominal value of supply voltage. Such meters are no longer used on public power supply systems, which are almost always alternating current (AC).

Single-phase AC meters

The basic AC watt-hour meter consists of a horizontal aluminum disk with an electromagnetic coil mounted above and below it. The driving torque is derived from the interaction of eddy currents induced in the disk and the flux from the two coils, which are arranged so that their fluxes are displaced relative to each other in both space and time. The speed of rotation of the disk is proportional to the amount of power passing through the meter, and a gear at the top of the disk spindle drives the counter dials.

In the simple single phase AC meter, the flux in the upper electromagnet is proportional to the supply voltage and that in the lower to the load current. The turning force, or torque, acting on the rotor disk is proportional to the product of the voltage and current and the power factor of the electric load being metered. Power factor refers to the amount by which the load current waveform lags behind or leads the supply voltage waveform. It depends on the nature of the load and can vary between 1 (zero lag or lead) and 0 (90 degrees lag or lead). Inductive loads have a lagging power factor and capacitive loads a leading power factor.

To translate the torque acting on the rotor disk into proportional speed of rotation, a permanent magnet brake is fitted that sets up eddy currents in the disk as it passes through an airgap in the magnet. These eddy currents are proportional to the speed of rotation of the rotor disk and, by Lenz's law, link with the permanent magnet flux to oppose the rotation. The full load speed of the disk is adjusted by altering the position of the brake magnet. The meters also contain various devices that compensate for variations in operating conditions so as to maintain overall accuracy within about 2 percent.

Polyphase kWh meters

Industrial power networks, either three-phase three-wire or three-phase four-wire, are metered by polyphase meters having two driving elements (three-wire) or three driving elements (four-wire), each acting on a separate rotor disk mounted on a common spindle. Alternatively, the drives can be concentrated on a single disk.

Kilovoltampere-hour meters

Kilovoltampere-hour (kVAh) meters register independently of the nature of the load, that is, independently of the power factor. One method

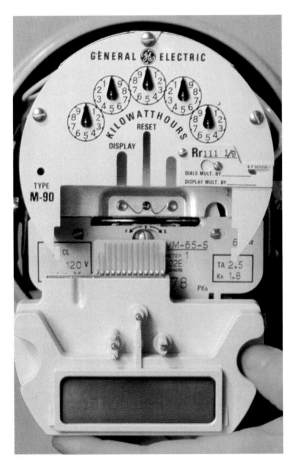

◀ A General Electric meter, which has an electronic demand register with liquid crystal display attached to an electromechanical meter base. It is not a home electricity meter but a demand register used by industry to plan peak-hour usage.

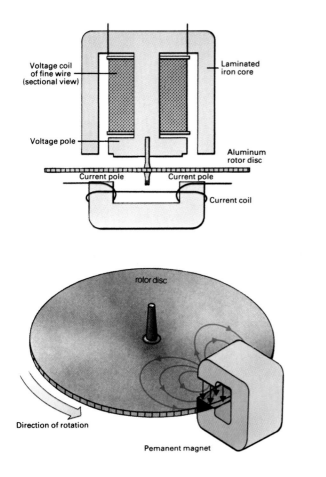

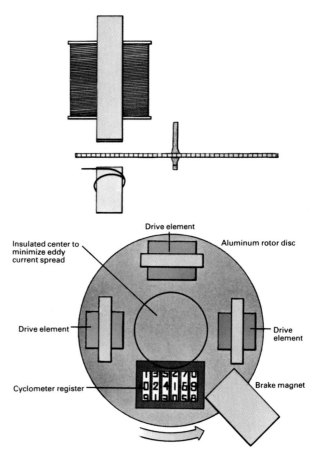

employs basically two polyphase kWh meters, one of which is cross-connected so as to cause it to meter the reactive, or wattless, component (kVArh) of the load. The two meters are mechanically coupled through a multiple differential mechanism that summates, or computes, the true kVAh. Another approach involves the conversion of the AC values of voltage and current to equivalent DC values. These are summated and reconverted to equivalent AC values, which are independent of load power factor and can be metered as kVAh.

KVAh metering is important where large industrial consumers are concerned, because the reactive component resulting from a power factor less than unity (1) will not be registered on an ordinary kWh meter, and so, in effect, energy would be consumed without being registered on the meter.

Maximum-demand indicators

Another complication that arises in the supply of electricity to large consumers is that of maximum demand. Actual energy consumed over a period of time is indicated by the kWh metering, but there may be peak loads at various points during the day, and the supply network must be capable of handling these peaks. Hence, the supply authority engages in extensive capital expenditure on plant and cabling to cope with the maximum

demand, and the consumer is billed for the actual power delivered plus a charge based on maximum demand.

The Merz pattern of maximum demand indicator (MDI), still widely used, embodies a pusher, or drive arm, that is continuously driven from the meter except for a few seconds (usually at 30-minute intervals) when the arm is decoupled and returned to zero by a spring. The drive arm controls the angular movement of a slave pointer, manually reset at regular intervals (usually monthly), so that this pointer will indicate on a circular scale the maximum value of kW or kVA averaged over any single 30-minute interval during the billing period.

Recent developments

It is increasingly common for electricity meters to be digitized using solid-state technology with LCD displays. In addition, meters are being developed that communicate directly with the electricity provider, avoiding the need for the costly manual reading of meters. These automated systems will also permit the introduction of more complex pricing tariffs for industry.

▲ The upper pair of diagrams show cross sections of a single-phase meter, seen from the front and from the side. The lower two diagrams show the eddy currents induced by the permanent-magnet brake and a plan view of a polyphase meter for three-phase, four-wire use.

| **SEE ALSO:** | DIGITAL DISPLAY • ELECTRICITY • INDUCTION • METER, ELECTRICAL • METER, GAS |

Meter, Gas

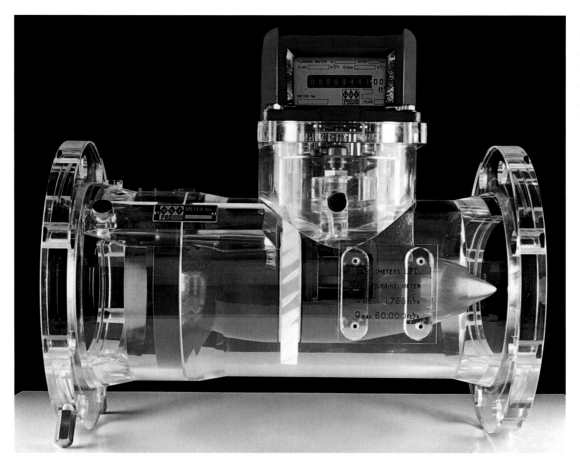

◀ A turbine gas meter, showing the internal components. The green cone directs the gas over the white turbine blades, causing them to turn. The turbine shaft can be linked to a rate counter.

Gas meters are instruments for measuring the volumetric flow rates of gases in the gas supply industry. Various types are available, depending on the application. Where large flow rates need to be measured, at the point of supply (the gas works) and by large industrial consumers, rotary (including turbine), orifice, and heat capacity meters are employed. These last three types are more accurately called flowmeters.

Small industrial consumers and homes today use positive-displacement meters. These are robust and accurate gas meters that can be suitably adapted for use with prepayment and coin-operated mechanisms.

The first gas meters were known as wet meters, because they depended on a quantity of water or other liquid to ensure that they worked. Wet meters were used in the gas industry for over 100 years but have now been superseded by dry meters. Wet meters consist of a rotating measuring drum, a casing, and a counter mechanism. The measuring drum is divided into three or four radial compartments. Apertures in the compartments alternately permit the introduction and expulsion of gas and water, resulting in a rotary motion of the drum. Knowing the volume of each chamber and counting the revolutions of the drum

with the counter mechanism enables the quantity of exhausted gas leaving the meter to be measured.

Positive-displacement meters consist of two chambers that are alternately filled and emptied. Their reciprocal actions are connected via a linkage mechanism to the inlet and outlet valves associated with each chamber to control the gas flow, and also to a counter mechanism. Knowing the displacement volume of each chamber enables the flow rate of the gas to be measured.

The main type of rotary meter—sometimes called a lobed impeller meter—consists of two or three precisely shaped and interlocking impellers (an impeller is driven by a fluid flow, whereas a propeller drives). They are positioned inside a carefully shaped chamber such that at no times can the gas flow straight through the meter unregistered. The pressure of the gas entering the meter forces the impellers to rotate, thus turning a counter mechanism. Each rotation of the impellers corresponds to a fixed volume of gas flowing through the meter. Turbine meters are a form of rotary meter used for industrial applications.

 SEE ALSO: COMPRESSOR AND PUMP • METER, ELECTRICITY • TURBINE

Meter, Parking

The control of the movement and parking of vehicles in urban areas has been practiced for at least 2,000 years. In ancient Rome, the authorities provided off-street parking areas for chariots, and traffic congestion became so bad that Julius Caesar banned vehicles from business areas of the city during certain hours of the day. This ban did not apply to vehicles on religious or state business.

The parking meter was invented by Carl Magee and first used in 1935 in Oklahoma City. Meters were first installed in New York in 1951 and in London in 1957. They are now commonplace throughout the world.

Mechanisms

The basis of the parking meter is a clockwork mechanism that is wound by an attendant about once a week, in the case of the automatic type, or by the user (by turning a knob after inserting a coin), in the case of the manual type. The manual parking meter also avoids the need for parking meter staff having to periodically wind the meters, and so reduces running costs. In either case, insertion of the coin begins the timing cycle, elapsed time being indicated by a pointer and scale arrangement. When the bought time period has expired, a penalty flag is displayed in the parking meter window.

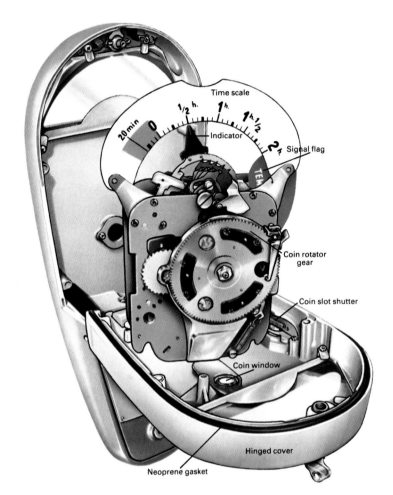

Electronic meters

Parking meters have not proven to be the panacea for all on-street parking problems. They are prone to vandalism and pilferage, and have a high cost of collecting many small quantities of coin. Such problems have prompted the development of a battery-operated, microprocessor-controlled meter that is activated by a stored-value magnetic card. Each insertion of a card buys units of parking, debits the equivalent units from the magnetic card, and displays the residual value of the card on a meter-mounted LCD.

Pay and display

Pay-and-display ticket machines are used as on-street parking meters in many cities throughout the world. Motorists park their vehicles in a vacant lot, walk to the pay-and-display meter, and purchase a ticket for a selected period of time. The ticket, bearing the time of departure, is prominently displayed in the windshield or side window (normally tickets are self-adhesive). Penalties are applied as with the traditional mechanical parking meters. Because one pay-and-display machine can serve 20 to 40 parking spaces, capital and revenue collection costs are reduced. Meters can include magnetic card readers while retaining the option of payment by coin for vehicle users who only occasionally use these parking spaces. Similar machines are used to control the use of numbered bays in a parking lot without the use of tickets.

Recent developments

Some of the latest electronic parking meters incorporate memories for data storage. The data collected may then be used by planners to improve their understanding of parking meter usage. This information may include how much money an individual meter takes and the frequency of use at different times. Some sophisticated meters are capable of sensing if a vehicle has vacated a parking space and, if so, automatically zero the meter to prevent another vehicle from using any remaining time. Other meters may even refund the user for any payed for time that has not been used.

▲ The mechanism of an automatic parking meter, which has to be wound only about once a week. Manual parking meters are wound by turning a knob when the money has been inserted. The coin gear, on the front, holds the last two coins that were inserted so that they can be seen through magnifying coin windows on the front of the case. This feature enables the attendant to check that the correct coins have been inserted.

 SEE ALSO: CLOCK • METER, ELECTRICITY • METER, GAS • TIMING DEVICE • VENDING MACHINE

Metronome

The metronome is an instrument used for visually and audibly indicating the tempo, or speed, of music. In its simplest, clockwork, form it consists of a pivoted pendulum; below the pivot is a fixed weight, and above it a sliding weight. The beat is altered by sliding the weight up and down.

The history of the metronome goes back at least to the 17th century, when the French musician and music theorist Étienne Loulié described in his *Eléments ou principes de musique, mis dans un nouvel ordre* (Paris, 1696) an instrument he called the *chronomètre*. It consisted of a metal bullet suspended on a cord so that it could swing from side to side. Provision was made to vary the length of swing to give 72 speeds.

Other people, such as the French physicist Joseph Sauveur, originator of the word *acoustics*, proposed similar instruments. Robert Bremner, the Scottish music publisher and instrument maker, wrote in 1756 that it was necessary to find a method whereby musical "time in all churches may be equal," saying that a pendulum 8 ft. 8 in. (2.67 m) long would by its double swing or vibration fix the length of the semibreve (the longest note in common usage). He suggested that such a pendulum be hung at the end of each school hall where church music was sung. The British horologist John Harrison, who invented the perfect

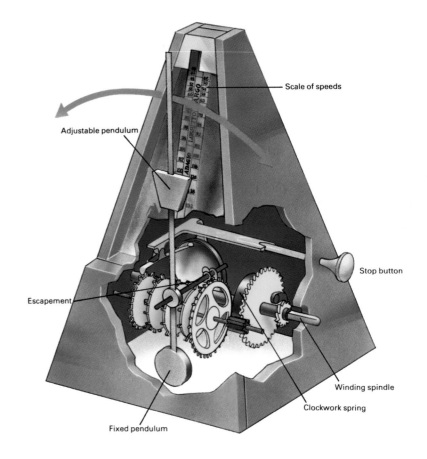

▲ Today's pyramid-shaped metronome. Its speed is adjusted by moving the top pendulum.

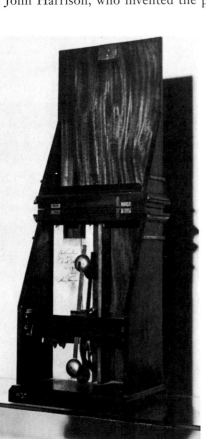

◄ A metronome designed by Dietrich Nikolaus Winkel in 1813. It has a double pendulum and a clockwise drive.

marine chronometer, noted the connection between timekeeping and the tempo of music, in 1775. In 1800, a German named Stöckel made a metronome that had a bell struck by a clock-type hammer.

Finally, around 1812, a German-born master organ builder living in Amsterdam, Dietrich Nikolaus Winkel, invented the first reliable metronome having the double pendulum feature. This design was copied in 1815 by the German inventor J. N. Maelzel, who patented the design in Paris and London.

Since then, many kinds of metronomes have been built. One popular 19th-century model, called Pinfold's Patent Metronome, was a pocket model with a pendulum that was reeled up like a tape measure; others can strike a bell at the first beat in a measure. Solid-state electronics have made possible small, extremely accurate metronomes; one model has a frequency generator that will emit a tunable A at the press of a button. Another model, which looks like a portable radio, can be set to beat any time signature, however complicated. An advantage of electronic metronomes is that, unlike the familiar pyramid-shaped Maelzel model, they do not have to stand on a level surface in order to work accurately.

SEE ALSO: CLOCK • PENDULUM • SPRING

Microbiology

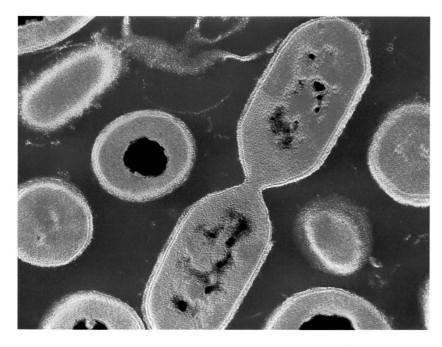

Microbiology as a science was born with the work of the French scientist Louis Pasteur in France in the 1860s. For centuries, scientists had speculated that disease resulted from "spontaneous generation," but Pasteur demonstrated that food spoilage was caused by microscopic organisms present in the environment and could be prevented by applying heat to kill them (as in the pasteurization of milk). Following up on Pasteur's work, Robert Koch in Germany and others discovered some of the actual microbes that caused disease.

Modern microbiology seeks a better understanding of how microorganisms—bacteria, fungi, viruses, and simple protozoa—behave. This understanding leads to improvements in clinical treatment, the exploitation of microorganisms in food production, industrial processes and research, and an appreciation of the important environmental role played by microorganisms.

Bacteria

Bacteria are tiny single-celled organisms. Typically, 1,000 cells laid side by side would measure only 0.04 in. (1 mm). Bacteria range in shape from common rod-shaped bacilli and spherical cocci to comma-shaped vibrios to unusual forms, such as the coiled spirochaetes. Bacteria have a rigid outer cell wall that maintains their shape; below this wall lies the outer cell membrane. Nutrients and waste products diffuse across the membrane, which may be folded to enclose cellular compartments with specialized functions, including photosynthetic activity. Bacteria belong to a class of organisms called

▲ False-color image of a colony of *Listeria* bacteria, magnified 30,000 times. The bacterium at center is dividing in two by binary fission.

prokaryotes, meaning they have no nucleus but carry their DNA in the cellular fluid, which is known as the cytoplasm. The cytoplasm contains subunits called ribosomes for protein synthesis and may often also contain particles, called inclusion bodies, carrying such material as stored fat. Mitochondria and chloroplasts, the "energy factories" of animal and plant cells, are also missing from bacteria.

Bacterial growth is rapid: under ideal conditions, the human gut bacterium *Escherichia coli*, for example, will replicate every 20 minutes. The rapid growth and relatively simple culture requirements of bacteria make them attractive for research and industrial applications. Specially tailored strains of *E. coli* are used in molecular biology and genetic engineering. Genes from other organisms have been inserted into *E. coli* to allow large-scale commercial preparation of products such as human growth hormone and insulin in a process called fermentation.

Growth conditions can be optimized in sealed, controlled culture vessels or fermenters. Nutrients, oxygen, acidity, and other factors can all be monitored and maintained at ideal levels to obtain the best yields. Commercial-scale fermenters allow huge volumes of cells—perhaps up to 25,000 gallons (100,000 l) at a time—to be cultured and harvested and their products collected.

Fermentation technology is applicable to other bacterial species, and to fungi. One class of bacteria, the filamentous actinomycetes, are of particular interest because they secrete antibiotics. Examples include *Streptomyces griseus* and *S. aureofaciens*, from which streptomycin and tetracycline, respectively, are produced.

Fungi

Fungi are more complex than bacteria, having a greater degree of cytoplasmic organization. Many fungal species also secrete antibiotics—penicillin, from *Penicillium*, being the best known example. Common fungi (molds) are shaped like filaments and grow from the tip. When you see mold on bread you are looking at colonies of fungi. Under a microscope you would see new growth occurring around each colony's outer edge.

Among fungal microorganisms, the yeasts have had some of the most widespread commercial use. Yeasts are single-celled organisms, again showing a higher degree of organization inside the cell than bacteria. The brewer's yeast *Saccharomyces cerevisiae*, for example, has its DNA packaged into 17 chromosomes, held together in

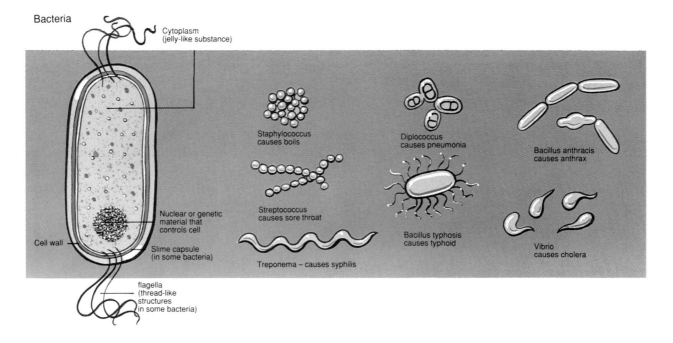

Bacteria

Cytoplasm
(jelly-like substance)

Nuclear or genetic
material that
controls cell

Cell wall

Slime capsule
(in some bacteria)

flagella
(thread-like
structures
in some bacteria)

Staphylococcus
causes boils

Streptococcus
causes sore throat

Treponema – causes syphilis

Diplococcus
causes pneumonia

Bacillus typhosis
causes typhoid

Bacillus anthracis
causes anthrax

Vibrio
causes cholera

a discrete nucleus. As eukaryotes (organisms with a nucleus), yeasts have a cell biology more in common with higher organisms than bacteria. Expression of cloned genes from higher eukaryotes is therefore often easier in yeasts; researchers are investigating the genetics of these organisms as an alternative to bacterial species for bio-manufacturing. *S. cerevisiae* and another yeast, *Schizosaccharomyces pombe*, are also being intensively investigated as simpler model systems in which to study processes such as cell division in higher eukaryotes.

Viruses

Both eukaryotic and bacterial cells may be infected by a third class of microorganism, the viruses. Viruses are much smaller than bacteria, and are made up simply of DNA or RNA surrounded by a protein coat known as a capsid. Sometimes viruses that infect animal cells will be found surrounded by pieces of membrane from previously infected cells. The DNA or RNA encodes the genetic information for making more copies of the virus, but the virus lacks the machinery for doing so; to replicate, the virus must enter a cell and "hijack" its systems for protein and nucleic acid synthesis.

E. coli is infected by a number of viruses called bacteriophages, of which perhaps the best-studied is known as lambda. Modified versions of lambda are used in molecular biology and genetic engineering as vectors to insert genes into bacteria. Lambda consists of a molecule of DNA 50,000 bases long, encased in a protein capsid. The tail of the capsid recognizes, and will attach to, the outer surface of *E. coli*, after which the DNA is injected into the cell. Lambda can then follow one of two

▲ Although bacteria, sometimes known as microbes, are popularly considered to be harmful, they have a wide range of uses. Those shown here cause diseases, but others are beneficial. Many antibiotics, including penicillin, are made naturally by bacteria and fungi found in the soil.

pathways. The DNA can integrate into the chromosome of the host, replicating in a benign fashion in tandem with its host, or it may initiate a process called the lytic cycle.

In the lytic cycle, bacteriophage genes are expressed to produce many copies of the bacteriophage DNA and of the proteins that make up the capsid. The DNA and proteins assemble into more copies of the virus, and after a time, the coup de grace is delivered: the infected cell is burst open or lysed by an enzyme also encoded by the bacteriophage DNA, releasing about 100 virus progeny that may then go on to infect more cells. Regions where lysis has occurred can be seen in bacterial growth on agar plates as clearings called plaques. Each plaque represents virus infection spreading from a single infective center.

The viruses that infect eukaryotic cells have more complicated growth patterns and grow more slowly than bacteriophages. For obvious reasons, great effort is expended in the field of virology in attempting to understand the workings of viruses that infect and cause disease in humans. In particular, the human immunodeficiency virus (HIV, the causative agent of AIDS) is the target of intense research.

Bacteria and human health

The human body is full of harmless bacteria. But a minority of external bacteria are capable of invading the body and causing disease. They have been responsible for some of the great scourges of humankind such as syphilis, tuberculosis, plague, cholera, and typhoid. With improved methods of diagnosis, such as the ability to locate and identify minute quantities of bacterial DNA by the polymerase chain reaction, it is likely that science will discover that many diseases for which no cause is currently recognized are, in fact, caused by bacteria. For example, in 1983, researchers first reported the association between bacteria (*Helicobacter*) and stomach ulcers. Such advances offer new hope in the treatment of disease.

Since the introduction of penicillin in the 1940s, antibiotics have greatly reduced the numbers of people dying or suffering disability from bacterial infections. However, many bacteria have developed resistance to antibiotics, particularly where they have been used indiscriminately, and some have developed into "superbugs." One of these superbugs, methicillin-resistant *Staphylococcus aureus* (MRSA), has become resistant to all forms of treatment except the antibiotic vancomycin. The search for new antibacterial agents continues in an attempt to combat the increase in resistance. Whereas the early antibiotics, such as penicillin, streptomycin, and chloramphenicol, were produced by bacteria or fungi, many newer agents are synthesized by chemists, either in part (modification of existing antibiotics produced by microorganisms) or whole.

A new class of synthetic drugs, the oxazolidinones, approved for use in 2000, is proving effective against MRSA and another superbug, vancomycin-resistant *Enterococcus faecium*. Provided their use is not abused, this class of drugs may hold back the superbug threat for some years to come.

Exploiting organisms

While they are often portrayed as being harmful, it is important to be aware that bacteria and fungi had been exploited by humanity in a number of valuable roles long before their nature was known. Yeasts, for example, are of great use in baking and brewing. Lactobacilli are used in the production of processed dairy goods, such as yogurt, while several species of fungi are exploited in cheese manufacture.

The ability of several microbial species to survive under hostile conditions and live on unusual nutrients is the key to their future exploitation in areas such as waste management. Some *Pseudomonas* bacteria can break down complex organic compounds found in toxic wastes. Specially tailored bacteria and fungi should help to control environmental pollution.

Microbiological breakdown of organic material has been exploited for a long time. Composting involves the concerted action of a succession of bacteria and fungi to decompose dead organic matter. Important to this process are fungi that produce enzymes called ligninases that break down the woody material in plants.

▶ Bacteria are often cultured on dishes of nutrient agar. The effectiveness of antibiotics can be tested by placing them on the dishes to see if they inhibit the growth of the bacteria.

Researchers are seeking to isolate improved ligninases for future application in waste processing and disposal.

Bacteria can be used in energy production. Species like *Methylobacterium* or *Methanococcus* generate methane, the principal component of natural gas, from decomposing waste. Other interesting ways of using the ability of bacteria to decompose a great variety of compounds are currently being developed. One of the most important of these is spraying oil spills with mixtures of bacteria selected for their ability to degrade hydrocarbons. These bacteria are grown in vast quantities (several tons of cells) in laboratories.

This approach, known as bioremediation, was used with some success on the beaches of Prince William Sound in Alaska, following the 11-million-gallon oil spill from the *Exxon Valdez* in 1989, and again in the Persian Gulf following the 1990 Gulf War. Mixtures of bacteria capable of degrading toxic chemicals, such as certain pesticides and herbicides, are also being developed. The environment may also benefit from the introduction of biodegradable plastics that have been manufactured from insoluble polymers produced by some bacteria and readily decomposed by others.

▶ Many scientists believe that only about 10 percent of the world's existing bacterial species have been classified to date. Apparently unimpressive algae, such as these organic laminae, can have their uses; they form a gene pool that scientists are currently investigating.

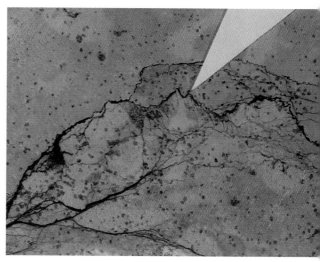

Unappetizing as the idea may initially seem to most of us, bacteria may also serve as a useful food source in the future. Again exploiting otherwise unusable material derived from petroleum, researchers are currently investigating the possibility of culturing bacteria on refinery waste to produce protein. The successful use of such material as cattle feed offers hope of a partial solution to the world's growing food demands.

Clues to the origins of life

Many bacterial species are remarkable in their tolerance of harsh conditions, including heat, cold, high salt concentrations, and desiccation. The ability to survive inhospitable conditions has been taken by evolutionary biologists to indicate that bacteria probably played an important part in the early development of life on Earth.

The best available current scientific theories of the origin of life suggest that the first organisms to appear, sometime within a billion years

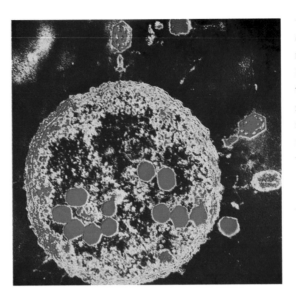

◀ A bacterium of *E. coli* (circular cell) infected by red T2 bacteriophages. Bacteriophages are viruses that infect only bacteria, some being specific to a single species. Having no reproductive machinery, they commandeer the bacterium to ensure self replication. The colors on this electron micrograph are false.

after Earth's formation, were simple bacteria scavenging nutrients from their environment. For the two billion years that followed, microorganisms remained Earth's sole tenants. Development of photosynthesis by one class of bacteria, the blue-green algae, led to important chemical changes in Earth's atmosphere: oxygen began to accumulate, paving the way for more complex life forms.

Archaebacteria, presumed to bear a close resemblance to early primitive bacteria, can still be found today, often in hostile oxygen-free environments that may resemble those in which cellular life first arose. One example is the hot-spring pools in Yellowstone National Park. Other surprising discoveries have included the presence of bacterial growth in the sulfur-rich hot environments around vents ("smokers") on the deep ocean floor, in regions such as the Mid-Atlantic Ridge where lava emerges from below Earth's crust. More startling still was the discovery, in 1992, of bacteria in drilled samples from great depths into Earth's crust.

Eukaryotic cells contain several small internal structures called organelles, each with some special function: ribosomes, for example, manufacture proteins, mitochondria process energy, and in plants, chloroplasts carry out photosynthesis. Several characteristics of mitochondria and chloroplasts suggest that they might once have been free-living bacterial organisms that became incorporated, perhaps via a symbiotic lifestyle, into the cytoplasm of more complex cells. Thus, microbiological research not only has important implications for understanding how modern bacteria function but also may yield important clues to how life itself arose and developed.

FACT FILE

- The gold nuggets, found in the silt of some riverbeds, that were responsible for several famed gold rushes may have been produced by bacteria. This surprise observation was reported in 1992 by a scientist who examined thousands of grains of gold found in Alaska.

- Using a scanning electron microscope, which can magnify objects many thousandfold, bacteria were seen in close association with the grains of gold, which appeared to be deposited around channels occupied by the bacteria.

- The proposed mechanism of gold deposition is not alchemy, but a well recognized bacterial activity known as biomineralization. Several minerals are known to be precipitated by bacteria after concentration of dilute soluble salts found in the environment. Thus, the bacteria would be responsible not for creating gold, but for concentrating it from soils rich in gold salts.

- Exactly how and why the bacteria perform this trick has still to be explained, but several investigators will no doubt attempt to repeat it in the laboratory with a view to commercial exploitation of these bacteria.

SEE ALSO: Biotechnology • Cell biology • Fermentation • Immunology • Molecular biology • Vaccine

Microencapsulation

Microencapsulation can best be described as a packaging technique that involves putting minute particles of a solid or droplets of a liquid into tiny capsules. A microencapsulated liquid behaves like a powdered solid, and the liquid is released only when the walls of the capsules are ruptured, for example, by pressure or heating. The technique can be used to keep reactive materials apart until mixing is required, to prevent deterioration of unstable materials, to mask taste and odor, and to reduce volatility and flammability.

Encapsulation technology dates back to the late 1800s and was largely pioneered by the pharmaceutical industry, which developed the familiar large gelatin capsule used to administer measured doses of drugs. In the 1930s, two U.S. chemists, H. R. Kruyt and H. G. Bungenberg de Jong, devised a technique that they called coacervation. They discovered that under certain conditions, a colloid dispersed in a liquid to form two separate phases would form a thin wall around any third phase that was present. At the time, there was no practical application for this technology.

▲ Microencapsulated inks provide the basis behind the developing technology of electronic inks. By applying an electric current to an invisible metal grid coating the paper, the lunch sign above can be rewritten almost instantaneously. Unlike television and computer screens, or liquid crystal displays, the image is retained after the power has been switched off and can be viewed from a variety of different angles, even in poor light.

The first significant application of microencapsulation technology was NCR (no carbon required) paper, introduced in 1954. NCR paper used two colorless chemicals that reacted to form a dye. One of the components was suspended in an oil and encapsulated into tiny particles. These capsules were coated onto the back of one sheet of paper, and the other component was coated onto the top of another sheet. When the two sheets were fed into a typewriter together, the local pressure of the key striking the top sheet ruptured the capsules and released the first dye component. This then flowed onto the top surface of the second sheet and reacted with the other dye component to produce the dye color. A copy of the typed sheet was thus produced.

Manufacture

Microencapsulated products can be made in a number of ways, the method chosen depending on the nature of the material to be encapsulated and the desired properties of the capsule. The size, wall thickness, permeability, and conditions under which the encapsulated product is released may all be varied over a fairly wide range by careful control of the microencapsulation process and the choice of materials.

Microencapsulation techniques can be divided into two broad categories—physical and chemical. The chemical techniques include coacervation, polymerization, and solvent extraction. These techniques usually rely on careful alteration of the physical and chemical conditions of a mixture of the product and the capsule material; a third component causes the mixture to separate, and the products become encapsulated inside tiny spheres. The physical techniques coat the product directly. In fluid-bed coating, for example, the product particles are suspended and rotated in a jet of air. The capsule material is then sprayed directly onto them, with the thickness of the coating depending on how long the particles are exposed to the jet.

Uses

One of the most useful properties of microencapsulated products is the ability to provide sustained release of the capsule contents. Thus, tablets containing a microencapsulated drug such as aspirin can give continuous benefit over a period of many hours. Similarly, insecticides, herbicides, and fungicides can be microencapsulated to provide sustained release over a predetermined period of time and to increase their storage life. Certain food and veterinary products can be microencapsulated to protect any vitamins and minerals they contain and hide any unpleasant taste. Adhesives and sealants that are activated by mixing two components can be packaged in a single container by microencapsulating one of the components. Only pressure or heat will rupture the capsules and activate the material. Microencapsulated deodorants and antiperspirants are released only when a person's sweat mixes with the capsules.

Perfume and fragrances can be applied in microencapsulated form to printed leaflets or labels. The odor is released when the coated surface is scratched, thus providing an inexpensive way of distributing advertising samples of a perfume—or of informing people of the smell of natural gas so that they can spot a leak.

A recent microencapsulated product is electronic ink. In conjunction with special sheets of "paper," electronic inks provide a system that prints like ordinary ink but has the added advantage that the paper can be erased electronically and reused. For example, a thin rubber sheet is coated with microcapsules containing positively charged blue ink mixed with a small quantity of negatively charged particles of white ink. The

▶ The following pictures show the chemical microencapsulation process of coacervation in action. In this first picture, a droplet of oil that is to be encapsulated floats freely in the surrounding liquid.

▶ As the chemical conditions are altered, the coating material starts to build up around the oil droplet, although it remains uncoated.

▶ The thin lines around the edges of the droplets show the first signs of the buildup of the coating material onto the surface of the oil droplet.

▶ After a suitable time period, a thick layer of coating has built up around the droplet. The encapsulated droplets can now be separated from the liquid and dried to form a powder of the microencapsulated oil.

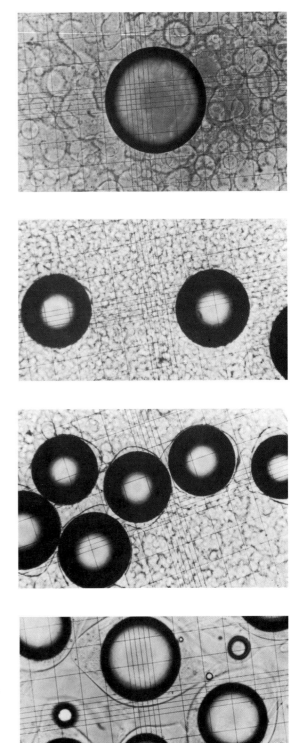

sheet is crisscrossed on both sides with a thin grid of electrodes, forming individual squares, or pixels. When a positive charge is applied to a particular pixel, the white ink is drawn to the top of the capsule turning it white. Reversing the charge on the pixel sends the white ink to the bottom, turning the pixel blue again.

SEE ALSO: ADHESIVE AND SEALANT • FOOD PRESERVATION AND PACKAGING • PHARMACEUTICALS

Microfilm

Microfilm is a form of data storage produced by recording on film a unit of information, such as an engineering drawing or the page of a book, and photographically reducing it in size.

The cameras that photograph documents, usually onto film either 16 mm, 35 mm, or 105 mm wide, are collectively called microfilmers, and they fall broadly into three categories: flat-bed, flow type, and computer output.

Whereas the flatbed and flow-type micro-filmers produce microimages from data recorded on paper, the computer-output microfilmers convert data directly from the electronic format used in a computer into human readable microimages on microfilm. Computer output microfilmers (COM) write data by laser onto dry laser film designed by Kodak to meet this special need. Development of the film is by heat alone. COM machines can produce their microfilm output in either fiche or 16 mm roll film format, and some can produce both simultaneously. Also, the 16 mm roll film can be automatically encoded for retrieval by computer-assisted retrieval (CAR) equipment.

Microforms

Microimages can be retained in various micro-forms. The most commonly used microform, especially in financial and business systems, 16 mm or 35 mm roll film, is retained in lengths up to 225 ft. (69 m) on spools approximately 4 in. (10 cm) in diameter. Magazines or cassettes are mainly used in 16 mm systems requiring frequent high-speed reference to information. The plastic magazine protects the microfilm and facilitates automatic loading of the viewing unit.

Where it is essential to maintain information in specific groups while retaining the ability to add or delete at any future date, microfilm jackets are used. They consist of two thin transparent sheets, sealed together to form channels accommodating either 16 mm or 35 mm film, or a combination.

Microfiches are used in micropublishing where it is necessary to distribute a large number of microfilm copies, such as in the dissemination of information to libraries and the engineering parts and servicing industry. A sheet microform, usually 6 by 4 in. (15 x 10 cm) or 80-column punched card size, contains between 60 (20:1 reduction) and 200 (40:1 reduction) microimages.

The aperture card, often used in engineering drawing microfilm systems, is a data-processing 80-column punched card containing one or more holes specially designed to accept 16 mm or 35 mm microimages.

Viewing microfilm

As the microimages cannot be read with the unaided eye, a microfilm viewer or reader is needed to magnify the very small image to a size that will be comfortable and easy to refer to. In addition to viewing the microimage, it may be necessary to make a paper print of the screen image; reader-printers are available for this purpose.

Intelligent microfilmers can film documents in totally random order. An integral micro-processor not only controls the microfilming operation to ensure the maximum quality in the microfilm, it also allocates a unique microfilm address to each document and encodes the micro-film with special marks that can be identified later by the intelligent terminal when it is searching for that particular document. The contents of the document and the unique address will be held in a computer.

Videomicrographics

Videomicrographics, such as the Kodak Image Management System (KIMS), enable CAR systems to operate with only one central microfilm file. The rolls of microfilm are selected by robots operating under computer control. Instead of the document image being viewed on a microfilm viewer, the image is presented to a charge-coupled device (CCD) scanner, which digitizes it. The digitized image can then be fed into a local area network (LAN) from which it can be accessed by any number of workstations attached to the network and sent across the country or, through satellite links, around the world.

▲ The microfiche display on the left is obtained from a tiny, transparent photograph of a book. This requires the reader to view the book in a library using specialized equipment. The computerized version, shown on the VDU on the right, is stored electronically and may be disseminated over the Internet.

SEE ALSO: CAMERA • DATA STORAGE • INFORMATION TECHNOLOGY • PHOTOGRAPHIC FILM AND PROCESSING

Micromachine and Nanotechnology

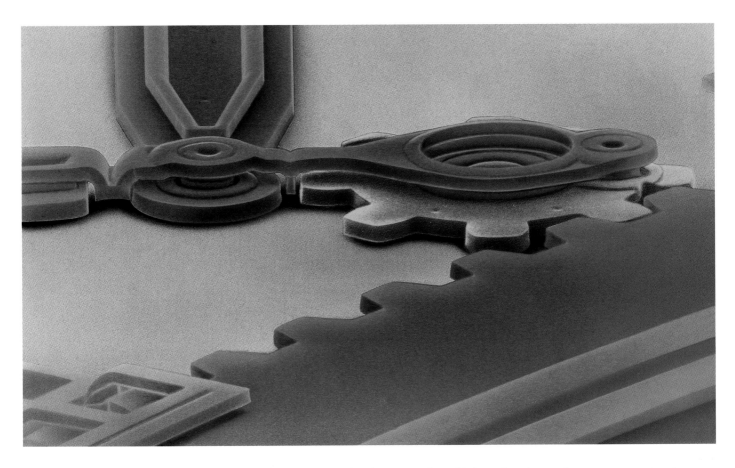

A micromachine is an electromechanical or mechanical device whose dimensions are of the order of a few microns, or millionths of a meter (one micron—1 μm—is around 4 x 10⁻⁵ in.). Such devices include MEMSs, or microelectromechanical systems. Nanotechnology is frequently defined as the construction and deployment of devices whose dimensions are less than 100 nm (1,000 Å), though some experts in the field prefer to set an upper limit of 50 nm (500 Å).

In comparison, the sizes of atoms—stated as the interatomic distance in a condensed sample of an element—range from 0.074 nm (0.74 Å) for hydrogen to 0.53 nm (5.3 Å) for cesium. Typical construction materials in nanotechnology include carbon (0.14 nm, 1.4 Å, in graphite) and silicon (0.24 nm, 2.4 Å). Hence, the usual definition of nanotechnology embraces devices whose dimensions are those of a few hundreds of atoms.

The original proposal of nanotechnology was made by the U.S. physicist Richard Feynman in his 1959 talk *"There's Plenty of Room at the Bottom,"* given to the American Physical Society at the California Institute of Technology. Feynman spoke of fabricating molecules by directing their constituent atoms to the appropriate positions for subsequent chemical bonding to occur. Moreover, his proposal included a rigorous description of nanotechnology: one by which molecular-scale machines could be designed and built so that each atom has a distinct role in the function of the machine of which it forms part.

Feynman challenged his fellow physicists to develop microscopes that would be able to "see" individual atoms and thereby help biologists understand the structures and actions of biological agents such as bacteria, viruses, and proteins. He proposed that the contents of works such as *Encyclopaedia Britannica* could be written on a pinhead using letters, each formed by a few atoms. Feynman also envisaged computers that would be far faster and more compact than then-current machines as a result of replacing the transistors at their processing cores with nanometer-scale electronic components. Such components would be made by evaporating, conducting, semiconducting, and insulating materials and condensing them onto a base material in an ordered fashion.

Some of Feynman's predictions have been realized already, at least in part. Extremely high-powered microscopes are now capable of resolving individual atoms in complex structures, and one such device has been used to shunt xenon atoms around the surface of a nickel crystal to form the IBM company logo. Also, modern computers use central-processing units that are built

▲ This scanning electron micrograph shows part of a micromotor. The image has been computer enhanced by adding false color to improve clarity. The small gear (orange) has a diameter smaller than that of a human hair. It is driven by two minute engines (not visible) and causes the larger gear (green) to move through one revolution per second. The device was built from a single crystal of silicon using photolithographic techniques similar to those used to create electronic circuits on silicon chips.

on the surfaces of slices of crystalline silicon using methods similar to those imagined by Feynman. The finest details of current state-of-the-art computer circuits are between 1,000 Å and 2,000 Å (100–200 nm) in size—a scale that is near the limit of what is possible by current technology but is many times greater than that of the nanometer-scale circuits predicted by Feynman.

Other predictions made in the same speech by Feynman have yet to be fulfilled and are the current goals of nanotechnological research. One such field of research aims to develop techniques for assembling molecules by mechanical means; another has the ultimate goal of producing nanometer-scale robots, or nanobots, that will be capable of being programmed to perform tasks.

Developments in microscopy

Whereas electron microscopes are adequate for studying the structure of micromachines, which may be many thousands of atoms wide, the study of the products of nanotechnology require instruments that are able to resolve individual atoms. Three types of such microscopes now exist.

Introduced in 1981, the scanning-tunneling microscope, or STM, is used to form images of the surfaces of conducting materials. An STM has a sharp metal probe that is one atom wide at its tip. A potential difference is established between the probe and the object of interest, and the probe is lowered to the surface of the object. As the tip of the probe gets close to the surface, electrons start to pass between the probe and the object in a quantum-mechanical process called tunneling. The ease of tunneling depends strongly on the distance between the probe and the object. Consequently, the amount of current increases sharply when the tip of the probe approaches the surface of an object.

As an STM scans the surface of an object, its control circuitry instructs servomechanisms to adjust the height of the probe above the object to maintain a constant tunneling current. Since this procedure effectively maintains a constant distance between the tip of the probe and the object surface, the probe position can be charted to produce a map of the object's surface in which each atom is clearly represented as a bump.

A related device is the atomic-force microscope, or AFM. Instead of monitoring the tunneling of electrons between a probe and the surface of an object, the control circuitry of an AFM monitors the repulsive force that develops as the electrons in the tip of the probe start to impinge on the electrons in the surface atoms of the object. As with the tunneling effect, the interatomic repulsive force increases sharply as the

separation between the probe and the surface diminishes, so an accurate map of an object's surface is put together by scanning the surface and adjusting the probe height to maintain a constant force. The AFM has the advantage over STM that it can be used to map the atoms in the surfaces of insulating materials, since no current needs to flow between the probe and the object.

Scanning-probe microscopes, SPMs, are the third type of microscopes that can resolve at the atomic scale. They measure the frictional resistance to the motion of a probe tip across a surface, and they are also capable of moving atoms around on the surface of an object.

Photolithography

The technique that has achieved the greatest amount of success in the production of micromachines is photolithography. This technique is related to the photoengraving techniques used to produce integrated circuits on silicon chips.

A single crystal of silicon is first coated with a light-sensitive emulsion that cures to form an impermeable barrier when exposed to ultraviolet light. Areas that are to be preserved in the finished article are then protected by selective exposure to ultraviolet light through a mask. Dark areas of the mask prevent the ultraviolet light from reaching certain parts of the crystal, and uncured emulsion in those parts is then washed away to leave them exposed.

The next stage of the procedure is etching, whereby a chemical agent that removes silicon as soluble compounds eats into the crystal where it has not been protected by cured emulsion. The depth to which silicon is removed from exposed parts of the surface depends on factors such as temperature, the concentration of the etching agent, and the duration of the etching process.

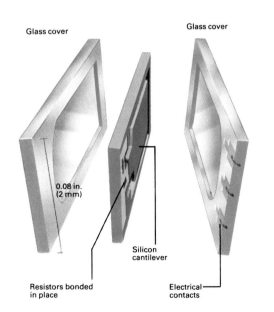

Glass cover Glass cover

0.08 in.
(2 mm)

Resistors bonded
in place

Silicon
cantilever

Electrical
contacts

◀ This microaccelerometer has a silicon cantilever with a conducting strip at its mobile end. Given a rapid acceleration in the appropriate direction, the cantilever swings from its neutral position, and the conductor bridges contacts on the protective glass plate so as to close a circuit. This type of accelerometer triggers the inflation of automobile air bags during the rapid deceleration of a collision.

Even the orientation of the crystal structure relative to the exposed surface has an influence on the rate of etching. Each of these factors can be used to control the shape of the finished article.

One of the key micromechanical components is the silicon cantilever, which resembles a microscopic diving board, secured at one end to a silicon frame that surrounds it. Such devices are made by bonding together two layers of silicon with different crystal orientations and then using photolithography to remove silicon such as to form the spaces around and beneath the cantilever. The cantilever is relatively flexible, so it is used as a mount for movable mirrors and switch contacts, among other applications. Cogs, shafts, and casings are other components that are made from silicon by photolithography.

Other techniques

Other techniques for sculpting micromachine components from blocks of starting materials include laser machining, whereby the energy of photons vaporizes surface atoms. Excimer lasers are particularly suitable for this process, since they produce higher-energy photons than do other lasers and achieve finer resolution. Electrochemical and electric-discharge machining have also been used with some success, as have beams of high-speed electrons.

There are three basic deposition techniques for use when material has to be added to a workpiece rather than removed from it. In the simplest, additional material is vaporized in the presence of the workpiece and forms a uniform surface layer by condensation. In chemical vapor deposition, the workpiece is heated in an atmosphere that contains one or more reactive compounds, each of which contains the substance that is to be deposited. When molecules of these compounds strike the hot surface of the workpiece, they decompose to deposit the coating material. Chemical vapor deposition is useful for applying materials that are not themselves volatile but that form suitably volatile compounds. In electrochemical deposition, a solution of an ionic compound is electrolyzed to deposit material on the workpiece, which is one of the electrodes of the electrolytic system. This technique can be used only to apply materials to conducting surfaces.

Assembly and heat treatment

Once the components of a micromachine have been fabricated, they are assembled using high-precision handling tools. Cogs and rotors are placed in bearings, which are holes etched into their supports. Inductor coils, electromagnets, capacitors, and resistors are secured in their respective positions by an adhesive—typically an ultraviolet-curing epoxy compound.

Once assembled, a micromachine must be heat treated at around 1650°F (900°C). This process removes the internal stresses generated during the component fabrication and assembly stages. Without heat treatment, the cogs and shafts of a micromotor would eventually deform and prevent smooth operation, for example.

Types of micromachines

The simplest micromachines are around 0.04 in. (1 mm) square, and 2.4 x 10^{-4} in. (6 μm) thick. Such devices include accelerometers, such as those that trigger the inflation of air bags in automobile collisions, and pressure sensors. More complex machines, including micromotors that can drive external cogs, are usually three times as thick as the simpler devices, since they are made by forming a three-layer composite structure.

First-generation micromachines received their power and control signals from external sources through wires. "Smart" micromachines are now made by mounting assembled and heat-treated electromechanical component in a trough cut into a silicon chip that is then used as the basis for building an integrated control circuit. The electromechanical portion is embedded in silicon dioxide to protect it during the construction of the chip and to provide a flush surface that does not hinder those operations. Once the integrated circuit is complete, the silicon dioxide is dissolved away to reveal an intact micromachine that shares a chip with its control circuit.

The problem of providing a micrometer-scale power source is still to be completely resolved, although solar cells made from hydrogen-modified amorphous silicon have produced

▼ These tiny air-pressure sensors are made from etched silicon, which is bonded to glass. They are used in General Motors' computerized fuel economy and pollution control system. The sensors are small enough to fit inside an engine inlet manifold.

▶ A colored scanning electron micrograph of a chip of acrylate resin floating in a human artery. The chip was built up in layers 10 μm (0.0004 in.) thick by using computer-guided lasers to initiate the polymerization of simple alkyl acrylate (ethenoate) monomers. Such chips could one day form the basis of nanorobot "submarines," fitted with tiny propellers and tools that could detect and repair damaged blood vessels in the human body.

promising results. Another possible power source might capture the charged beta or alpha particles emitted by the decay processes of radionuclides. The small scale of micromotors means that they have minute power demands—typically around one milliwatt. Hence, the capacity of micrometer-scale power sources need only be feeble.

Starting from the bottom

The long-term ambition of nanotechnologists is to be able to produce custom-built molecules and structures by manipulating individual atoms and molecular fragments. This type of procedure is well beyond the capabilities of micromachines and will require nanomachines, mechanisms with dimensions around one-millionth those of micro-machines. Nevertheless, researchers are already exploring how such machines could work.

As mentioned, scanning-probe microscopes are capable of moving atoms and molecules around on even surfaces, such as those of metal crystals. One branch of nanotechnology aims to join molecular fragments by plucking one hydro-gen atom off each of a pair of parent molecules and allowing a new bond to form between the points from which the hydrogen atoms have been

taken. The latter part of the process will occur spontaneously provided the component molecu-lar fragments are sufficiently close and in an appropriate relative orientation to one another.

The tool that is likely to perform the task of removing individual hydrogen atoms is likely to be the ethynyl radical ($-C\equiv C\cdot$), bonded to the tip of a scanning-probe microscope for the purposes of tests. Researchers have calculated that the energy barrier to the abstraction of hydrogen atoms from certain types of organic molecules is practically zero and that the energy released when a hydrogen atom bonds to an ethenyl radical is so great as to make the reaction irreversible.

One of the challenges of the ethynyl radical is that its formation requires a great deal of energy. This energy might be supplied mechanically, by pulling apart a group of atoms that preferentially snaps at the point that yields the required radical. Another challenge is to find a way to regenerate the ethynyl radical tool after use.

It is possible that amorphous solids will be converted into perfect crystals by nanobots equipped with tools for pushing atoms into place. In a similar way, the impurities in crystals could be distributed according to specified patterns, and molecules could be constructed by pushing atoms into place. This technique, which uses mechanical force to break chemical bonds, is sometimes called called mechanochemistry.

Assemblers and nanobots

Nanotechnology currently uses macroscopic devices, guided by human instruction, to perform tasks at the nanometer scale. The technology will have reached fruition only when these tasks are performed automatically by machines whose own dimensions are tens of nanometers.

The key to the achievement of this goal will be the construction of assemblers: machines that are capable of making exact copies and scaled-down replicas of themselves. The first generation of assemblers will be made by macroscopic devices operating near their lower limits of scale. Then, the first-generation machines will make second-generation machines, which will make yet smaller third-generation machines, and so on. When the desired scale has been reached by progressive miniaturization, the resulting nanobots will continue to make further machines, but with no change in scale, in a process called replication. In fact, some programming element will have to be included to prevent replication from getting out of hand. It might be done by switching off replication when the average distance between nanobots falls below a threshold, for example.

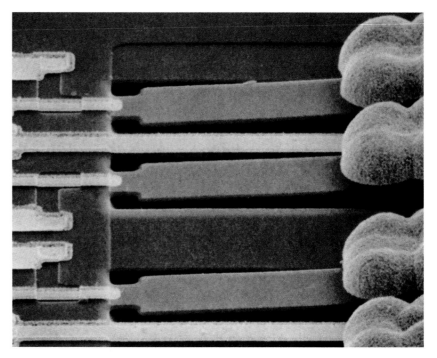

▲ These accelerometers are only 275 µm long. Smart sensors such as these are finding many new applications, including development of the "intelligent" automobile in which microprocessors control the automobile's performance.

The final-generation assemblers—nanobots—will be mechanically identical to the first generation machines. However, they will be able to perform tasks beyond the capabilities of larger machines because their tools will be of the appropriate sizes for the tasks. The most likely programming mechanism will use mechanical switches, based on rods whose positions indicate the zero and one of binary logic, that will interact by a mechanical interlocking system. A typical tool will be a rigid but jointed carbon nanotube arm whose pivots allow its tip to move in three dimensions and rotate around three perpendicular axes.

Given the appropriate tools, programming, and raw materials, it is hoped that the capabilities of nanorobots will be vast. Some will build molecular and quantum computers whose processing power will vastly exceed that of current devices. This will be an important advance, since the trend for processing power to increase continually is due to stop completely in 2010, when current technology will reaches its lower scale limit.

Other potential applications will be in the automatic degradation of toxic materials, such as dioxins, and in medicine, where nanobots floating in the bloodstream are hoped to be able to remove cholesterol deposits and tumorous cells efficiently and without the need for surgery. Nanobots will also be able to perform exact chemical syntheses with no waste products, thereby helping preserve natural resources.

FACT FILE

■ The earliest micromechanical devices were multiple tungsten electrodes some 50 µm (500 Å) in diameter. Made in the mid 1960s, these devices, whose individual electrodes were around 5 µm (50 Å) in diameter, served to detect signals from individual cells in a human brain. They therefore allowed neurologists to perform direct measurements of the firing patterns of nerve cells.

■ Carbon nanotubes, discovered in 1991, are hollow, rod-shaped molecules whose walls are formed by nets of carbon atoms arranged in hexagons. These tubes are excellent conductors, around 100 times as strong as steel, and the finest are 30 nm (300 Å) in diameter. Such tubes have been mounted on silicon-cantilever "springs" to form extremely tough tips for scanning-probe microscopes. They are likely to be the material of choice for the arms of nanometer-scale robots.

SEE ALSO: COMPUTER • INTEGRATED CIRCUIT • MICROPROCESSOR • MICROSURGERY • ROBOTICS • TRANSDUCER AND SENSOR

Micrometer

A micrometer caliper is a measuring device widely used in engineering to measure the diameter of round objects or the thickness of flat pieces. It consists of an accurately ground screw or spindle that is rotated in a fixed nut. The end of the spindle advances or retracts, opening or closing the distance to an anvil.

The thread grinding to the spindle is done with an almost diamond hard stone grinding wheel, and the thread is inspected rigorously. The pitch diameter taper tolerance and the uniformity of thread and pitch must be held to within 0.00005 in. (1.20 microns). With the micrometer assembled, the anvil and spindle faces are ground parallel and then lapped. The tolerance to which lapping must be held is about three lightbands, with flatness tied to within one lightband. (A lightband is a unit of measure used in interferometry, the measure of very small distances by the use of light. A lightband is the wavelength of sodium, a yellow color: 0.000011 in., or about ¼ micron.) Anvils are frequently faced with tungsten carbide for longer life.

A micrometer spindle that measures in inches has a pitch of 40 threads to the inch, so one complete turn of the spindle advances the spindle face exactly one-fortieth, or 0.025 in. The spindle revolves inside a fixed nut covered by a sleeve marked with a longitudinal line having 40 graduations. The outside shell of the micrometer spindle is called the thimble and has a beveled edge that covers these graduations as it is turned; on the beveled edge are 25 graduations corresponding to thousandths of an inch.

When the micrometer is closed, only the zero line can be seen on the sleeve next to the beveled edge of the thimble. A measurement is taken by reading the number of longitudinal graduations

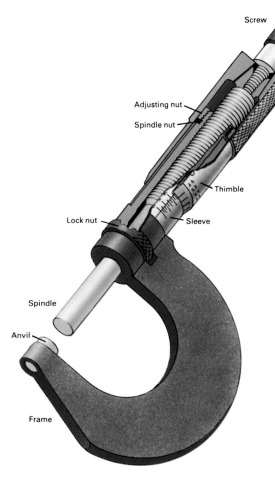

◀ To take a measurement using a micrometer, the object must be placed between the anvil and the spindle. The screw is then turned to bring the spindle down onto the object. Final adjustment is made by turning the thimble, and the measurement is read by adding together the readings on the sleeve and on the thimble.

▼ A machinist's micrometer that measures from zero to one inch in thousandths of an inch; it is open to 0.335 in. (8.5 mm).

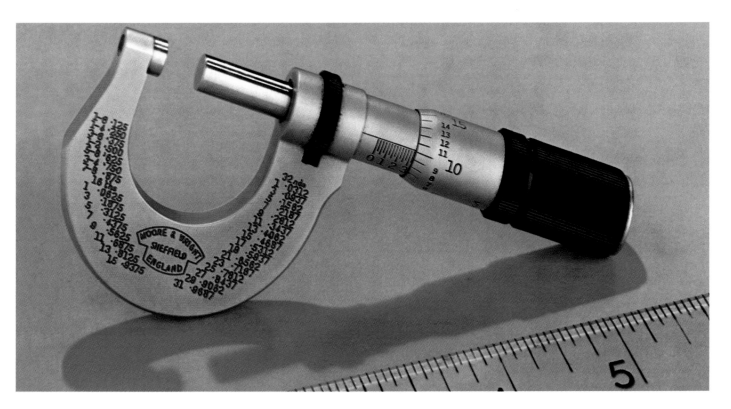

uncovered and adding the number of thousandths above the zero mark on the thimble. Thus, for example, measuring the size of a piece of metal of uniform cross section 0.259 in. in thickness, ten longitudinal lines will be uncovered on the sleeve (10 x 0.025 = 0.250, or ¼ in.) plus nine lines on the beveled edge of the thimble. Adding these two results together gives the total measurement.

Metric micrometers are used the same way. The pitch of the spindle thread is 0.5 mm, one revolution of the thimble advancing or retracting the spindle 0.5 millimeters. The longitudinal line on the sleeve is graduated from zero to 25 millimeters, and each millimeter is subdivided in half. The thimble is graduated in 50 divisions so that each graduation equals ⅕₀ of 0.5 mm, or 0.01 mm.

Micrometers are made in graduated sizes. The most common micrometer measures zero to one inch (or 0–25 mm); the next size is for measuring one inch to two inches, (or 25–50 mm), and so forth. Thus the spindle, thimble, and other parts are identical on all micrometers, and the size of the body of the instrument is the variant. When learning to use a micrometer, some practice is necessary to get the feel of the device—for example, the thimble is never tightened as though it were a clamp. Doing so would result in excess wear of the threads and inaccurate measurement. The object being measured should slip between the anvil and the spindle face without looseness

but without excessive tightness. A friction ratchet may be used to obtain uniform feel.

Adjustment to the micrometer is seldom necessary, but with constant use, play sometimes develops in the spindle because of wear of the spindle nut. By backing off the spindle, an adjusting nut becomes accessible, and by slightly tightening this nut, play is eliminated. Sleeve adjustment is possible by having the spindle and the anvil faces in contact and rotating the sleeve very slightly by means of a tiny wrench, supplied with the micrometer, until the line on the sleeve coincides perfectly with the zero line on the thimble.

Today, micrometers are often made with a liquid crystal display (LCD) or a light-emitting diode (LED) display, which saves the user the effort of having to add the measurements on the spindle and the thimble. Many micrometers are also made that can give both metric and standard measurements.

Micrometers are used by motor mechanics, instrument technicians, toolmakers, inspectors, and many others. An employee in a wire-rope factory will carry a micrometer and use it often to check the size of wires to be used in the cable-winding machinery.

▲ An electronic micrometer, which can measure up to 1 in. (25 mm) with great accuracy. Readings are clearly shown by means of a light-emitting diode (LED) display.

SEE ALSO: DIGITAL DISPLAY • MACHINE TOOL

Microphone

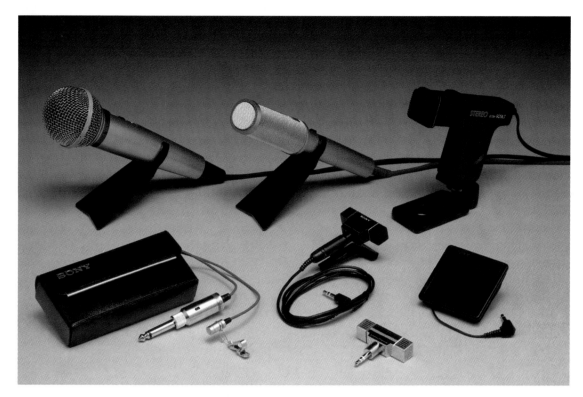

A microphone is a device that converts sound into electrical energy; as such, a microphone is a type of transducer, converting energy from one form into another. In general, a microphone contains a flexible diaphragm that responds to the changes in air pressure that constitute sound waves and produces an electrical signal whose amplitude follows the variations in air pressure of a sound.

There are various types of microphones, each converting sound energy into electric energy by a different mechanism. The principal types are carbon, moving-coil, ribbon, condenser, and crystal microphones. The choice of microphone for a given application is influenced by cost, size, sensitivity, directionality (ability to select sounds from specific directions), and frequency response.

Carbon microphones

The sound detector of a carbon microphone is a chamber that contains carbon granules between a flexible diaphragm and a rigid cup. The diaphragm and cup are both conductors, but they are electrically isolated from one another. One terminal of a direct-current supply is attached to the diaphragm, the other to the cup.

When sound waves strike the diaphragm, their pressure variations cause it to vibrate, thereby imposing a fluctuating pressure on the carbon granules. Since the conductivity of the mass of carbon granules increases when the granules are forced together, the fluctuating pressure causes

variations in electrical resistance (resistance is the inverse of conductivity). As a result, the current that flows between the cup and the diaphragm oscillates about a mean value in step with the pressure variations of the sound waves. This varying current is in effect the sum of an alternating current and a direct current, and the component that alternates is extracted by a transformer.

Since the carbon microphones respond to pressure variations on only one side of their diaphragms, they are called pressure-operated devices. In contrast, pressure-gradient-operated devices respond to differences in pressure between the two sides of a diaphragm.

Carbon microphones are sturdy and cheap to produce, making them the microphone of choice for telephones for many decades. Their frequency response is limited, however, and the granules are prone to clogging, which causes noisy signals. As a result, they have been largely superseded by superior and more compact condenser microphones in recent years.

Moving-coil and ribbon microphones

When a springlike conducting coil expands and contracts repeatedly in a magnetic field, an alternating electric current flows in the coil. Moving-coil microphones use this effect to create signals from the oscillations of a flexible diaphragm. The coil is attached to the diaphragm at one end and a permanent magnet at the other, causing the coil to expand and contract in the magnetic field in time with the vibrations of the diaphragm. The current thereby induced in the coil is directly related to the incident sound wave.

Ribbon microphones also use electromagnetic effects to produce electrical signals from sound. A corrugated metal ribbon strung between the poles of a permanent magnet acts as the diaphragm, and receives an induced current related to the incident sound wave. A ribbon microphone is an example of a pressure-gradient-operated device, since it responds to differences in pressure between the two faces of a ribbon.

Condenser microphones

Condenser microphones, found in many telephones and used with some computers, are so called because their key components are condensers, or electrostatic capacitors. A capacitor consists of two parallel conducting plates separated by an insulating material, such as air. When the plates are connected to the two terminals of a direct-current supply, opposite charges accumulate on the two plates, where they experience mutual attractions.

The density (number per unit area) of charges that accumulates on the plates of a capacitor is governed by the distance between the plates and the voltage. In a condenser microphone, the capacitor forms part of a circuit that keeps the voltage across its two plates constant. One plate of the capacitor is a flexible diaphragm that vibrates in response to incoming sound waves. As it vibrates, the mean distance between the two plates oscillates in time with the vibration. When the gap between the plates diminishes, charges rush to the plates; when the gap increases, they disperse to some extent. In this way, an alternating current arises when the diaphragm vibrates, and this current forms the basis of the microphone's output signal.

Condenser microphones are more compact than other types of microphones, respond consistently to a wide range of audible frequencies, are rugged, and are inexpensive to manufacture. These properties have enabled them to gain widespread acceptance in a variety of applications.

Electret microphones are related to conventional condenser microphones and work in a similar way. In place of the standard capacitor of a condenser microphone, they have capacitors in which one plate is an electret—a film of material whose two surfaces carry permanently opposed

▼ The four types of microphones illustrated here are, from top to bottom, carbon granule, moving coil, ribbon, and electrostatic (condenser). Each has its own way of converting sound into an electrical signal.

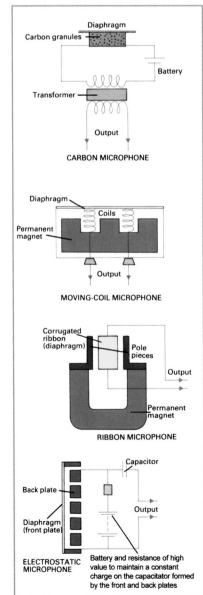

CARBON MICROPHONE

MOVING-COIL MICROPHONE

RIBBON MICROPHONE

ELECTROSTATIC MICROPHONE

charges from manufacture. This charge separation induces the other plate of the capacitor to accumulate a charge of opposite sign to that carried by the closer face of the electret. As the diaphragm vibrates under the influence of incoming sound waves, an alternating current is set up in the external circuit in the same way as occurs with a conventional condenser microphone. The advantage of an electret microphone is that it requires no power source to create the voltage across the plates of the capacitor.

Crystal microphones

Crystal microphones use the piezoelectric effect to produce electrical signals that correspond to sound waves. A piezoelectric material develops opposite charges on opposing crystal faces when subjected to compression. As such, incoming sound waves cause a fluctuating potential difference between opposing faces of a piezoelectric crystal that can be used to produce a signal.

Frequency response

An ideal microphone would respond to all audible frequencies with equal sensitivity so as to give a true representation of detected sound. In reality, a microphone's sensitivity varies across the frequency range, and this variation is called its frequency response.

The frequency response of a microphone is assessed by subjecting the device to sounds of various pitches (frequencies) but constant intensity while monitoring the strength of its output signal. The values of the output signal are converted into decibels (dB)—units used to compare sound intensities—and plotted graphically against the frequency of the calibrating sound.

The plot of sensitivity against frequency for an ideal microphone would be a horizontal line—a "flat" frequency response. While an ideal response is not achieved, high-quality microphones include circuitry that yields a reasonably level frequency response for audible frequencies.

Obstacle effect

The frequency response of a microphone is not merely a matter of overall sensitivity: the relative sensitivity to sounds from different directions also varies with frequency. This variation is due to a phenomenon called the obstacle effect.

The obstacle effect occurs because the ability of an object to reflect sound is significantly enhanced if the wavelength of that sound is shorter than the dimensions of the

DIRECTIONAL MICROPHONES

For a sound source of a fixed frequency and intensity, the sound energy detected by a microphone depends on the distance between the source and microphone. In general, this energy also depends on the angular position of the source relative to the centerline of the microphone. This dependence is called directionality.

Polar diagrams show the directional properties of microphones. In such diagrams, gradients of shading or arrow lengths can represent the sensitivities along different radii from a microphone. A series of diagrams can indicate sensitivities in horizontal planes above and below that of the microphone, or the data for several planes can be combined to produce a three-dimensional map on a computer screen. Each diagram may have several versions, depicting sensitivities at different frequencies.

Microphones that have spherically symmetrical polar diagrams are described as omnidirectional (from the Latin *omnis*, meaning "all"). They are used to detect ambient sounds, such as crowd noises.

Unidirectional microphones are highly selective in favor of sounds that come from one direction only. As such, they are useful in isolating the sound from a point source from background noise, such as comments from a targeted speaker in the audience of a televised debate.

▶ These polar diagrams portray the directional properties of four types of microphones: omnidirectional (1), highly unidirectional (2), cardioid (3), and bidirectional (4). The depth of color at each point represents that type of microphone's sensitivity to sound waves from that point.

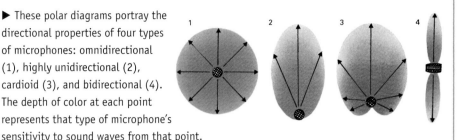

▼ A multitube line microphone (left) is highly unidirectional, since sound waves that strike its tubes from the front reach the detector in phase, whereas those that strike the tubes from the side are split into several phases by the different tubes, and these phases eliminate each other as a result of destructive interference at the detector.

A pressure-gradient-operated microphone (right) is bidirectional, since sound waves that strike from the front or rear create the pressure difference between the two surfaces of the diaphragm necessary for sound to register. Sound waves that strike from the side create the same pressure on both sides of the diaphragm, so no sound is detected.

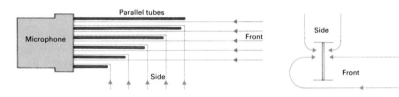

Cardioid microphones are so called because their polar diagrams are heart shaped (the Greek for "heart" is *kardia*). Such microphones have a heightened sensitivity to sounds from the forward direction, while detecting more sound from the sides and the rear than is detected by a highly unidirectional microphone. Such microphones are used

when it is desirable to emphasize sound from one direction while not completely excluding ambient sounds.

Bidirectional microphones have polar diagrams that are figure-of-eight shaped. They favor sounds from opposing directions to an equal extent and are therefore useful as table microphones for head-to-head debates between two speakers.

---

object. For a typical microphone, enhanced reflectance sets in at frequencies greater than around 1,000 Hz. Consequently, a pressure-operated microphone may be equally sensitive to sounds from all directions below that frequency, but increasingly selective in favor of sounds from one direction as frequency increases.

Long-range microphones

Under certain circumstances—surveillance work and wildlife observation are examples—it is necessary to detect sounds from faint or distant sources. In such cases, it is usual to employ a high-sensitivity microphone with an acoustic device that eliminates sounds from directions other than that of the target source. In general, the acoustic devices use destructive interference to eliminate background noise while constructive interference boosts sounds from the target.

In one such device—the rifle, or line, microphone—a number of parallel tubes guide sounds to the microphone. Sounds that arrive along the axis of the tubes follow paths of equal lengths through all tubes and arrive in phase at the microphone. Sounds from other directions follow paths of different lengths and cancel themselves out.

Sound from a single direction can be magnified using a parabolic reflector. Sounds that arrive parallel to the axis of the reflector converge in phase at its focal point, which is the location of the microphone. Sounds from other directions arrive with diverging phases at the focal point, so they cancel each other out. A typical reflector is around 3 ft. (1 m) in diameter.

SEE ALSO: ACOUSTICS • CAPACITOR • ELECTRET • ELECTROMAGNETISM • SOUND • SOUNDTRACK • TELEPHONE SYSTEM

Microprocessor

Microprocessors are complex integrated circuits that process binary information from input devices and provide instructions for the operation of electronic and electromechanical devices. Microprocessors are also called processors or, in computing, central processing units (CPUs).

The degree of complexity above which an integrated circuit can be described as a microprocessor has no distinct definition. The term *microprocessor* was first used to describe Intel's 4004 circuit of 1971, which had 2,300 transistors and was capable of performing 60,000 logic operations each second. The 4004 performed as the "brain" of an electronic calculator but was unable to support the calculations necessary for the operations of even the most basic computers.

Microprocessors started to develop more processing power with the introduction of large-scale integration (LSI), whereby 10,000 to 20,000 components were included on a single silicon chip. Very large scale integration (VLSI, 100,000 components or more per chip) soon followed, and current top-end microprocessors have many millions of components linked by tiny aluminum or copper wires. Such microprocessors can perform billions of logic operations each second.

The progressive miniaturization of integrated circuits, coupled with increasing economies of scale in production, has caused a relentless reduction in the cost of processing power. This cost reduction has had a twofold effect: it has made powerful computers affordable within the budgets of many families and has led to microprocessors finding uses in applications other than computing. For example, the engine-management systems used in some modern cars have microprocessors at their core. Instead of taking their inputs from devices such as keyboards, these microprocessors use signals from sensors to determine the ideal fuel-to-air ratio. On this basis, they provide control signals for the operation of the engine's fuel-injection system.

Basics

The basic element of a microprocessor is the MOSFET—metal-oxide-semiconductor field-effect transistor, so called because it consists of a trilayer of metal (conductor), silicon dioxide (insulator), and doped-silicon semiconductor. A voltage applied to the metal contact creates an electrical field in the doped silicon. The field redistributes the charge carriers in the semiconductor and thereby enables it to conduct. Removing the voltage returns the semiconductor to its nonconducting state. The two states of a MOSFET—conducting and nonconducting—express the 0 and 1 of binary logic.

When groups of transistors are combined in appropriate circuits, the output signals of such circuits depend in a logical manner on the combination input signals. (In fact, the NOT circuit has a single input: its output is the inverse of its input, so 0 becomes 1, and 1 becomes 0.) Combinations of such circuits provide the decision-making capability of a microprocessor.

Internal architecture

The designers of microprocessors refer to the layout of an integrated circuit as its internal architecture. The design of this architecture is the most expensive element of microprocessor development, and it has a far-reaching impact on the performance of a microprocessor.

The way logic circuits are distributed on the surface of a silicon chip has an enormous impact on microprocessor performance: the signals that pass between circuits in the course of a calculation are carried by electrons, so the speed of calculations is influenced by how far those electrons must travel between circuits. Progressive miniaturization has helped improve this performance aspect by reducing the sizes of components and therefore shortening the paths between them.

▼ This enlarged photograph of a microprocessor chip shows the complexity of the circuitry. Thousands of circuit elements are contained in a tiny area—and with improved production methods, the number is expected to increase several times. Computer-aided circuit design will also ensure that future chips are more efficient and cheaper to produce than at present. The biggest factor in reducing costs, however, is the vast number of microchips that will be needed in the future, enabling design, development, and manufacturing costs to be spread over a large number of chips.

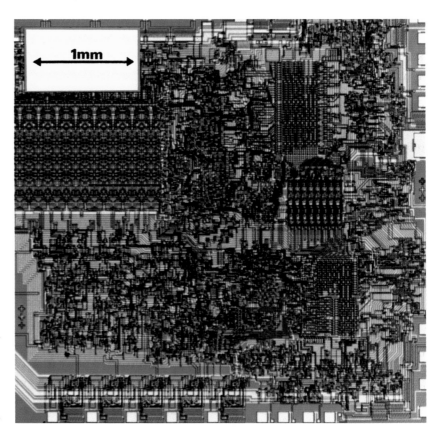

1mm

Microprocessor designers strive to achieve optimum performance from a chip by minimizing the distances between circuits that will be in most frequent contact. Computer simulations are of great help in evaluating and comparing different circuit-layout options.

A microprocessor designer must also decide what proportion of logic circuits have permanent connections—hardwired logic circuits—as against those that form within a matrix of transistors as a result of program instructions. In general, simple microprocessors destined to perform a limited range of tasks have more hardwiring, and thus have the advantage of great reliability. Such microprocessors are used in the control systems of washing machines, for example. In contrast, microprocessors for use in computers have little hardwiring. Therefore, most of their transistors are available for forming circuits according to programmed instructions—an approach that results in extremely versatile processors.

A further design choice concerns the amount of random-access memory (RAM) that will be included in the microprocessor chip. A microprocessor uses RAM to store data between calculations. Integrating RAM with a microprocessor reduces its dependence on external RAM, which responds more slowly because of the greater lengths of wires between the processor and the RAM. In practice, this choice tends to be made by the marketing team of a microprocessor manufacturer: RAM is expensive, and the pressure for lower unit costs can outweigh the benefit of increased performance brought by integral RAM.

Production

When the circuit design has been established—often after several years of work—the design must be converted into real integrated circuits on silicon chips. Such chips are manufacture by a series of etching and deposition processes. Selective etching is achieved by protecting the majority of the surface of a silicon chip with a light-cured resin. The chip is first coated with an emulsion of the resin, and the areas that are to be protected are exposed to light to cure a protective film. The uncured resin is then washed away and the unprotected areas are etched by a chemical reagent.

Each etching process therefore requires a mask that allows light to pass to the areas to be protected from etching. These masks are first produced on film at around 250 times the scale of the circuits that will be formed on the actual chip.

The creation of such films is facilitated by computer programs, and the dimensions of the etched components must take into account the physical limitations of the etching process,

▶ Semiconductors being loaded into a carrier ready for doping, in which semiconducting regions are formed.

▲ A designer drawing a circuit for etching onto a microchip. He can make modifications to the design using a light pen and sophisticated computer software.

because light can only produce well defined areas of cured film if the dimensions of those areas are greater than the wavelength of the light used for curing. The greater the frequency of the light (and thus the shorter the wavelength), the finer the detail that can be achieved on the finished chip.

Once the large-scale masks are complete, they are reduced in scale for use in the photoetching of the chips. Several hundreds of chips are produced on a single wafer of silicon by etching and deposition. The chips are then tested individually, and those that fail to function within the established specifications are marked for rejection. The wafer is then cut into chips, and the approved chips pass to the next manufacturing stage.

The final stage in the production of a microprocessor is its preparation for use in a larger system. This stage entails the addition of conductive leads through which the processor will communicate with external circuits and enclosure in a protective plastic casing. The conductive leads protrude through the casing or form part of a board that fits a slot with matching electrical contacts, or they are left free to be welded into contact with the conductive traces on a circuit board.

Uncommitted logic arrays

The cost of producing a new microprocessor can be reduced to some extent by designing the processor to be made from an off-the-shelf component called an uncommitted logic array, or ULA. Such devices are silicon chips on which numerous unconnected logic elements have been produced. A microprocessor designer selects the appropriate elements for a given function and indicates how they should connect to give the desired circuit. The connection process involves only the production of a mask for the final metal layer of the chip and is therefore much less expensive than a fully custom-made chip. However, a high proportion of the logic elements on a ULA may remain unused, and the circuit layout may be less than ideal for agile processing.

Instruction sets

The commands that a microprocessor subcircuit can obey depend on the details of its component logic circuits and are called its instruction set. Most computer languages are written at a higher level, with each instruction corresponding to several logic operations, and must first be translated by dedicated circuits into signals that can be interpreted by the logic subcircuits. Such signals are called machine code.

For a while, there were two divergent schools of thought directed at achieving optimal performance from a microprocessor: CISC and RISC. In CISC—an acronym of *complex instruction set computing*—each instruction performs a complex logic operation; in RISC—*reduced instruction set computing*—the logic operations are less complex than CISC operations. They are therefore less productive but take less time. At present, the consensus appears to be to adopt a middle ground of intermediate speed and complexity of operations.

MMX processors gain processing speed by using a single instruction to perform the same operation on multiple sets of data. This approach is particularly effective in the handling of audio and video data, and thus, the label MMX has been widely accepted as deriving from *multimedia extensions* (extension here referring to an extension of the basic instruction set). An alternative derivation of the acronym MMX is *matrix-math extensions*, a phrase that refers to the mathematical basis of MMX processing.

Central processing units

The processing core of any computer is a microprocessor called its central processing unit, or CPU. Instead of using simple on-off binary instruction signals, CPUs process "words" that consist of several binary digits, or bits. Most current CPUs work with 32-bit words for processing and for communication with memory chips and peripheral devices such as disk drives, keyboards, monitors, printers, and scanners.

A CPU consists of three main elements: a control unit that performs the program instructions, an arithmetic-and-logic unit (ALU), and a set of storage registers. These elements are linked together with external system components by conducting paths called buses. Each bus consists of several connectors or lines, the number of which depends on the function of the bus.

In the case of data buses that transfer digital data between the operating elements, the number of lines corresponds to the word length used by the microprocessor (32 lines in a 32-bit device, for example). The address bus carries signals from the control unit to direct the data to specific memory locations, or addresses, and an 8-bit processor would have 16 lines, allowing up to 2^{16} (65,536, or 64 k) locations to be accessed. A control bus has 10 or more lines carrying signals that control functions such as the reading and writing of data from individual elements or the direction of flow along the data bus.

In operation, the control unit transfers the first part of a set of instructions (program) from memory to an instruction register via the data bus. The control unit then decodes the first word of the instruction using a series of logic units to produce the internal working commands. These commands include control signals to read additional material from memory when required and instructions to transfer or process data, and they are directed to the appropriate working elements along the control bus.

The data being worked on in any given step are held in the registers, with the accumulator being a special register used to hold the results of arithmetic operations. Another specific register, the program counter, is used to keep track of the program steps so that they are carried out in the proper order. Processing of the data is carried out

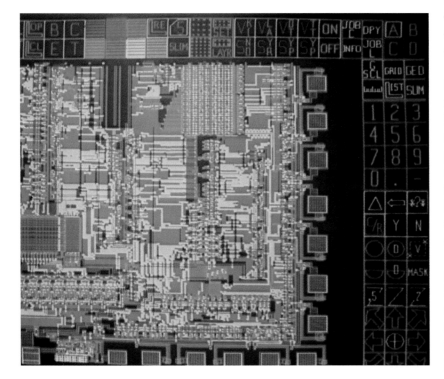

▼ A computer screen shows the planning stages of a microchip. Once the circuit has been finalized, it is transferred to a solid material to form a mask. Light is then shone through the mask onto the silicon, and the chip is finally formed during a series of etchings and chemical washes.

LANDMARK PROCESSORS

During the last three decades of the 20th century, the pace of development of microprocessors for computers was set by the Intel Corporation. Some notable innovations are listed here.

1971: 4004
The first commercial microprocessor, this circuit was the processing core of the Busicom electronic calculator.

1972: 8008
This model had twice the processing power of the 4004 and was used in a primitive home computer in 1974.

1976: 8088
This model became the core of IBM's revolutionary PC (personal computer), which established a market for home computing.

1982: 80286
The "286" was a processor of the class of computer that would sell more than 15 million units before being superseded.

1985: Intel386
The "386" had more than 100 times the transistors of the 4004 and could multitask—run several programs at one time.

1989: Intel486 DX
Use of a dedicated mathematical co-processor boosted performance by freeing the main processor of calculating tasks.

1993: Pentium
The Pentium was designed specifically to have enhanced performance when handling sound and photographic images.

1997: Pentium II
The Pentium II included MMX data handling to improve performance, particularly with video and audio data.

▲ A close-up image of circuit components on a Pentium microprocessor. Pentium chips vastly increased the ability of home computers to handle multimedia data.

1999: Pentium III
A total of 9.5 million transistors increased yet further the Pentium's capacity for multimedia data streams from the Internet.

2001: Pentium 4
Intel entered the 21st century with a processor geared for three-dimensional gaming and digital multimedia files.

in the arithmetic and logic unit, which enables addition and subtraction of both binary and decimal numbers together with the logic operations AND, OR, and Exclusive OR.

Clock speed and performance

The rate at which processors perform calculations and logic operations is governed by a clock signal, which synchronizes the movement of data within the chip. Clock speeds, quoted in megahertz and gigahertz, are the nominal frequencies with which processor operations occur. The clock is not the only measure of performance, however, since different processor and system designs can result in wide variations in processing speeds for the same value of processor clock speed.

Pipelining is one technique that improves performance for a given clock speed. A pipelined processor has several channels that can process information in parallel, so that five such channels can give a fivefold increase in processing speed for a given clock speed, for example.

The availability of RAM also has an influence on performance at a given clock speed. The speed of RAM access determines how many clock cycles will be missed while waiting for data from the RAM—a situation complicated by the fact that some RAMs run by clocks that are slower than the main clock. In general, a processor that has its own RAM cache will miss fewer cycles than a processor that relies on external RAM. In contrast, a processor that uses virtual RAM—hard-drive space configured as RAM—will suffer greater delays while waiting for information from the hard drive.

A number of benchmark tests exist for comparing the performances of processors. Such tests should be viewed with caution, however, since processor manufacturers tend to promote tests that are favorable for their own products.

SEE ALSO: COMPUTER • COMPUTER GRAPHICS • ELECTRONICS • INTEGRATED CIRCUIT • SEMICONDUCTOR • TRANSISTOR

Microscope, Electron

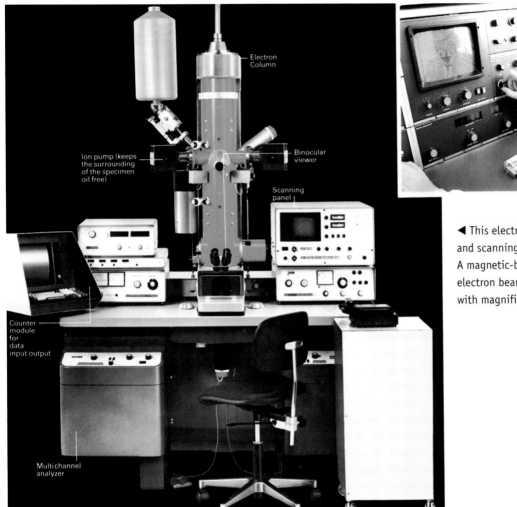

Electron Column

Ion pump (keeps the surrounding of the specimen oil free)

Binocular viewer

Scanning panel

Counter module for data input output

Multichannel analyzer

◄ A scientist tunes in the image on the screen of the scanning electron microscope. It has 30 times the power of optical microscopes and 300 times the depth of field.

◄ This electron microscope provides transmission- and scanning-electron-microscope images. A magnetic-beam alignment system centers the electron beam, and a digital system matches focus with magnification.

The electron microscope was developed to examine specimens in much greater detail than had been previously possible using an ordinary microscope, more correctly known as the light microscope. It has proved extremely useful in studying metals as well as biological samples, such as cultures, viruses, and cancerous tissue.

In 1873, a German physicist, Ernst Abbe, proved that in order to distinguish clearly between two particles situated closely together, the light source must have a wavelength no more than twice the distance between the particles. This theory therefore applies to adjacent points in a specimen.

The ability to clearly distinguish two particles is called resolution, which should not be confused with magnification. No matter how many times something is magnified, if its image is blurred it will always be so. The wavelength of visible light is approximately 5,000 angstroms (500 nm). Thus, the minimum details resolvable under a light microscope would be 2,500 angstroms (250 nm) units apart.

In the search for a new type of microscope, scientists began to study the electron, and found that accelerated electrons travel with a wave motion similar to that of light but over 100,000 times shorter. Researchers found that either electrostatic or electromagnetic fields could be used to control an electron beam, these lenses behaving in much the same way as a glass lens does in focusing a beam of light. Gradually, during the 1930s, the electron beam and its control by magnetic lenses were developed to produce shadow pictures of specimens until, in 1939, the first commercial electron microscope, capable of resolving 24 angstroms (2.4 nm), became available. Since the first commercial instrument, designers have worked toward higher resolutions until today's instruments are capable of resolving 2 angstroms (0.2 nm) as a matter of routine.

The electron microscope is an example of accelerated 20th-century technology reaching an advanced stage of development in less than 20 years, whereas it had taken 300 years to perfect the light microscope.

Transmission electron microscope

The first electron microscope was known as a transmission electron microscope, because the electron beam was passed through an ultrathin sample. The variation in density of the specimen resulted in a variation in the brightness of the corresponding area of the shadow image. The transmission electron microscope consists of a vacuum column, which is essential for the free passage of the electrons. A tungsten hairpin filament, the cathode, is heated to a point at which it emits electrons. By applying 20,000 to 100,000 volts between the cathode and the anode, the electron beam is accelerated down the column. (This system is called an electron gun.) Condenser lenses control the beam size and brightness before it strikes the specimen, which is mounted on a three-millimeter diameter copper-mesh grid. The electron beam is focused and magnified by the objective lens before being further magnified and transferred onto a viewing screen by the intermediate and projector lenses.

Most instruments cover the magnification range of x50 to x800,000. The screen is made of phosphorescent material (zinc phosphide), which glows when struck by the electron beam, and beneath the screen is located a camera for recording the image. Micrographs are not usually recorded at the highest magnification of the particular electron microscope, as it is easier to enlarge them later by photographic processes.

The limitation of the transmission electron microscope (as well as the conventional microscope) is that it can focus on only a limited depth of field of the specimen.

Scanning electron microscope

In 1965, a second type of electron microscope became available with a depth of field enabling the study of specimens in three dimensions. This new instrument was known as the scanning electron microscope. It employs a column very similar to that of the transmission instrument, consisting of an electron gun and condenser lenses, which are used to bounce the electron beam off the surface of the specimen. Situated in the condenser lenses are a pair of coils that deflect a small beam spot across the surface; linked to this scanning system is a cathode-ray tube (CRT), and its electron beam is scanned across the screen in sequence with the scanning beam in the microscope. The electron beam hitting the surface of the specimen drives off secondary electrons, which are drawn toward a detector that, via an amplifier, sends a signal to the grid of the CRT. The greater the number of electrons leaving the specimen, the brighter the corresponding spot on the CRT. The magnification of the image

◀ This false-color micrograph of hollyhock pollen has been produced using a scanning electron microscope. Because electron microscopes do not use visible light, the images they produce are monochrome. Therefore, color is often added artificially to highlight certain parts of the image.

depends on the relationship between the size of the area scanned and the size of the CRT, varying between 10 and 200,000 times. The image can be processed by the operator for brightness, contrast, and display of either a negative or positive image. A conventional polaroid camera or a roll-film camera can be used to record the scanned image.

The smaller the size of the scanned spot, the higher the resolution achieved, but as the spot is decreased, the energy that it contains decreases. A balance between the energy required to drive off the secondary electrons and the minimum spot size results in a resolution limit of 10 angstroms (1 nm) in present-day instruments.

Scanning transmission electron microscope

A third type of microscope, first developed in the 1960s and commercially available in 1973, is the scanning transmission electron microscope, or STEM. It combines the most prominent features of its predecessors. The STEM has a new type of electron gun called a field emission source. The instrument scans the electron beam across the specimen, causing the sample to emit electrons that are then collected by a detector, and the image is produced through a conventional scanning display system. The field emission source enables a high-energy beam, as fine as a few angstroms in diameter, to be produced. Thus, the instrument is able to provide resolution as high as the transmission electron system with the flexibility and image display of the scanning electron microscope.

High-voltage electron microscopes have been made that operate at voltages up to 1,500 kilovolts and produce electrons of enormously high energy. This ability enables scientists to study specimens many times thicker than those studied with conventional instruments.

Specimen preparation

In electron microscopy, specimen preparation is divided into two categories: transmission, including scanning transmission, and surface scanning. Biological transmission specimens usually undergo a complex preparation before being cut into very thin sections with an expensive instrument called an ultramicrotome; the conventional specimen thickness range extends between 400 and 1,000 angstroms (40–100 nm). Metallurgical specimens are usually thinned down to less than 1,000 angstroms by means of electrochemical polishing. Sometimes metal specimens containing particles can be examined as suitably transparent replica films, formed by deposition onto a thin plastic film that has been previously coated on a specimen grid. On the other hand, specimens for surface scanning are often examined with little or no preparation, but if a sample is nonconducting, a thin layer of gold may be deposited upon its surface to provide good contrast with the scattering of electrons.

Scanning tunneling microscopes

Scanning tunneling microscopes (STM) were developed in 1981 and enable scientists to create images of the atomic structure of surfaces. A tungsten needle is placed close to the surface of the sample, and a small voltage is applied between the two, causing electrons to tunnel across the gap. The needle is scanned across the surface of the sample, and any differences in the tunneling current are measured and used to create an image of the material's surface.

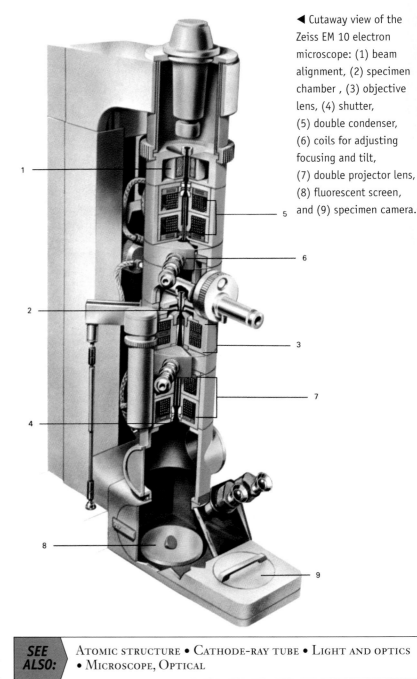

◀ Cutaway view of the Zeiss EM 10 electron microscope: (1) beam alignment, (2) specimen chamber , (3) objective lens, (4) shutter, (5) double condenser, (6) coils for adjusting focusing and tilt, (7) double projector lens, (8) fluorescent screen, and (9) specimen camera.

SEE ALSO: ATOMIC STRUCTURE • CATHODE-RAY TUBE • LIGHT AND OPTICS • MICROSCOPE, OPTICAL

Microscope, Optical

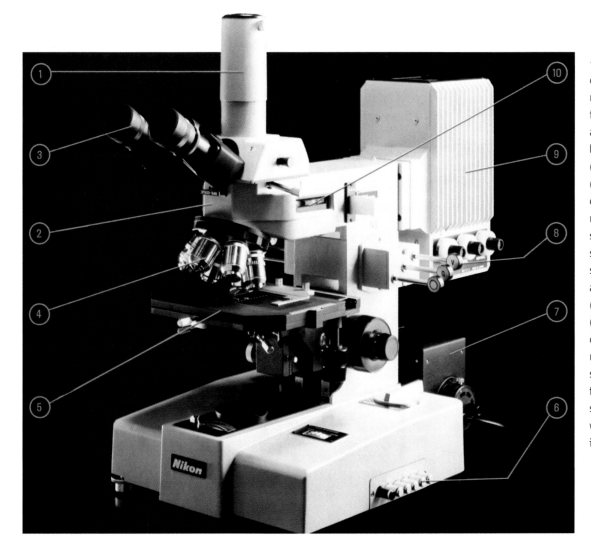

◄ Some of the features of the fluorescence microscope: (1) phototube for optional camera attachment, (2) UV light-absorption filter, (3) stereo eyepiece, (4) carousel, which allowes objectives of different magnifications to be selected, (5) stage for specimens, (6) base selectors, which allow a choice of filters, (7) halogen light source, (8) focusing control of collector lens, (9) mercury-vapor light source, (10) excitation filter, which allows selection of exact wavelength for illumination.

The use of two lenses gives the light microscope its alternative name of compound microscope. It is based on the principle that the image formed by one lens (the objective, next to the specimen) is further magnified by a second lens (the eyepiece) to give much higher magnifying powers than could be obtained by a simple magnifying glass alone. The microscope, which has uses in all branches of science and technology, is one of the most valuable instruments ever invented.

The compound microscope was probably invented by Dutch spectacle makers, Hans and Zacharias Janssen, in about 1600. It became well known through the work of a British scientist, Robert Hooke, in England, especially through publication of his book *Micrographia* in 1665. During the 18th century, the instrument was largely a plaything, but by 1830, the objective had been improved from a simple lens to a high-quality achromatic system (where the image is free from false colors), largely through the work of a British scientist, Joseph Jackson Lister. Many

other people contributed to the perfection of the instrument in the next 50 years, and by 1880 the German physicist Ernst Abbe pushed the microscope to its practical limit—a usable range of magnification from about x30 to x2000.

This maximum useful magnification cannot be exceeded, because of the nature of light itself—a form of electromagnetic radiation. Light is a wave motion, and it is the nature of a wave, for example, a water wave on a pond, that it is unimpeded by an obstruction smaller than its wavelength. If a wave is not altered in any way by an obstacle, then as far as an observer detecting the wave is concerned, nothing can be seen. For this reason, no microscope that uses light can pick out an object smaller than the wavelength of its light. Therefore, although it would be possible to make a microscope that would magnify more than x2000 (for example, just by using a stronger eyepiece), because the resolution (ability to separate fine detail) is fixed not by the instrument but by the nature of light itself, further magnification would not give better resolution. Thus, to resolve details closer together than 2,500 angstroms, or 0.00025 mm, an electron microscope must be used. Electrons, which are usually considered particles, can behave as waves. This wave-particle nature is a fundamental property of all matter and radiation. Electron waves have much shorter wavelengths than light waves.

Illumination

The microscope is arranged for either transmitted illumination, where the light goes through the specimen, or for reflected illumination, where the light bounces back from the specimen. Transmitted lighting is more usual today. The light source for most work is an electric lamp, as daylight is not intense enough. In some instruments, the light is built into the stand itself, making use of the microscope more convenient. If a separate lamp is used, the light has to be carefully directed up through the specimen by means of a mirror. On advanced instruments, the lamp is complicated, with a lamp condenser and lamp iris controlling the light from a compact-filament bulb.

For the best results, a substage condenser is used to concentrate a beam of light accurately on

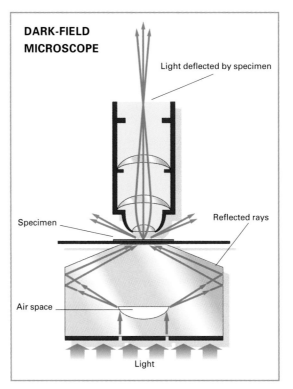

DARK-FIELD MICROSCOPE

Light deflected by specimen

Specimen

Reflected rays

Air space

Light

◄ In a dark-field microscope, the only light seen is that which is scattered off the specimen. Various parts of cell structures will scatter the light differently and can be distinguished in this way.

the specimen on the stage. Although for low-power work the condenser is not vital, for other requirements, the illumination is not sufficiently intense without a condenser, which also has an iris diaphragm used to control the angle of the light reaching the specimen. After passing through the specimen slide, the light reaches the objective. This lens system may be very complicated and expensive, containing as many as 14 separate lenses, some only 1 mm in diameter, very carefully arranged relative to each other. The higher the magnification of the objective, the more complicated it becomes; in addition, there are special types, such as flatfield objectives for photomicrography and apochromatic objectives—having both chromatic aberration and spherical aberration (where the image is not focused at a point, but fuzzy) corrected to a high degree. For convenience, several objectives are usually carried on a revolving nosepiece.

On a modern research microscope, the range of powers of the objectives might be x3, x6, x10, x20, x40, and x100. At the top end of the body tube is the eyepiece, which is also available in various powers. A usual range today would be x6, x10 and x15. The total magnification is given simply by multiplying the power of the objective by that of the eyepiece, so the range of magnifications available, with the six objectives and three eyepieces mentioned above, would be from x18 to x1,500. Stereoscopic microscopes, which provide a binocular view of specimens through the use of pairs of lenses, are useful in areas such as microsurgery and dissection of biological specimens.

FACT FILE

■ The electron probe microanalyzer is a modified electron microscope that causes its target to emit X rays by bombarding it with electrons. Varying X-ray energies indicate different chemical elements, and the composition of specimens can be mapped without sampling or destroying the substance being analyzed.

■ The oil immersion lens, invented by Ernest Abbe in the late 19th century, had a thin layer of cedarwood oil covering the specimen. The oil barrier decreased distortion caused by bending light, allowing focus closer than 1/25 in. and magnification of up to x 2000.

■ Before the microscope investigations of Antonie van Leeuwenhoek in 17th-century Holland, it was generally believed that many life forms were spontaneously generated from their physical environment. Van Leeuwenhoek proved that weevils and fleas do not spring from corn grains or dirt and dust but are hatched from eggs.

For practical reasons, however, these microscopes can magnify only between x5 and x50.

When setting up a microscope, the alignment of the optical components, from the lamp to the eyepiece, is of great importance; modern microscopes have the most useful arrangement preprogrammed. Similar principles apply if the instrument is used with reflected light, for example, when studying the surfaces of metals.

Other methods

In addition to the straightforward types of illumination mentioned above, which have not changed in essence since the instrument was first invented, the 20th century has seen the addition of three new techniques. Phase-contrast illumination allows specimens that appear almost invisible by normal illumination to be seen clearly and is thus of major importance for direct investigation of living cells. Stains that may enhance the contrast between different parts of a specimen may also kill it if it is living. The system was invented by a Dutch physicist, Frits Zernicke, in the 1930s and relies on condenser and objective pairs arranged in such a manner that light going through part of the condenser is slowed down relative to the rest and is thus put out of phase. In normal circumstances, this phase shift is undone at a phase plate in front of the objective. But when a specimen is introduced, variations in refractive index across its surface cause delays in some of the light. These delays mean that some light is shifted to positions on the phase plate where its phase shift is not undone. The differences in refractive index across the specimen, therefore, show up as differences in light and shade.

Interference microscopy also relies on the interference of light beams with each other and was developed after the phase-contrast microscope had shown the advantages of the method. The beam of light is split into two, one of which goes through the specimen and is modified by it before being recombined with the first beam. Differences in the light-retarding properties of the specimen show up as differences in light and shade again. The advantage is that actual precise measurements of the thickness of objects and other dimensions can be made.

Fluorescence microscopy requires the minimum of specialized equipment but does need

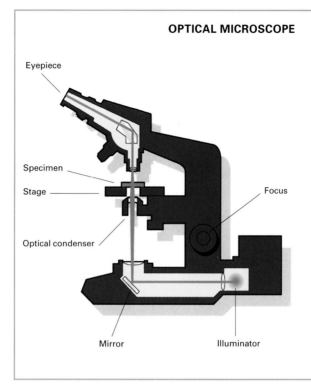

OPTICAL MICROSCOPE

Eyepiece

Specimen

Stage

Optical condenser

Focus

Mirror

Illuminator

▲ Objects to be viewed with an optical microscope have to be either thin or translucent so that light can pass through them. The light is provided from underneath the specimen by means of a mirror or lamp. Compound microscopes have two main lens systems. Objective lenses near the stage produce a magnified version of the specimen. The ocular lenses in the eyepiece then further enlarge the image produced by the objective lens. The image is brought into focus by adjusting the stage up or down, which alters the distance between the specimen and the lenses.

staining techniques developed for this method. The principle is that blue or ultraviolet illumination is used to make parts of a specially treated specimen emit light of various colors. Barrier filters absorb the light used to illuminate the specimen, which shows up only in the colors generated by the technique.

Mounting specimens

The modern microscope is versatile and relatively simple to use; many of the accessories thought essential in the last century are now being superseded. By itself, though, the instrument may be of little use: preparation of specimens for viewing through it is also most important, for most things are far too large to be viewed directly. The most usual technique is to make a slice of a specimen so that it is thin enough to be transparent. It will then need staining with colored dyes to make the structure clear, and it will need mounting on a protective slide surrounded by a resin such as Canada balsam to give it the correct characteristics for viewing.

Other means of illuminating specimens show to advantage with some older slides. Two techniques have come down from Victorian times, dark-field illumination and polarized illumination, and they can still give useful results. In dark-field work, all direct light is cut off by a disk under the substage condenser so that only very oblique rays are bent upward by the specimen to enter the objective. As a result, the specimen shows up brilliant white on a black background, an effect especially useful for extremely small living things.

Polarized lighting requires polarizing filters, one below the specimen and one somewhere above, and relies on one of the properties of light as a wave motion, which is that wave displacement occurs at all angles to the line of direction of the beam. Use of a polarizing filter cuts off all angles except a very few. If two such filters are used at right angles to each other, no direct light can pass, but if the specimen is a crystal, it may be able to alter some of the waves to enable them to pass through the second filter.

SEE ALSO: Lens • Light and optics • Microscope, electron • Microsurgery • Photomicrography

Microsurgery

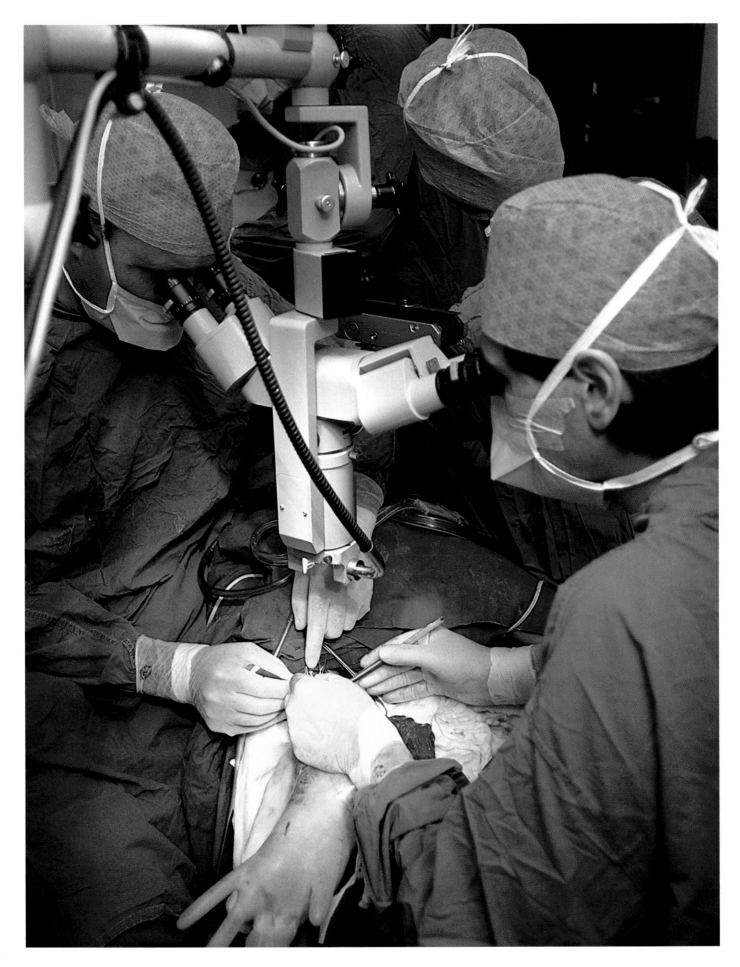

Microsurgery is a specialized surgical technique based on the use of a surgical microscope to give an enlarged view of the very small elements, such as blood vessels or nerves, being worked on.

A major application is in the transplanting or restoration of damaged tissue where small arteries and veins have to be joined up to restore the blood flow to and from the tissue. This technique of joining arteries is known as anastomosis and is regularly used on the larger blood vessels, down to a minimum of around 3 mm in diameter. It was found that below this size, naked-eye operations were impracticable owing to the problems of accurately positioning and manipulating the vessels, even when they could be identified. A further difficulty lay in the fact that the instruments used were of a comparable size to the vessels concerned so that, for example, the holes left by a needle during stitching were large enough to cause significant damage and subsequent leakage. Development of microsurgical techniques from the 1960s onward made it possible to carry out the procedure on significantly smaller veins and arteries, down to 1 mm in diameter.

Another application of microsurgical techniques is in the joining of nerve fascicles (bundles), a procedure known as a fascicular repair. The same principles can be applied to reverse the effects of a vasectomy. Microsurgery also allows surgery to be carried out on areas that were previously very difficult to get at, such as on parts of the eye, the spinal cord, and the brain. A related technique is arthroscopy, in which instruments are inserted into joints through surface incisions to examine them and carry out whatever surgery may be necessary.

Microsurgery is a very delicate technique that calls for considerable manipulative skills on the part of the surgeon and regular practice to maintain standards. Every effort is made to ensure the potency (strength) of repairs, since the failure of a single anastomosis can lead to failure of the whole operation. Extensive use is made of animal subjects for training and for the development of new techniques.

Equipment

The most important single piece of equipment is, of course, the operating microscope, with magnifications of around x15 to x25 being common. Binocular eyepieces are fitted with two or even three sets of eyepieces, allowing the principal surgeon and assistants to view the progress of the operation at the same time. Light sources are built in with fiber-optic systems taking the light down from the source to the microscope head, where it is projected to illuminate the image area. The microscope is carried on substantial support with articulation to allow for easy positioning over the patient. Foot-operated controls may be provided for adjustment of the magnification with zoom-lens systems and for focusing, while motorized positioning is also used. Although not capable of giving such high magnifications, use is also made of magnifying eyepieces, or loupes, that can be fitted to eyeglass frames and thus move with the wearer's head.

In general, the instruments used for microsurgery are simple and of a size to fit comfortably in the hand, even though the working end may be very small. Typically, they may be 3.9 to 4.7 in. (10–12 cm) long for easy manipulation, although longer instruments are sometimes used in conjunction with a support.

The basic implements are forceps, for holding and manipulation, similar to jewelers' tools though the tips have to be particularly well smoothed to avoid snagging and damage to the tissue being worked on. Curved forceps are used to hold and control the needle, which may be as small as 50 microns in diameter with a monofilament thread (normally nylon) of around 20 microns. Cutting is carried out with scissors, while clamps are used to stop the blood flow in the veins and arteries being worked on. Double clamps on a frame are used to hold the cut ends to be joined in alignment.

During an operation, the exposed internal area of the body is kept free of blood by hemostasis, or stoppage of bleeding. While clamps are used for a temporary stoppage, more permanent methods involve tying off vessels or cauterizing them with a heated wire. Coagulation, or clotting, of the blood to close off a vessel can be achieved with the bipolar coagulator, which

◀ Microsurgeons perform a delicate operation under a microscope that allows two of them to view the site of the operation at the same time. Operating microscopes use a condenser lens to produce a high-intensity light that is directed by prisms to where it is needed. The light is reflected back via an objective lens, magnification changer, and prisms to the binocular eyepieces.

▼ Microsurgeons work with special instruments that have cutting edges small enough to repair the smallest blood vessels and nerves, yet large enough to be handled comfortably. Typically instruments may be 3.9 to 4.7 in. (10–12 cm) long but can be extended for use in areas that are more difficult to reach.

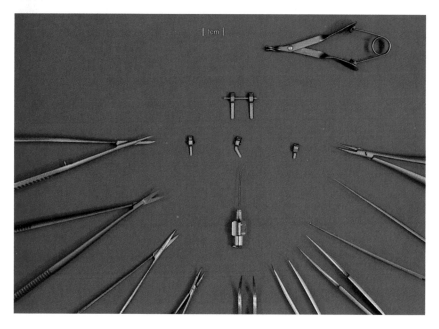

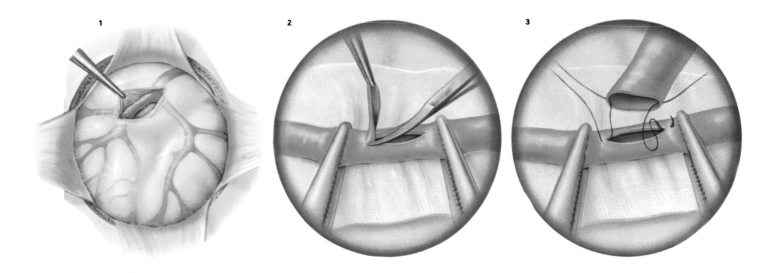

▲ In an operation on the brain of a stroke victim, the blocked cerebral artery is by-passed by a scalp artery, which assumes its task. Incisions are made in the scalp and skull (1), then the surgeon, working with a microscope, cuts an opening in the artery (2) and starts to sew the scalp artery to it (3, 4), until they are fully joined (5).

passes a current between two jaws on either side of the vessel, the heating effect of the current providing the seal.

Techniques

The techniques used are broadly similar to those in general surgery except that the scale is much smaller and precise movements are needed—even a slight tremor of the surgeon's hands can be enough to spoil the work. An idea of the general principles involved can be gained by considering the joining of two blood vessels—for example, when grafting tissue.

The first stage is to identify the vessels to be joined and then dissect them free of the surrounding tissue before clamping where the connection is to be made. The vessel is cut (assuming that it is complete) to make an end for the connection, and this free end is dilated (stretched) in preparation for the anastomosis (joining). The two vessels are lined up, taking care to avoid any kinks or twists, and clamped with their ends together and aligned with one another.

Using the forceps, the point of the needle is inserted through the wall of one vessel, close to the end, passed along inside to the other vessel and back out through the wall. Pulling the needle through takes the filament with it, and the ends of the filament are knotted together by manipulation with forceps to give a fine loop suture, or stitch, that pulls and then holds the two vessel ends together. This process is repeated several times (say, ten or more, depending on the vessel diameter) around the circumference of the two vessels to give a complete closure. Note that the sutures lie along the inside walls of the vessels and do not cross the central bore. When the joint is complete, the holding clamps are released and blood is allowed to flow along the joined vessel as

soon as possible. Any leakage of blood around the joint will result in a buildup of platelets that will seal the leaks. A slightly different technique uses a smaller number of sutures to hold the two vessels together with a fibrin (blood-clot) glue being applied around the joint to provide a seal.

Rapid restarting of the blood flow minimizes the risks of clotting in the vessel and also restores the blood supply to the tissue being worked on. The efficiency with which the blood flow has been restored to the tissue can be checked using a laser Doppler technique. Laser light is carried by a fiber-optic system to penetrate the tissue, where some of the light is scattered by reflections from red blood cells. This scattered light is detected by a set of photocells and processed, with Doppler changes in the light frequency giving a direct measurement of movement of the cells and so of the blood flow.

Anastomosis can be carried out between vessels of different sizes provided that the variation is no more than 50 percent. Where the mismatch is greater, a section of intermediate diameter is transplanted to make the connection.

Tissue transplants

Application of microsurgery techniques has had a considerable effect on the practice of plastic surgery, allowing the development of procedures that are not otherwise practicable. A typical example is in the transfer of large areas of skin and tissue from one part of the body to another. With previous techniques, such movements were limited to sideways steps by the need to keep existing blood vessel connections in place, but with microsurgery, a complete skin flap can be detached and reconnected in a new position. Typical donor areas for such skin flaps include the groin, upper chest and shoulder (delta-pectoral

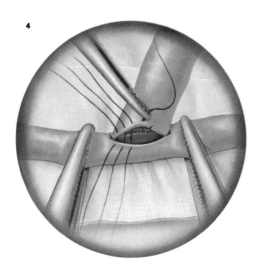

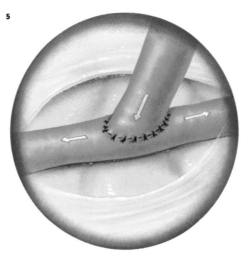

region), and the top of the foot or the forehead, while recipient areas include the head and neck, chest, arms, hands, and legs.

The recipient area has to have a suitable arterial blood supply, together with the venous return, and when selecting the donor area, the skin type and hair growth are matched to the donor area as closely as possible. Having identified the donor site, a suitable-size skin flap is selected, care being taken to ensure that it has good circulation. The circulation can be checked by isolating the flap before it is removed from the donor site, just leaving the connections to the vessels that will be used in the transplant.

A similar technique, used to transplant neuromuscular flaps, involves the connection of nerve bundles as well as the blood vessels. Free muscle has been transplanted in a similar manner.

Digit and limb replacement

One of the more spectacular examples of microsurgery lies in the replacement of digits and even complete limbs that have been severed in accidents. High success rates have been achieved; for example, over 60 percent of digital replacements are successful—and in many cases a failure is likely to be due to the poor condition of the replaced member rather than the operating technique. In such a case, the procedure involves shortening of the bones to allow tension-free joining of the skin, soft tissues and nerves, and blood vessels. As many vessels are reconnected as possible, the blood flow is restored rapidly to prevent tissue degeneration. Once the blood supply is restored (with any small unconnected blood vessels sealed to prevent bleeding), the nerves are aligned, along with the soft tissues and the tendons. Finally, the skin is closed after checking that the blood flow has been restored

and that there is no bleeding. Such operations do not always result in full restoration of the motor functions of the damaged member, and secondary operations may be required, though full success is not always possible.

In cases where a severed digit is lost or in an unsuitable condition for replacement, it is sometimes possible to use a substitute; a typical example is the replacement of a lost thumb with a big toe. This operation is only possible when some of the lower section of the thumb (below the second joint) is still present, since the end of the big toe has to be left in the foot to give stability when standing. Proper connection of the tendons and nerves—as well as the blood vessels—results in a working replacement for the thumb, although full articulation is not achieved because there is only one joint. If the first segment of the thumb is present, however, it is possible to just transplant the end of the toe, resulting in a fully functional digit.

Following successes in the reattachment of the patient's own limbs and digits, surgeons began to explore the possibility of transplanting limbs. In 1998, an international team of surgeons managed to transplant a hand from a dead body onto the arm of a man who had lost his arm 14 years previously. One year after surgery, the recipient could write, use a knife and fork, and hold items securely. However, after two years, the patient became unhappy about the hand and asked for it to be removed. Despite this early setback, a number of people have since had successful single and even double hand transplants.

Arthroscopy

In arthroscopy, a special type of endoscope, the arthroscope, is used to examine the condition of joints by passing it through a surface incision into

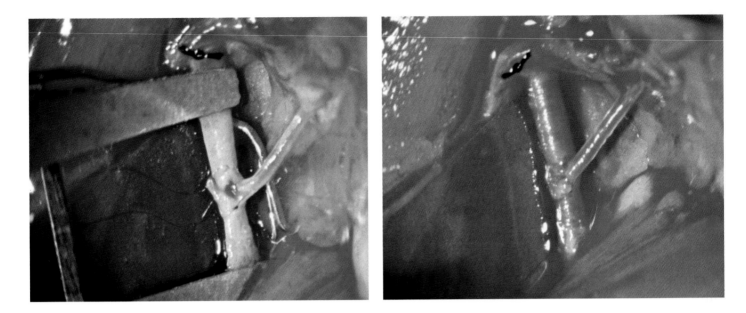

the joint. Light is carried down the arthroscope with a fiber-optic system to illuminate the joint, and in some designs, it is possible to feed instruments along the endoscope to work within the joint. More commonly, though, instruments are introduced directly and viewed using the arthroscope with typical operations including the repair of damaged cartilage and the removal of foreign bodies. It is also possible to use video techniques whereby an image of the inside of the joint is shown on a television screen. This technique has the advantage that both hands are then free to carry out the intra-articular surgery.

On-screen microsurgery

The painstaking care and attention needed for microsurgery makes it a very physically demanding procedure for the surgeon, who may have to spend several hours looking through the eyepiece of a microscope. The miscroscopes have to be positioned centrally over the operating area and are adjusted for the comfort of the leading surgeon. This setup may put the assistant at some disadvantage and may also block the view of other theater personnel. Some of these problems can be overcome with loupe glasses, which allow the surgeon more freedom of movement but are limited in magnifying power.

Instead, a video-microscope system is being developed that will allow surgeons to view the operating area on a video monitor. The three-dimensional on-screen microsurgery system (TOMS) uses two cameras to produce a stereoscopic image that gives an accurate perception of depth, which is vital where such small structures are involved. Although prototype TOMS suffer from problems with image resolution, loss of illumination, and reduced width of field, the system has received approval from microsurgeons.

 Left: microclips are used to interrupt the flow of blood while two arteries in the arm are sutured together with nylon thread. Right: blood flows through the newly joined arteries when the clips are removed.

Advances in technology are expected to resolve these problems, and the comfort of being able to view the operating area without fatigue makes TOMS a positive step forward for the future of microsurgery.

Robots in microsurgery

Another potential leap in the development of microsurgical techniques is the use of robots to carry out some minimally invasive procedures in eye, ear, nose, throat, hand, face, and cranial surgery. NASA's Jet Propulsion Laboratory in collaboration with MicroDexterity Systems has developed a robot-assisted microsurgery (RAMS) workstation, which uses a six-degrees-of-freedom telemanipulator with programmable controls. The robot arm was designed to work in a one cubic inch volume on features 100 microns in size, with the aim of producing an arm capable of working on 20 micron structures. A successful simulation of an eye operation by one of the prototypes was followed by a dual-arm configuration developed to test the system's ability to perform suturing at a microscopic level. Further development of RAMS is now underway to turn it into a viable and commercial medical tool.

Robots have already assisted in some cranial surgery procedures where the site is difficult to see. Stereotactic brain surgery, where a probe is inserted into the brain through a hole in the skull, requires careful positioning to avoid damaging vital parts of the brain. A robot can be programmed to align a guide to the target and entry points and to the correct depth. The surgeon can then safely insert instruments along the guide.

SEE ALSO: Endoscope • Microscope, optical • Operating room • Plastic surgery • Surgery • Transplant

Index

Page numbers in **bold** refer to main articles; those in *italics* refer to picture captions.